Praise for
TOO DUMB

"This book is far from a standard D.C. 'if only they listened to me' critique...Conservatives who feel dismayed at the current state of affairs should run out and buy Lewis's book."

—Henry Olsen, *Weekly Standard*

"Lewis...has probed the true makeup of today's GOP."

—*Washington Post*

"Lewis's book offers a wise and far-reaching and brave take on how we got here and what conservatives must do to enlist the 'accumulated wisdom of the past to make our future even brighter.'... *Too Dumb to Fail* is worth reading and pondering because we are watching many of the themes Lewis pinpoints play out in real time... *Too Dumb to Fail* is a great summing up. It's also practical and specific. Earnest, witty, and well-meaning, Lewis is more of a truth teller than a diplomat or glad-hander. He names names... This will not make [Lewis] popular. After the November 2016 elections, however, it may make Matt Lewis something of a prophet."   —*Washington Times*

"Lewis's knockabout style is a relief... [He] argues that conservatives must recover the enthusiasm for ideas they had in the Reagan era."

—*New York Times Book Review* (cover review)

"I've been reading Matt for a long time. He's always incisive and thoughtful, and this book is both. Anyone who cares about the future of the Republican Party should read it."

—Peggy Noonan, *Wall Street Journal* columni*

"A good book... Lewis writes with panache." —*Buffalo News*

"*Too Dumb to Fail* provides the Republican Party a roadmap to get back to its intellectual foundations. With the rise of Donald Trump and Sarah Palin, the book perfectly represents the state of the Republican Party and where it's headed if it doesn't return to its core beliefs... Prescient."

—Christian Schneider, *Milwaukee Journal Sentinel*

"*Too Dumb to Fail*... functions as a smart, sobering premortem on 2016. Now most books about 'fixing' conservatism are written by liberal concern-trolls who secretly want to kill it. But Lewis is an actual, real-deal conservative... This, ultimately, is what Lewis really wants: a conservative movement that honors its intellectuals, that works through its ideological problems honestly, and that doesn't rush to glorify hucksters... If you put Donald Trump or Sarah Palin back in 1980, they couldn't last a week in the ring with the Gipper. Because back then conservatives expected more from their leaders. Matt Lewis thinks we should expect more today, too. He's probably right."

—Jonathan V. Last, *Weekly Standard*

"Matt K. Lewis takes the most unconventional possible approach to Washington journalism: he's completely honest all the time. Not everyone likes him for it, but that's their problem. Like Matt himself this book is cheerful, smart, and insightful as hell. Buy two copies."

—Tucker Carlson, editor-in-chief of The Daily Caller, cohost of *FOX & Friends Weekend*

"Matt K. Lewis has fought in the trenches of some of our hottest political battles, occupying a unique position at the intersection of conservative politics and the popular culture. He brings a rare perspective to everything he writes about, and manages to look at what everyone else is looking at and see what no one sees."

—Yuval Levin, editor of *National Affairs*

"Matt K. Lewis has written an insightful book about the roots of the conservative movement and just how far Washington Republicans have diverged from that proud past. *Too Dumb to Fail* is a major achievement from one of conservatism's most important voices, and it could not come at a more critical time."

—Joe Scarborough, host of
MSNBC's *Morning Joe*

"Matt K. Lewis is one of the sharpest and most principled political commentators of our day. *Too Dumb to Fail* is a lively and fascinating read for any person confounded by the state of today's Republican Party. Lewis provides some much-needed tough love as well as a clear way forward for the GOP. If Republicans are smart, they'll make this book mandatory reading."

—Kirsten Powers, *New York Times*–bestselling
author of *The Silencing*

"Very few books about politics get my 'must read' stamp, but Matt Lewis's is one of them. Every conservative feeling as though the movement has collapsed, every Republican despairing of ever winning the White House, every independent who has no idea what to do or whom to support, should read this book immediately."

—Hugh Hewitt, host of
The Hugh Hewitt Show

"*Too Dumb to Fail* traces the evolution of conservative philosophy from Aristotle to Burke to the present in a clear and readable way that reminds us why conservatives need big ideas—and why America needs conservatism."

—Arthur C. Brooks, president, American
Enterprise Institute

"Right from the beginning, Lewis shows the courage to take on conventional wisdoms in modern conservatism, and that alone makes his book essential." —Craig Shirley, *Newsmax*

"A great read...Really worth reading and thinking about."
—Newt Gingrich (via Facebook)

TOO DUMB TO FAIL

How the GOP Went from
the Party of Reagan to the
Party of Trump

MATT K. LEWIS

NEW YORK   BOSTON

Cover illustration by Robert Karl Blake
Author photograph © Thomas Van Veen
Cover copyright © 2016 by Hachette Book Group, Inc.

Hachette Books
Hachette Book Group
1290 Avenue of the Americas, New York, NY 10104
hachettebookgroup.com
twitter.com/hachettebooks

Originally published in hardcover and ebook by Hachette Books in January 2016
First Trade Paperback Edition: September 2016

Hachette Books is a division of Hachette Book Group, Inc. The Hachette Books name and logo are trademarks of Hachette Book Group, Inc.

The publisher is not responsible for websites (or their content) that are not owned by the publisher.

The Hachette Speakers Bureau provides a wide range of authors for speaking events. To find out more, go to www.hachettespeakersbureau.com or call (866) 376-6591.

Library of Congress Cataloging-in-Publication Data

Names: Lewis, Matt K., author.
Title: Too dumb to fail: how the GOP betrayed the Reagan revolution to win elections (and how it can reclaim its conservative roots) / Matt K. Lewis.
Description: First edition. | New York: Hachette Books, [2016] | Includes bibliographical references.
Identifiers: LCCN 2015039421| ISBN 978-0-316-38393-6 (hardcover) | ISBN 978-1-4789-6095-9 (audio download) | ISBN 978-1-4789-1043-5 (audio cd) | ISBN 978-0-316-38391-2 (ebook)
Subjects: LCSH: Conservatism—United States—History. | Republican Party (U.S.: 1854–) | Elections—United States—History. | Political campaigns—United States—History.
Classification: LCC JC573.2.U6 L49 2016 | DDC 324.2734—dc23 LC record available at http://lccn.loc.gov/2015039421

ISBN: 978-0-316-38392-9 (trade paperback)

Printed in the United States of America

RRD-C

10 9 8 7 6 5 4 3 2 1

To Burke and Becket

CONTENTS

PART ONE:
The Great Thinkers Who Invented Conservatism

PART TWO:
The Great Betrayal

PART THREE:
What a Mess

TOO DUMB
TO FAIL

FOREWORD

Hockey great Wayne Gretsky once famously advised his son to "skate where the puck is going, not where it has been."

Too Dumb to Fail followed that advice—perhaps a little too much so. The 2016 Republican primaries skated right past the puck and straight into the penalty box.

Too Dumb to Fail's hardcover edition arrived with much anticipation in January 2016—*before* Donald Trump had garnered a single primary or caucus vote. When I began writing the book, few observers thought Trump would run at all, let alone seriously compete. Scott Walker and Jeb Bush (remember them?) were the front-runners, and everyone assumed Ted Cruz (or maybe Mike Huckabee or Rick Santorum) would galvanize (most likely in vain) the inchoate middle-American populist angst that has come to dominate today's conservative politics.

As it turned out, *Too Dumb to Fail* presciently nailed the conservative meltdown best epitomized by the surprise Trump juggernaut. As Dr. Russell Moore, president of the Southern Baptist Convention's Ethics & Religious Liberty Commission, quipped, "I don't believe in gambling, but if I did, I would have encouraged Matt Lewis to play the Powerball lottery."

And yet there was something unfulfilling about having been right. *Too Dumb to Fail* warned readers of the approaching storm, but nobody heeded those warnings quickly enough to avoid an incredibly ugly primary process. It's no fun to say "I told you so" while standing on the deck of the *Titanic*.

While pundits fumbled for a definitive explanation for Trump's popularity (a weakened economy, an anti-Obama backlash, and so on), so many of the trends described in this book—the death of experience, weakened political institutions, the "celebritization" of politics, the rise of content-craving 24-7 cable TV, the "conservative echo chamber," the lowering of barriers and democratization of politics brought on by social-media platforms like Twitter, and the general dumbing down of politics (and, yes, American culture in general)—conspired to lift Trump to the pinnacle of a chaotic 2016 GOP field.

While the hardcover edition of this book included plenty of talk about Donald Trump, I felt compelled to address Trump's historic rise since its publication. By embracing populism, nativism, protectionism, and the zero-sum politics of scarcity, Trump's pernicious, if increasingly popular (at least on the Right), worldview threatens to redefine American conservatism and the GOP for a generation, making it more akin to European politics. If Don Rickles and Marine Le Pen had a son, he would indeed look very much like Donald Trump.

Of course, Trump's status as a front-runner didn't occur in a vacuum. His rise required unexpected (and unplanned-for) help along the way. Conservative talk radio had to provide him cover—overlooking his liberal policies and personal peccadilloes while praising him for taking on the establishment and political correctness. The other candidates had to cooperate, too. Scott Walker had to turn into the Tim Pawlenty of 2016. "Low-energy" Jeb Bush had to allow The Donald to emasculate him. "Lyin'" Ted Cruz had to buddy up to Trump for months, thus providing him cover (before ultimately turning on him). Ben Carson had to be along for the ride and make The Donald look well-informed by comparison. And sadly, too many people had to die in Paris and San Bernardino and Brussels (my theory is that anything bad that happens in the news ultimately helps

Donald Trump in the polls). These are just a few of the ingredients that gave rise to the toxic stew that is Trump.

On the verge of catching fire in New Hampshire, the GOP's most articulate conservative spokesman since Ronald Reagan—Marco Rubio—transformed into one of the "empty-headed talking-point reciters" that *Too Dumb to Fail* had cautioned against. For his part, Chris Christie savagely ensured that no one missed this Rubio implosion.

Each time a non-Trump Republican threatened to emerge as the alternative, someone else would pull him down. (This has been compared to how crabs behave when you put them in a bucket; they pull back down any potential escape artists.)

Still, none of this would matter if a sizable chunk of the GOP base wasn't buying what Trump was selling. His forceful, if often discordant and incoherent, message resonated with many frustrated Americans. *Too Dumb to Fail* urges conservatives to reacquaint themselves with conservative philosophy to insulate themselves from that raucous siren call, and I am still optimistic that this book will win the day. Eventually.

Although Trump is sui generis and is aided by the culmination of unique cultural and technological trends, it's also true that populism in America is cyclical—it emerges roughly every twenty or thirty years, lurching from Left to Right, from a William Jennings Bryan to a Huey Long to a George Wallace to a Pat Buchanan and a Ross Perot to The Donald.

I was recently reminded of just how deeply embedded Trump's rhetoric is when I went back and reread a speech delivered at the Republican National Convention in 1992 by "Pitchfork Pat" Buchanan. Having battled and been ultimately defeated by George H. W. Bush, Buchanan sought to keep the party from coming unglued by urging them to co-opt at least part of his message. As he said,

My friends, even in tough times, these people are with us. They
don't read Adam Smith or Edmund Burke, but they came from
the same school yards and playgrounds and towns as we did.
They share our beliefs and convictions, our hopes and our
dreams. They are the conservatives of the heart.

They are our people. And we need to reconnect with them.
We need to let them know we know they're hurting. They don't
expect miracles, but they need to know we care.

The 2016 GOP establishment didn't seem to care about those
people, and Donald Trump seemed to. At the very least, he voiced
their resentments, fears, and frustrations—and he used *their* language. Unfortunately, they mistook bad grammar for truth and bad
manners for honesty.

Trump was further aided by a backlash against Barack Obama's
liberal policies and executive overreach, political correctness run
amok, and an impotent, inert, and insincere Republican establishment that promised action and provided excuses.

That's not to let Trump (or his followers) off the hook. Trump
promises to bring new people into the Republican fold, but his "big
tent" doesn't just include hardworking, salt-of-the-earth Americans who are mad that their manufacturing jobs have been shipped
overseas. His rise has inspired enthusiasm from the fringes. David
Duke, former grand wizard of the Ku Klux Klan, endorsed him (it
took Trump multiple news cycles before he got around to completely
disavowing that support). And online, throngs of supporters that fit
under the umbrella term *Alt-Right* (a designation that loosely seems
to include young male gamers, men's-rights advocates, and white
nationalists) took it upon themselves to police social media, label-
ing conservatives who dared to speak out against Mr. Trump as
"cuckservatives"—a derisive portmanteau that combines the words
cuckold and *conservative*.

Women who dared challenge Trump had it even worse. *Fox*

News' Megyn Kelly was attacked by Trump over her menstrual cycle (there was "blood coming out of her eyes, blood coming out of her wherever"). Breitbart reporter Michelle Fields (a former colleague of mine) was grabbed by Trump's campaign manager, who was later charged (though never prosecuted) with battery, when she tried to ask a question about affirmative action. Ted Cruz's wife, Heidi, had an unflattering picture of her (juxtaposed with a flattering one of Trump's wife, Melania, a former model) retweeted by Trump himself. And the list goes on.

With all of Trump's political bobbing and weaving, the term that best describes what's afflicted the GOP since *Too Dumb to Fail's* January 2016 debut is *sucker punch.* That's more than a metaphor. It's also an all-too-tangible reference to seventy-eight-year-old Trump supporter John McGraw, who sucker punched a young protester at a Fayetteville, North Carolina, rally. (A month earlier in Las Vegas, Trump said of another protester, "I'd like to punch him in the face.")

McGraw's shot to the face has become a window into the soul of Trump's candidacy: *nasty, angry, authoritarian, demagogic, and utterly stunning.* Step by ugly step, Trumpism advances from words in Las Vegas to a punch in Fayetteville to charges filed in Jupiter, Florida (Trump's campaign manager was charged with battery against a female reporter).

But it's not just Trump who looks bad. The political establishment, the commentariat, and the media also suffered second-hand black eyes as a result of Trump's embarrassing tactics.

If the Red Sox rocket from worst to first, nobody thinks this discredits the many sportswriters who picked another team to win the World Series. There's a big difference between being a good reporter and being a Cassandra. Predicting the full force of Trump's perfect storm required being a truly great prophet. It's not surprising that so many pundits didn't see it coming. But they should have seen the numerous symptoms that *Too Dumb to Fail* warned about.

As of this writing, Donald Trump is the presumptive GOP

nominee. Regardless of that outcome in November, he has lit the fuse that might blow up the GOP. The long-standing but uneasy conservative coalition—evangelicals, neocons, businesspeople, suburbanites, Southerners, and so on—may finally unravel.

Trump has certainly sullied the name of conservatism—a neat trick for someone who is not actually a conservative. It is now more important than ever for real conservatives to unite and rescue our movement from anti-intellectualism, opportunism—and just plain, sheer nastiness.

Of course, as I write this foreword for the paperback, I am left with the same dilemma I was confronted with back in January: the lack of a satisfying denouement. We do not yet know who will emerge as president in November. As I type this, it is looking increasingly likely that this could be a real race, and that Donald Trump could actually win. I wouldn't bet on it, but the assumption that he would lose in a landslide might serve to be as incorrect as the notion that he could never win the GOP nomination.

Part of the reason for this is that outside forces matter a great deal in politics, and one of those outside forces is the fact that around 70 percent of Americans are dissatisfied with the direction of the nation. This number might suggest that a candidate like Hillary Clinton, who is essentially cast as the status quo "establishment" politician hoping to win a third term for Democrats, is at a disadvantage when it comes to facing an unpredictable, insurgent outsider like Donald Trump.

This disadvantage is compounded by the fact that Hillary Clinton, unlike her husband, is a bad (and not especially likable) candidate. Long after Donald Trump became the presumptive GOP nominee, Clinton was still struggling to fend off Democratic insurgent candidate Senator Bernie Sanders for her party's nomination—a struggle that showcased her abject vulnerability and inability to close the deal. Trump might not be beloved, but neither is Clinton. What is more, despite Sanders's refusal to make an issue of it, questions linger about the appropriateness of her use of a private e-mail server while serving as secretary of state.

Conventional wisdom still suggests that demographic shifts and the electoral map both heavily favor Clinton, but Trump is banking on the fact that the game has changed. A Trump victory would likely require him to (among other things) flip some Rust Belt states by turning out additional working-class white voters who might otherwise stay home. It would be an impressive feat, to be sure, but having watched him outmaneuver so many Republicans to get here, don't be so quick to underestimate his powers of persuasion.

I don't want to give you the impression that this book is just about the horse race. Far from it. It would be a mistake to view this book as being solely (or even mostly) about 2016, or the rise of Donald Trump and Ted Cruz. *Too Dumb to Fail* aims to pull the GOP back from the precipice of populist protectionism and comb-over authoritarianism and help modernize it into a vessel of optimistic, intelligent conservatism. What's the alternative? Well, when the Whig Party collapsed, not every former Whig immediately transmogrified into a Republican. A substantial number of them (led by Millard Fillmore) enlisted in the Know Nothing Party. That strategy didn't work any better than stand-for-nothing Whiggism did.

But here's the good news: once our philosophical ancestors got the Know Nothing poison out of their system, four years later they truly became the party of Lincoln.

Read on, and I'll explain how something akin to that can happen again.

—*Matt K. Lewis, April 2016*

INTRODUCTION

"Wisdom is the principal thing; therefore get wisdom:
and with all thy getting get understanding."
—*Proverbs 4:7*

In September 2010, I took part in a conservative think tank panel discussion on the rise of a new phenomenon known as the Tea Party—a loose-knit group of aspiring activists who previously were not engaged in the political process. In contrast to the other panelists, I argued that, while the entry of new activists and voters into politics was usually a welcome development, the characteristics that came to define the Tea Party posed significant challenges to the Republican Party: doubling down on anti-intellectualism, courting isolationism, and taking cues from amateurs who lacked experience and professionalism. My comments, though delivered in a tone I considered measured and thoughtful, evoked murmuring and at least a few audible gasps. The question hanging on the lips of many audience members was clear: Why wasn't a conservative writer blindly cheerleading this seminal moment in conservative movement history?

One of the forum's other speakers was an avuncular and sharp conservative leader who had worked for Ronald Reagan and George H. W. Bush, and he was now the head of an important conservative organization. At the event, he bristled at my remarks. "That's just what people said about the Christian Coalition in the 1980s," he charged, winning the crowd's approval.

A few days later, while direct messaging with one of his aides on Twitter, I learned the truth. "He agreed with everything you said," the aide confided. "He just thought it was foolish to say so out loud."

This is the dirty little secret of the conservative movement in America today: everyone knows that it has lost its intellectual bearings. Empty-headed talking point reciters, rookie politicians who've never managed anything in their lives, media clowns such as Donald Trump, dim bulbs in tight pants or short skirts, professionally outraged shout-fest talking heads, and total political neophytes dominate conservative airwaves and the Right's political discourse.

It wasn't always like this. A half century ago, the presidential candidacy of Barry Goldwater was nearing a disastrous end. Lyndon Johnson, Goldwater's Democratic opponent in the 1964 election, had bludgeoned the Arizona senator as a conservative extremist who would recklessly start a nuclear war. Trailing in every poll with time dwindling, Goldwater's supporters (led by an auto dealer named Holmes Tuttle) decided to spend a small fortune for thirty minutes of TV airtime. To make the case for Goldwater, they chose a former actor and Screen Actors Guild president named Ronald Reagan. Officially titled "A Time for Choosing," the spot became known simply as "The Speech." The story of how it came to be is interesting. Reagan (who was then serving as cochairman of Californians for Goldwater) traveled the state, stumping for his candidate. After addressing a fund-raiser in Los Angeles, Reagan recalled that he was approached by "a delegation of high-powered Republicans" who asked if he would deliver the speech on TV if they funded it. "I said yes and suggested that, instead of just having me in a studio alone, they bring in an audience to get a little better feel," he recalled.[1]

Reagan began his address by remarking that he had chosen his own words and would be discussing his own ideas. Back in 1964, neither of those facts was especially startling. Political speakers frequently wrote their own speeches, and the political arena still welcomed the debate of big ideas. Goldwater and his team initially opposed the plan, fearing Reagan would overshadow Goldwater.[2] Of course, he did. But "The Speech" also helped raise millions of dollars for Goldwater's campaign. And, of course, it ultimately served as the catalyst that would make Ronald Reagan the president sixteen years later.

At a time when the electorate was still comfortable with Franklin Roosevelt's big government philosophy and the United Nations was seen as maintaining global peace, Reagan's promotion of free market principles and hawkish foreign policy challenged conventional wisdom of the day. But what was not unusual is that "The Speech" had *substance*. In his first minute and a half, Reagan effortlessly cited eight statistics. In the next half hour, he cited forty more. Behind his command of details and data was an elevated rhetoric that challenged his listeners to consider "the long history of man's relation to man" and "his long climb from the swamp to the stars."

Reagan's address fell short of reversing Goldwater's descent, but it propelled Reagan's own election win two years later as the next governor of California, when he vanquished the once popular two-term New Deal Democrat Pat Brown. Twenty years later, when he was elected to his second term in the White House with the support of forty-nine states, he could look back at the words he chose in October 1964 and "The Speech" that started the Reagan Revolution.

Today, almost everything about Reagan's address is inconceivable. No political consultant would advise a struggling campaign to buy thirty minutes of airtime for an ideological monologue. We assume the modern attention span demands information in thirty-second installments or less, preferably with alternately ominous and bathetic music and computer graphics (the video-sharing service Vine features looping videos just six seconds long, and the service is wildly popular).

Today, no aspiring politician would deliver a speech that wasn't poll tested, consultant crafted, and focus group approved. Reagan's speech had instead been honed by decades of Reagan's reading, thinking, and writing about history, economics, and international relations. Who has time for all *that*?

As it turns out, the answer is...just about every significant political leader in American history, including the likes of John Adams, Thomas Jefferson, Daniel Webster, Henry Clay, Stephen Douglas, Abraham Lincoln, William Seward, Thaddeus Stevens, William Jennings Bryan, Theodore Roosevelt, Woodrow Wilson, Calvin Coolidge, Franklin Roosevelt, Barry Goldwater, and Ronald Reagan.

As unimaginable as it sounds, there was once a time when Americans could turn on their televisions and not expect to hear a parade of tired and trite talking points spewed forth from a split screen of four screaming pundits with no experience or expertise in whatever ratings-driven controversy cable news had manufactured for that day. Ideas mattered. Men and women fought over ideas and thought before they spoke. Politicians speaking on television and writing in newspapers (ask your parents) were judged by their expertise and eloquence, not their ability to outshout the medley of other amateur gasbags vying to entertain and excite an audience that long ago surrendered any hope of being informed or inspired.

The Republican Party is called the Grand Old Party for a reason. It was founded on big ideas: abolishing slavery and holding together a federal republic. But the dumbing down of the GOP has gone on for so long that nearly half of Republicans don't know what that acronym stands for.[3]

I am not suggesting that liberals are immune to these problems. They faced similar struggles in past decades and settled for simplistic solutions. Over the years, liberals came to believe a university president could keep us out of war, a plain-speaking peanut farmer could restore honor to Washington after Watergate, and a community organizer could unite America. Democrats went through their own time in the wilderness, losing three consecutive presidential elections from 1980 to 1992. But their identity crises didn't coincide with a time when respect for institutions was declining, when outside groups made it possible for backbench politicians to usurp a leader's authority without fear of retribution, and when a technological revolution meant any Tom, Dick, or Harry could have a megaphone and a printing press on his smartphone.

Palinized?

Perhaps it's not fair to compare the mediums, but—just for a second—juxtapose Ronald Reagan's 1964 speech and one of former Alaska governor Sarah Palin's infamous posts to her four million-plus fans on Facebook, which concluded with the words, "Thank you, prayer warriors! I love you!" Until Palin came along, Reagan was the last Republican to generate euphoric excitement within the Party. And he was not without flaws. But from his first televised address to his last, he appealed, in his words, "to your best hopes, not your worst fears; to your confidence rather than your doubts."[4] He did not, as Palin does, blame the "liberal media" for his problems. In fact, he was not quick to blame *anyone* for his problems—or for yours. Solutions mattered more than indictments; ideas mattered more than enemies; and his nation mattered more than his ego. The product of a generation that prized actions over words, he showed his love for our country by serving it, not closing his statements by calling out, "I love you!" For Reagan, "God bless America" did just fine.

Somewhere between Reagan's thirty-minute speech in 1964 and the most recent government shutdown, the conservative movement became neither conservative nor a movement. Hijacked by the divisive and the dumb, it now finds itself hostage to emotions and irrational thinking. It became more personal and less principled—more flippant and less thoughtful. It became mean. It became lazy. It became its own worst enemy. Where once the movement drew strength from its desire to win the philosophical argument over its adversaries, it now wears its lost causes as badges of honor—expected, like Coriolanus, to show these battle scars as a means of vote mongering.

This is the story of how that happened, and how the Republican Party has become the latest victim of a dumbed-down popular culture. Far from burying the conservative movement, I hope with this book—to borrow from Shakespeare—to save it.

Too Dumb to Fail

So why call it *Too Dumb to Fail*?

The title is a play on words—an allusion to Andrew Ross Sorkin's *Too Big to Fail*, about the financial crisis of 2008. The crisis was brought on in part by the fact that individual actors (in this case, financial institutions) behaved unethically and ignored warnings that bubbles would eventually burst. And when they did, some of the actors were deemed too big and too interconnected to be allowed to fail, and were, thus, bailed out by the taxpayers.

As Sorkin described it, this climate created what economists called a "moral hazard," meaning that future companies (knowing they will be bailed out when things go wrong) now had an incentive to take even greater risks.

Today's Republican Party faces similar perverse incentives. It's in everyone's best interest to ignore the potential looming crisis. For example, the fact that Republicans have lost the popular vote *in five out of the last six* presidential elections should be cause for grave concern. Instead, it's barely mentioned. Part of the reason is that individual actors (instead of financial institutions—think political candidates, organizations, etc.) are prospering. They have little reason to change their behavior because they profit, regardless of whether a Republican candidate wins the presidency. (In fact, they may profit more if a Democrat wins.) And, of course, although there are continual threats of third parties, the notion of abandoning the "too big to fail" GOP seems highly unlikely.

Speaking of a moral hazard, rather than addressing the serious problems (demographic, as well as rapidly shifting public opinion on a spate of social issues) facing the GOP, almost all the incentives—including fund-raising and media attention—reward a sort of dumbed-down, red meat–hurling style that kicks the can down the road. This book is about the irony that the dumbing down of conservatism has (so far) resulted in the worst offenders failing forward. They are, in essence, *too dumb to fail*.

Now, a few words about what this book is *not*.

This book is not an argument for a small, elite group of the best and brightest to rule us by using their sophisticated formulas and technocratic ways. While I was writing the book, a scandal erupted and revealed that Jonathan Gruber, one of the architects of Obamacare, had boasted that the health care law benefited from a "lack of transparency" and the "stupidity of the American voter." This is the kind of snobbishness that fosters American skepticism about the "ruling class," the "Washington cartel," and the so-called "experts."

I'm the son of a prison guard. I grew up in a place called Wolfsville, Maryland—situated between Frederick and Hagerstown, about eight miles from Camp David. (Our other claim to fame is that the 2002 DC sniper was apprehended at the Myersville McDonald's, which is about five miles from where I grew up.) Today, Wolfsville is basically a bedroom community for people who commute to DC or Baltimore; but not that long ago, it was about as rural as you could get. I went to school with a kid who didn't have indoor plumbing until we were in middle school. In elementary school, when they asked us what we wanted to be when we grew up, the number one answer was "farmer" and the number two answer was "truck driver." (I wanted to play for the Baltimore Orioles.) Later, my dad, who had been a country musician as a younger man and played for a band called Irene and the Country Rascals, taught me how to pick country and bluegrass guitar. When I went to high school in Middletown, Maryland, I was immediately labeled a redneck by virtue of coming from the sticks. In short, I'm the last person to promote elitism. My book is instead a call for a meritocracy where our political and opinion leaders earn and deserve our loyalty.

Too Dumb to Fail is not an argument that intelligence is more important than wisdom or courage. Were that the case, Jimmy Carter, a nuclear engineer and graduate of the US Naval Academy in Annapolis, Maryland, would have been preferable to Ronald Reagan, a humble graduate of Eureka College, and Bill Clinton, a Rhodes scholar, would have won my vote over Russell, Kansas's, Bob Dole. In this regard, I agree with Theodore Roosevelt, a Manhattan intellectual turned roughriding cowboy: "Exactly as strength comes before beauty, so character must stand above intellect and genius."

This book is not a criticism or an indictment of the many God-fearing good conservative activists and individuals who attend rallies and want to take their country back. Nor is it an attack on rural Americans (among whose number I counted myself for the first twenty-four years of my life) or Christians (I'm an evangelical).

Lastly, this book is not an argument for *credentialism*—the theory that says two-term Wisconsin governor Scott Walker, who, by all accounts, appears to be both serious and competent, wasn't qualified to be president just because he doesn't have a college degree. With my humble West Virginia–based BS degree, I am the last person to believe politics should be the exclusive province of Rhodes scholars and Ivy Leaguers. Lincoln never went to college. Harry Truman never graduated.[5]

What I am suggesting, though, is that the current challenges confronting conservatism have to do with a deficit of both intellect *and* wisdom—as well as discipline, humility, and prudence. What we need, in short, are *adults*. But somewhere along the way, the adults started acting like kids; they started wanting to be popular—to be liked, rather than feared or respected.

This book is also an indictment of the charlatans, organizations, and political candidates who attempt to exploit good conservative Americans and hijack the conservative movement. As such, my rhetorical crosshairs are reserved exclusively for those who would manipulate conservatives and besmirch their conservative cause—all for ulterior motives (cash, not least among them).

Intellectuals, the Establishment, and Populism

I want to define a couple of terms that get bandied about in this book. For our purposes, the word *intellectual* is defined in philosophically neutral terms. In my mind, the word refers to "a learned person who thinks about big ideas, endeavors to study history and philosophy, and engages in critical thought and reflection." This is close to historian Richard Hofstadter's definition that an intellectual is someone who "in some sense lives for ideas—which means he has a sense of dedication to the life of the mind which is very much like a religious commitment."[6] Most of the people discussed in this book might also be thought of as *public* intellectuals, inasmuch as they sought to inject their ideas into politics and the broader culture.

It is important to concede that the word *intellectual* is often assumed to have an ideological connotation. For example, in British historian Paul Johnson's appropriately titled book *Intellectuals*, the brilliant men he profiles (including Rousseau, Sartre, Shelley, Marx, Tolstoy, and Hemingway—Ernest *not* Mariel, for you folks in Rio Linda) tend to be ruthless, selfish, secular men of the Left, who "preferred ideas to people." Having emerged from an era where the church and the earthly (if divinely appointed) monarchies were assumed to have all the answers—not just theologically, but also philosophically and *scientifically*—it was perhaps natural for the newly unshackled great minds of the time to rebel. And rebel they did—in many cases, stubbornly so.

I want to debunk the notion that to be an intellectual is to be a liberal secularist. This may prove to be an uphill battle. The Left promotes the stereotype that to be conservative is to be stupid. Dan Quayle and Sarah Palin have been served up (often unfairly) as examples of this. But unfortunately, especially since the 1960s, conservatives—many of them highly educated in their own right—have been complicit in advancing this trope by playing the populist card and mocking "pointy-headed intellectuals." You'll rarely hear a conservative boast that he (or a friend) is an *intellectual*. And this has nothing to do with humbleness. The word has a negative connotation on the Right. A liberal might be an intellectual, but a smart conservative—if he can help it—is a "man of letters."

The term *establishment* also deserves an asterisk. By definition, it means "the power structure," which is a philosophically neutral term. Today, it is not uncommon for "leaders" of the conservative movement to constantly lament the so-called "establishment." Ironically, many of these men and women have lived in the Washington, DC, area (sometimes for decades) and have made millions of dollars during that time. In what world are they not part of it?

Then there is the term *populist*. What does it mean? If it means someone who favors the American people over big government and the crony capitalists who rig the system to benefit big business over the little guy, then count me in. Amitai Etzioni, professor of international relations at the George Washington University, calls this kind of populism "popular populism." And that's a pretty descriptive name. As Etzioni wrote in a January 2015 column for the *Atlantic*, about half of us think politicians are corrupt.[7] "Very low on people's 'trust' lists are all those perceived as powerful, including not just the government but also banks and corporations and labor unions," he wrote. "This kind of populism appeals to both those on the left, such as the Occupy Wall Street folks, and to Tea Partiers."

If, instead, populism represents the demagogic politics of nativism, xenophobia, resentment, know-nothingism, victimhood, bitterness, envy (specifically on the Left, in the form of redistributionism[8]), and/or protectionism—used as a rhetorical cudgel to manipulate the masses—then count me (and most of the public) out. Unfortunately, it sometimes *does*. Populism often requires scapegoats. As *National Review*'s Jonah Goldberg has noted, "It should be no surprise that populism is a conducive medium for anti-Semitism. America's nineteenth-century populists were always quick to blame 'the Jews' for their troubles."[9] When you pander to the whims and passions of the public, you are bound to find that the majority isn't always correct or even moral. Then, what's a leader to do? "The people of Nebraska are for free silver and I am for free silver," populist William Jennings Bryan is said to have declared in 1892. Compare that to Edmund Burke's speech to electors at Bristol, November 3, 1774: "You choose a member indeed; but when you have chosen him, he is not a member of Bristol, but he is a member of parliament." The dichotomy is stark: Bryan's populist politics was really followship; Burke's conservative politics was leadership.

In the chapters that follow, I will come down hard on this *negative* brand of populism. I admit it. I've come to believe that this strain of populism has become synonymous with "conservatism," and is therefore partly to blame for the dumbing down of conservatism. As Peter Wehner wrote in a *New York Times* column titled "Conservatives in Name Only," "What often masquerades as conservatism these days is really populism. There is room for populism within conservatism, but it should not define conservatism. In fact, it is often in conflict with it." Sadly, in recent years, populist conservatives have invoked a sort of class warfare. Thus, the "ruling class" versus "country class" rhetoric has come to define one's political identity, replacing the "Left" versus "Right" paradigm. One's political philosophy, as such, is less important than one's perceived status as an outsider who "tells it like it is."

One of the ironies of the dumbing down is that it often stems from the work of highly intelligent people. There seems to be a misconception about well-traveled and highly educated people that suggests they are more open-minded and tolerant than the rest of us. Not only have I found little correlation between intelligence and open-mindedness, I wonder if the two may even be mutually exclusive. Some of the smartest people on either side of the aisle are also the most biased. They simply use their intellect to more effectively argue their biases. Some of the most pompous, partisan blowhards on the Right and the Left also tend to be the most intelligent and highly educated. What explains this? "It doesn't matter how intelligent you are if you don't use your brain," says Daniel Flynn, author of the book *Intellectual Morons*.

"Intelligent people aren't necessarily rigorous thinkers. In fact, many of them are mentally lazy. Ideology provides a way for lazy people to respond to issues, ideas, people, and events without thinking."[10]

I would take this argument one step further: many of the great ills in the world (let's take Communism, for example) were not the result of ignorant or stupid people. Some of history's greatest evils have sprung from very smart people who lacked *wisdom*. In *Intellectuals and Society*, Thomas Sowell put it thus: "The opposite of intellect is dullness or slowness, but the opposite of wisdom is foolishness, which is far more dangerous." My purpose here is to encourage conservatives to seek both knowledge and wisdom, along with other virtues such as courage, authenticity, empathy, discipline, consistency, and humility. Intelligence is important, but without these other attributes, it is more dangerous than ignorance.

Who Am I to Judge?

Fears about a dumbed-down America are nothing new. Richard Hofstadter warned us about *Anti-intellectualism in American Life* fifty years ago (his book won the 1964 Pulitzer Prize for General Non-Fiction). But when Hofstadter wrote his book, John F. Kennedy—who combined style with intellectual substance—was president. The Kennedy administration rewarded intellectualism and boasted of its own intellectual vigor. It brought top-notch artists and authors and thinkers to the White House and actually celebrated them. One could only imagine what Hofstadter would think now.

Today's media environment is hostile to serious people who offer thoughtful ideas. We refuse to embrace complexity in major public policy decisions. We reward and elevate leaders who lack either the depth or the experience to address major national problems (and yes, this is a criticism *not* just of the Right, but also of Exhibit A: Barack Hussein Obama). As a result, our culture is dumb. And our leaders are unprepared and often unfit for the offices they hold.

So why am I, a conservative-leaning journalist, writing this book when there are so many worthy topics out there? "Why not write a book talking about all the sins committed by liberals?" you might ask. My task may be a thankless endeavor. This business of constructive criticism is always fraught with danger. Because the mainstream media has long covered conservatives with the distortive filter of latent liberal bias, there is a sense that center-right journalists ought to eschew criticizing the Right, and instead, devote themselves solely to a tit-for-tat exchange with the mainstream media. In other words, I should be in the business of seeking revenge. Many of my friends on the Right believe center-right journalists should exist solely to boost conservative candidates and causes—and to attack liberal ones. Whether this is a desire for payback or simply a push for journalistic parity is moot. These are their expectations of conservative media.

I work at the *Daily Caller*, the website co-founded by conservative writer and commentator Tucker Carlson and Vice President Dick Cheney's former aide Neil Patel. The *Daily Caller*'s writers have to cope with these expectations every day. Some of the biggest stories we've broken—such as the Republican National Committee's spending at a "bondage-themed nightclub" or the revelations about Jon Huntsman's "love letters" to Barack Obama (before the former governor launched a presidential campaign to oust the president in 2012)—have been examples of center-right media holding Republicans accountable. Despite such overt displays of intellectual honesty, the Left continues to cast us as partisan hacks, while the Right sometimes considers us apostates. Being fed a steady stream of leaks that can be spun into clickable scoops (in return for doing a politician's bidding) is surely a more profitable business model. It would also be boring and intellectually dishonest. What's the contrarian conservative to do?

Perhaps, as some have suggested, we are headed back to the days when newspapers cast aside any pretense of objectivity and overtly aligned with political parties. I hope not. The notion that any journalist, even an opinion journalist, should serve solely as a mouthpiece for his tribe is not only a dismal view of journalism, but also ultimately self-destructive. Sometimes, your friends need an intervention. Sometimes, you have to allow them to hit rock bottom. New media (websites, blogs, social media, etc.) might be ideological (by admittedly having a point of view), but that's entirely different from being reflexively *partisan*, which is to carry water for your "side" with no regard for larger principles. Without intellectually honest center-right journalists holding Republicans and conservative leaders accountable, their bad deeds will metastasize to the point where the mainstream media has a field day exposing them. If we are stupid in one thing, we will soon be stupid in others.

Conservative opinion leaders mostly looked the other way when the George W. Bush administration decided to invade Iraq—save for a few scribblers such as famed conservative writers Patrick Buchanan and Robert Novak, who were called "unpatriotic" at the time. Conservatives were equally silent when Bush-era Republicans increased the size of government and ran up the debt, while Bush refused to veto most spending bills. In the long run, protecting your friends doesn't work any more than shielding your kids from all the realities of the world. Yes, let's give little Johnnie or Jennifer a medal for just showing up. There's a plan.

Holding our own side accountable isn't just about exposing ethical scandals or betrayals. The question is whether you want to be loyal to your friends or to a greater cause—including your readers and the general public. I would argue that anti-intellectualism, coupled with an unconservative brand of hubris, is among the most insidious diseases this generation of conservatives must eradicate.

Anti-intellectualism and its natural by-product of scorched-earth populism have been around for a long time and have been exploited by both parties. However, today's conservatives are disproportionately susceptible to it. The conservative movement's weakness for these rabble-rousing tactics poses serious long-term problems for both the movement and the Republican Party. Demographic trends imply there will be more young, urban, college-educated Americans who will be repelled by obscuritanism, and proportionately fewer older, white, non-college educated Americans who grouse at what they might deem to be elitist lecturing.

Beyond the electoral consequences, the very viability of conservatism is at stake. There's no reason a free market philosophy cannot compete and win in a free market of ideas. It's immeasurably more complex and less naive than the King Canute–style economics of the Left. But conservatism cannot thrive if its own champions do not treat it seriously. To those who doubt conservatism qualifies as an intellectually rigorous school of philosophy, a brief history of the conservative movement is in order, and my book aims to provide it.

If you're a liberal looking forward to a fun diatribe and a healthy dose of schadenfreude, put the popcorn away. This is not me playing Eeyore, engaging in "navel-gazing," "pearl-clutching," or even what the Twitter era has dubbed "concern trolling" (insincere advice meant to disrupt or arouse a reaction). I don't want to "fundamentally transform" conservatism. I'm proudly pro-life. My goal isn't to argue that conservatives can win by suddenly changing our position on abortion, or the minimum wage, or taxes. Instead, my goal is to offer *constructive* criticism that will help conservatism rediscover its intellectual roots. To criticize constructively is to *love*. The car aficionado will not ignore the pinging sound in his 1965 Ford Mustang. He will immediately try to identify the problem and fix it. A real lover of classic cars wants to *restore* the thing he loves, and that's precisely what conservatism needs today. To ignore problems is not a sign of affection. I take solace in the words of Aristotle, who, in criticizing his revered mentor Plato, said he loves his friend, but he loves the truth more.

In short, I essentially have two enemies: heretics and lunatics. Heretics are those people who think the only way conservatives can win is by becoming more liberal. Lunatics are those people who are hoarding Confederate flags and worried about black helicopters. This book rejects both extreme ends of that spectrum.

A child of the 1980s, I grew up loving Ronald Reagan. My dad turned me on to listening to Rush Limbaugh around 1988. For the first four years of my professional career, I worked at a nonprofit called the Leadership Institute—a top-notch organization, founded by veteran conservative movement leader Morton C. Blackwell, that trains conservative activists.

My wife, Erin, is a conservative fund-raiser whose projects have included an annual dinner honoring conservative movement leader Paul Weyrich, and whose clients have included some of the most conservative elected officials in America. Her mother formerly served as the volunteer head of the West Virginia chapter of Eagle Forum, the conservative pro-family women's group founded by Phyllis Schlafly. Our eldest son is named Burke Blackwell, after conservative Edmund Burke—and Morton *and* Ken Blackwell, the former secretary of state and treasurer of Ohio. Our youngest is named Becket Wilberforce, after Thomas Becket, who stood up to the King of England in defense of religious liberty, and William Wilberforce, who led the fight to ban the British slave trade. (And, we joke the Lewis surname is in honor of Christian author C. S. Lewis.) If there's a third offspring, it will not be named Delano or Rodham.

What follows will be interpreted by some of my friends as harsh. I may become persona non grata in some conservative circles. However, to the extent I identify villains in this book, my criticisms are in no way directed at the vast majority of decent, hardworking conservative Americans who are legitimately frustrated by the direction of our country. My scorn is directed at the politicians, organizations, and grifters who have mastered the art of manipulation, and who have effectively hijacked parts of the conservative movement that I love and admire.

My interest is in seeing that conservatives get their house in order, and to begin that process, we must remember that conservatism began as a serious and thoughtful philosophy.

PART ONE

THE GREAT THINKERS WHO INVENTED CONSERVATISM

1

A HISTORY OF BRILLIANT CONSERVATISM

"I coulda had class. I coulda been a contender."
—*Marlon Brando,* On the Waterfront

Conservatism's roster of historical leaders should be—and is—a genuine pantheon of intellectual rigor and moral fiber, not the clown car it is too often portrayed as today. That this book must begin by (re)establishing this very premise is quite telling. But a casual observer of modern politics would be forgiven for not realizing how deep the intellectual roots of conservatism go. As such, any argument for a return to those roots must first establish that those roots, indeed, *exist.* And the only way I know how to do this is to begin at the beginning.

While patriotic conservatives rightly revere the Constitution and the Founding Fathers, conservatism is not merely an American invention. It is a fundamental political philosophy that can be traced back to antiquity. And while some conservatives prefer to talk about the conservative *sensibility, worldview, disposition, temperament,* or even *persuasion,* I don't shy from using the word "philosophy," which can be defined as the seeking of wisdom. And *that* exercise is a very conservative pursuit. Along those lines, conservatives can take great pride in knowing that the father of political conservatism is none other than Aristotle—and that its modern champion was the great eighteenth-century politician and thinker Edmund Burke.

384 BC: Ancient Greece

A star is born: Aristotle, destined to become one of the most important philosophers in history. At eighteen, he moves to Athens to attend Plato's Academy, where he matriculates for nearly two decades. (Imagine his student loans!) His brilliance is so undeniable that King Phillip II of Macedon invites Aristotle to tutor his son, whom we know today as Alexander the Great. Returning to Athens, Aristotle inaugurates his own school, the Lyceum, where he continues to study, teach, and contribute major advances to the worlds of science, education, ethics, philosophy, and politics—essentially every field of human intellectual pursuit.

He wasn't always right or virtuous (he endorsed slavery, for example) but the depths of Aristotle's accomplishments are undeniable. As such, it should come as a relief to many conservatives—those who might lament the old trope about being "the stupid party" (which also says that the Democrats are the "evil party")—that Aristotle is also considered by many to be "the father of political conservatism."

Aristotle's political philosophy was rooted in fundamental principles that all real conservatives—whether they realize it or not—inherently believe. He rejected the moral relativism of his day, insisting instead upon *a priori* moral truths. He held that families and communities were not abstract constructs, but rather, natural and intrinsic. As he asserted in *The Politics*, "The city belongs among the things that exist by nature." This flies in the face of the utopian notion that civilization developed arbitrarily, and could thus be cavalierly uprooted.

If the notion that our social order wasn't merely a human invention seems obvious to you, it wasn't for a lot of philosophers and world leaders throughout the ages. In some ways, the story of the twentieth century amounts to a huge argument over something Aristotle figured out thousands of years ago. He believed that the way civilization developed was not random, but rather, natural. Man, it follows, is not malleable. As such, change (the logic continues) must be slow, organic, and cautious. (As we shall see, many of these assumptions fell out of favor with the arrival of the Enlightenment and modernity.)

You might be thinking, "What does this have to do with the real world, and what does this even have to do with conservatism?" To us moderns, living in twenty-first-century America, Aristotelian philosophy may seem an esoteric idea—and it is. It's easy for us to think of conservatism as merely a doctrine that is pro-national defense, anti-tax, and pro-life—or even a philosophy of self-reliance or rugged individualism. But these downstream ideas derive from deeper, more existential concepts. Aristotle's foundational conservative truths speak to the very ideas on which humanity rests—and on which nations rise and fall. If you absorb his worldview, you will usually arrive at conservative policies. But get his fundamental ideas wrong, and the consequences can be dire.

The Great Debate

In the centuries after Aristotle's death, others (most notably Thomas Aquinas, a thirteenth-century Catholic priest and saint who wrote several important commentaries on Aristotle) would help keep his ideas alive. But Aristotle's modern political scion is the Anglo-Irish Edmund Burke. Burke's philosophy was very much in keeping with Aristotle's, inasmuch as it argued that Western civilization was not the result of luck or happenstance, but rather, the result of human nature evolving by virtue of trial and error.

Born in Dublin in 1729 and educated at that city's Trinity College, Burke was the son of a Protestant father and a Catholic mother (in his day, these details mattered greatly). Moving to London, Burke emerged as a philosopher, lobbyist, author, reformer, statesman, and Whig politician who served in the British House of Commons for three decades. There, he famously advocated for better treatment of the American colonies, arguing to respect America's unique traditions of freedom and independence—and that Great Britain should accommodate her rebellious cousins across the pond. But Burke's most important contributions to history and conservatism derive from his opposition to the French Revolution. To some, this opposition came as a surprise. His pro-American stance incorrectly led Thomas Paine, a patriot and a radical, to believe that Burke would likewise support revolutionary attempts to quash royal oppression elsewhere. Instead, as Yuval Levin writes in his book about Burke and Paine, *The Great Debate*, the French Revolution exposed a yawning chasm of worldviews—arguments that would define the modern Right and Left for centuries to come, with Burke representing the former.

Paine's ideology serves as a perfect foil to illuminate Burke's conservative worldview. Paine's more radical writings include themes of primitivism (a notion that civilization enslaves us) and utopianism (the quixotic idea that this enslavement might be remedied on earth). Such views overlapped with the intellectual father of the disastrous French Revolution, the Geneva-born Enlightenment philosopher Jean-Jacques Rousseau.[11] (Anyone who doubts the ubiquity of Parisian primitivism can ask themselves why a wise and cosmopolitan man such as Benjamin Franklin would, when wooing the French to the American cause, don a coonskin cap. Boston-born Benjamin Franklin was many things, but he was neither Davy Crockett—nor Mike Huckabee.)

Without any basis in history, Rousseau invented a creation myth out of whole cloth. In his pre-social original state, man—a "noble savage"—was content and peaceful. He went where he wanted and had sex when he wanted. (It has been said that all heresies originate below the waist.) It was, Rousseau contended, only after the invention of the concept of private property and the rise of civilization that greed and jealousy and war crept into his secular Eden. As such, Rousseau viewed institutional intrusions between the government and the individual—for example, the family and the church—as artificial ingredients that had essentially paved paradise and put up a parking lot.

Again, you might be thinking, "What does this have to do with modern conservatism?" but stick with me. Primitivism might sound quaint, if naive, but followed to its logical conclusions (as in the French Revolution and elsewhere), this belief led to the guillotine and the gulag. Returning to man's natural state requires toppling—by force—organic institutions that took centuries to develop. To accomplish this, the ends justify the means, and patience is not a virtue. As with Rousseau, Paine's focus on noble-sounding principles such as liberty and equality came at the expense of tradition, institutions, and faith, which were deemed not only superfluous but also counterproductive.

Against this backdrop, a clash of philosophies emerged. "We have it in our power to begin the world over again," Paine famously averred.[12]

Burke saw things differently. His worldview, more traditionally Christian, assumed a fallen world could not be perfected or begun over again. It could only (if we were lucky) be managed. He thought us fortunate to inherit a Western civilization that functioned to the degree it did. Bad things would always happen, of course, and Burke spent much of his career advocating for wise reforms to redress chronic problems; however, he also believed we had been well served by respecting the accumulated wisdom and institutions that had slowly developed over years. To put it in modern parlance, he believed we had "crowdsourced" wisdom from our ancestors. From the signing of Magna Carta in 1215, through the Glorious Revolution of 1688, until Burke's present day, Britain's tale had been one of gradual change, where history's arc slowly bent toward justice. Burke believed we must work hard to preserve these freedoms gradually won over time, so that we might continue this positive evolution of civilization into the future.

Burke's advocacy for reform and preference for "ordered liberty" attempted to balance competing, but not mutually exclusive, values. He wasn't opposed to change, yet his philosophy stood in sharp contrast to radical attempts of the Jacobins to cast off the yoke of history. Burke was not a "reactionary" or even a conservative who solely wanted to preserve the past; he believed it was our responsibility to use our accumulated wisdom to wisely and prudently continue moving forward. (Modern conservatives who admire Burke should not hearken for the supposed "good old days" of the 1950s but instead go "back to the future," as it were.)

Aside from Aristotle and Christian tradition, we can only conjecture about Burke's motivation and influences. It would be convenient if we had a "Rosebud" sled moment to shed some light on this and possibly turn his story into a neat narrative. While there are no obvious answers, theories exist, says Burke scholar Yuval Levin. "I think that Burke's upbringing in Ireland—his witnessing of how love can overcome deep differences of dogma (in his parents' mixed marriage, say) and how neighborly trust and affection can allow people to live together in seemingly impossible circumstances left him thinking that life was just much more complicated in practice than it could ever be in theory, and that this was a good thing."[13]

Burke's prescient concerns about the French Revolution were quickly confirmed when talk of the "Rights of Man" led to a Reign of Terror in 1793, as cries of "Liberty, Equality, Fraternity" gave way to cries from the guillotine. Eventually, the Revolution turned on itself. Paine, who had done much to boost the revolutionary fervor (first from America and later from France), ended up imprisoned in Paris. Even revolutionary leaders Danton, Saint-Just, and Robespierre went to the scaffold. The Revolution not only devoured its enemies; it ate its own. A dictator named Napoleon arose. The revolution's denouement played out much the way Burke expected (and Aristotle might have predicted).

Burke in the Twentieth Century

Burke's sounding of the alarm about the French Revolution became even more prescient to twentieth-century Americans—many of whom were introduced to him in the early 1950s, when Russell Kirk published his seminal book *The Conservative Mind*. The geopolitical and economic context was as pertinent then as it had been during Burke's own life, and Burke's warnings about uprooting long-held tradition and institutions were arguably even more relevant. Burke, in retrospect, looked even more like a Cassandra—someone who was prescient and ahead of his time. The French Revolution, it turned out, wasn't an anomaly, but presaged a bloody trend. After all, what was the Soviet Union if not the bastard child of the French Revolution?

In between Rousseau and Lenin was Karl Marx,[14] another intellectual who had invented an abstract dogma divorced from human experience—an alternative, historical narrative that led to significant bloodshed. The notion that Communism would be the final and inevitable stage of history was, like Rousseau's creation story, conceived ex nihilo. As a bonus, achieving this mythic resolution would require completely toppling nearly every traditional institution of civilization. Just as King Louis XVI and Marie Antoinette had met the guillotine, Russia's Tsar Nicholas II would be forced to abdicate and then, along with his wife and children, summarily stood up against a basement wall and executed in 1918. The state would have an ideological objective of eliminating religion and confiscating the property of the Russian Orthodox Church. In one fell swoop, the Bolsheviks would upend centuries of tradition and institutions that had been deeply ingrained into Russian lives. While most conservatives are inherently skeptical of top-down planning (because life is too complex for a handful of elites to game out), Communism espoused the efficiency of a centrally planned economy. Burke's warnings about the French Revolution not only proved prophetic for the time; they also anticipated the rise of the Soviet Union. If conservatives needed an intellectual hero to help guide them forward in the 1950s, who better than Burke?

Burkean Conservatism versus American Individualism

It's worth noting that American conservatives have never fully embraced the notion that *conserving* good things from our past defines conservatism. This is, no doubt, due in part to the fact that America began with a revolution. More than their European brethren, American conservatives tend to focus more on individual rights and liberty than on tradition or order or virtue. These values are not mutually exclusive, but their relative weight creates tension. While the Traditionalist wing of the conservative movement hews closely to a Burkean philosophy, the more libertarian wings of the movement do not. Craig Shirley and Don Devine argue that "modern American conservatism has roots in the ideas of philosopher John Locke, the founding fathers, and the notion that humans' natural state is freedom."[15] Burke, they argue, was wedded to a British system where power flowed downward rather than an American system where power flows upward. As Shirley also told me, "Reagan often quoted Paine. He rarely quoted Burke."

To illustrate how complicated and nuanced this debate can become, consider this question: Was Thomas Jefferson a conservative? Burkeans would say that Jefferson, a Deist and a Francophile, most surely was *not*. But Jefferson's emphasis on small government and agrarianism would probably fit in with today's conservative movement quite nicely. Indeed, if one takes a close look at the Tea Party movement, it's probably fair to say that today's American conservatives are perhaps closer to Jefferson and Paine than they are to Burke. I would argue that this dual alignment is indicative of the problem that this book aims to address. Others would see it as a prime example of American exceptionalism where even our version of what constitutes a conservative is uniquely individualistic.

There are other reasons why it's hard to define conservatism, and why the notion of preserving the good things of Western civilization lacks appeal for many. Some argue that a fetish for conserving the past is a rather nihilistic view that fails to take value judgments into account (just because something happened in the past certainly does not make it *good*). And even those who tout the importance of conserving the good things from the past may argue about *which* things are worth preserving (though the intent of the Founding Fathers, the Declaration of Independence, and the Constitution seem to be areas of obvious agreement). The absence of an agreed-upon definition of conservatism has negative consequences. If someone believes that the blessings of Western civilization were the product of ideas, he or she will come to different policy conclusions than someone who (I would argue, incorrectly) thinks a white racial majority is the key— or that the real battle is to preserve Jeffersonian agrarianism and that the yeoman farmer was the key to virtue and independence. Or, perhaps a conservative is someone who wants to conserve changes that just a generation ago were seen as radical. Perhaps a modern conservative is someone who wants to return us to the liberal consensus that dominated American thinking in the 1950s and early 60s. This brings to mind the G. K. Chesterton quote: "The whole modern world has divided itself into Conservatives and Progressives. The business of Progressives is to go on making mistakes. The business of Conservatives is to prevent mistakes from being corrected." This lack of a foundational philosophical agreement has led to the confusion and contradictions that now confront conservatives.

Writing about Burke presents another dilemma; radicals such as Paine and Rousseau present a more gripping biography. Just as their philosophy was romantic, their eccentric lives consisted of drama and turmoil. Conservatism, like Burke's life, is comparably boring and complex. To fully appreciate it requires going back to assumptions regarding human nature and the rise of civilization, not to mention comprehending the long-term implications that come from the chipping away of traditional institutions. But in a short-attention-span world where action is admired and simple solutions are required, the fact that one cannot easily sum up Burke's philosophy and slap it on a bumper sticker ("Stability We Can Believe In!" somehow doesn't cut it) poses a challenge for us. Then again, maybe his slogan could simply be summed up with the words *I told you so.*

The Rise of the American Conservative Movement

For most of American history, we have been a culturally conservative people, with strong religious traditions and deep resistance to decadence. Customs, mores, and values were decidedly conservative. In terms of economic liberty, no permanent or constitutional national income tax existed until 1913. There was also a prevailing sense that America's two great oceans could insulate us from the ideologies and entanglements of the world.

Events such as World War I, the 1925 Scopes Monkey Trial, and the Great Depression would shake our traditional collective perceptions about existence and our place in the world. America didn't become more liberal overnight. There were fits and starts. In the early twentieth century, progressive presidents such as Theodore Roosevelt and Woodrow Wilson began changing the size and scope and raison d'être of the federal government. Though this resulted in a brief conservative backlash ("normalcy"), most personified by Presidents Warren G. Harding and Calvin Coolidge, it was Franklin Roosevelt who landed the decisive knockout punch. With the Great Depression giving him wide leeway, FDR dramatically transformed Washington, creating a previously unthinkable welfare state. In a few short years, he increased the number of Americans dependent on the federal government while simultaneously redistributing income, encroaching on civil liberties, and implementing new ideas such as income tax withholding. While Roosevelt repeatedly won reelection, not everyone was happy—his margin of victory in later terms became much thinner. By the late 1930s, the New Deal had stalled. It was in this context that a nascent conservative movement began making inroads.

Because America remained culturally conservative until at least the 1960s, and because the Democrats were seen as more bellicose on foreign policy (remember, Democratic presidents presided over World War I, World War II, and Korea and, prior to the bombing of Pearl Harbor, the "Old Right" strain in the Republican Party was decidedly isolationist), modern conservatism's first breakthrough was fiscal. It rejected the New Deal welfare state[16]—instead advocating a return to the free markets that had transformed nineteenth-century America into an industrial powerhouse. Austrian immigrant Friedrich Hayek arguably provided this movement with its most significant voice. His 1944 masterpiece, *The Road to Serfdom*, emerged as a classic in the conservative canon. Arguing that central planning inexorably leads to authoritarianism, while competition and free markets spur economic growth, the book gained immense prominence after *Reader's Digest* published a condensed version.

Unlike most of today's contributions to conservative literature—which often seem to consist primarily of semi-comedic, off-color shtick from pundits, tomes ghostwritten for candidates, or demagogic polemics by talk radio hosts—*The Road to Serfdom* was a complex book about economics written by a foreigner, and the public gobbled it up. (In 2014, the Left turned obscure French economist Thomas Piketty's book *Capital in the Twenty-First Century* into a surprise best seller. But the current lack of anything from the Right that resembles Hayek's or Piketty's success suggests a problem.)

Though there was a hunger for free market ideas in 1944, Hayek and other likeminded twentieth-century economists[17] were really just updating a principle first preached by Adam Smith in his 1776 work *The Wealth of Nations.* By now, the heavy hand of government had replaced Smith's "invisible hand," a metaphor that suggested that competition and the pursuit of self-interest organically leads to salutary social benefits. Smith's ideas (sometimes called by the confusing name "classical liberalism") might have been utterly consistent with America's founding principles, but they were a radical departure in the mid-twentieth century, where the liberal intelligentsia had replaced Smith with economists such as John Maynard Keynes, who espoused liberal economic principles.

It's worth noting that Hayek did not label himself as a conservative, and his economic philosophy has only shaped one leg of the "three-legged stool" of modern conservatism. The two other coalition blocs were the anti-Communists (thought of today as national security or defense hawks) and the Traditionalists (sometimes used interchangeably with "social conservative," though there are nuanced distinctions). Each of these disparate wings began as intellectual movements. Although social conservatives sometimes get a bad rap, they make a very serious argument that goes back to antiquity: a good civilization must contain virtue, charity, community, ethics, honor, and a moral order. America's Founders believed that only a people who exhibit these traits could preserve our form of government.

Foreign Policy Becomes the "Glue"

Prior to World War II, the GOP and the "Old Right" were essentially isolationist entities that worried about balanced budgets and supported protective tariffs at home. But Pearl Harbor, the struggle against Nazi fascism in the 1940s, and the subsequent rise of the Soviet Union's Iron Curtain, rendered the isolationist worldview untenable, and the subsequent rise of America as a global economic power proved protectionism obsolete. With the rise of the Soviet Union after World War II, foreign policy positions were increasingly scrambled. Democrats were split into three factions: doves who wanted détente with the Communists, anti-Communist moderates who pursued a mix of diplomacy and military responses designed to "contain" the spread of the Soviet empire, and a diminishing band of Scoop Jackson Democrats (hawks named after the New Dealer who gamely ran for the Democratic presidential nomination in the 1970s despite his stubborn support for the Vietnam War).

Meanwhile—whether out of necessity or because the new political realities had opened their eyes to the fact that America could not retreat from the world—conservative Republicans evolved into fervent hawks, a development today's anti-interventionist, libertarian-leaning conservatives lament. Electorally, this evolution turned out to be incredibly fortuitous. For decades the struggle against Communism served as the glue binding the disparate elements of the conservative movement (which helps explain the problems conservatives have faced since the fall of the Berlin Wall, and why there was some belief that the war on terror might replace it). Each wing of the conservative movement had valid reasons for putting aside their petty differences and uniting to confront this existential threat. Fiscal conservatives railed against the Soviet's anticapitalist system of central planning. Christians despised the Godless atheistic empire and its gulags.[18] And for national security conservatives, there was obvious reason to fear the "Red Menace"—especially once they started pointing nukes at us.

Intellectual conservatives, too, argued that the Soviet Union posed an existential threat, and that the rise of the Iron Curtain necessitated an aggressive foreign policy to stop and roll back, not merely contain, the spread of Communism. They, of course, would not only win this argument, but also, eventually, the Cold War. For the purpose of concise retelling, I want to focus on perhaps the most prominent and important: Whittaker Chambers, whose tortured soul revealed more than the stakes involved in the anti-Communist fight.

Leaving "the Winning Side"

Now, you might think that an intellectual editor and writer for *Time* magazine—who had also served as a Communist spy and acknowledged he had numerous homosexual experiences—might make for an odd hero for the foreign policy wing of the conservative movement. In fact, you might think that, if this were fiction, this plot point would be thrown out on the grounds that nobody would believe it. But that's where this story begins.

Born Jay Vivian Chambers (Whittaker was his mother's maiden name) in 1901, Chambers emerged from a dysfunctional Brooklyn family. Defining biographical details include his grandmother's insanity and his brother's suicide—chaotic turns that seem to have made him susceptible to the authoritarian nature of Communism. But Chambers's brush with history began in August of 1948, when the House Un-American Activities Committee (HUAC) summoned Chambers, then a senior editor at *Time*, to verify the testimony of Soviet spy Elizabeth Bentley. With painful personal reluctance, Chambers testified that he knew Alger Hiss, who had served in the State Department under FDR, when the two were fellow Communists a decade earlier. Hiss was no low-level functionary. He accompanied Roosevelt to the infamous Yalta conference, where some critics felt a dying president gave away Eastern Europe to Stalin. He was also the secretary-general of the 1945 San Francisco Conference that created the United Nations.

Hiss was eventually convicted of perjury, and while debate persists over whether or not he was a Soviet spy, the preponderance of evidence suggests Chambers was correct. The Hiss trial, coupled with the Rosenberg atomic spy case that followed in the early 1950s, made it increasingly difficult for anyone to argue that Communist infiltration wasn't at least a potentially serious problem. Aside from the obvious national security implications, the Hiss affair also suggested that liberal intellectuals were being manipulated and turned into unwitting dupes or "useful idiots." As Chambers wrote in his book, *Witness*, "While Communists make full use of liberals and their solicitudes, and sometimes flatter them to their faces, in private they treat them with that sneering contempt that the strong and predatory almost invariably feel for victims who volunteer to help in their own victimization."

To most Americans, the Soviets had become an existential threat. Supporting their ideology was tantamount to treason, and whichever political party could be the most anti-Communist would stand a better chance of winning future elections, and, presumably, the future. The fight against Communism turned out to be a winner for conservatives—despite Senator Joseph McCarthy's infamous and sometimes demagogic Red-baiting, which ultimately led to his downfall—and a loser for liberal intellectuals. Ultimately, America would win the Cold War—a result Chambers did not envision, as he told the House in 1948 that he feared he was "leaving the winning side for the losing side."[19]

But Chambers's contribution didn't end there. The Hiss ordeal also turned him into an influential public intellectual, whose writing shaped the foreign policy thinking of conservatism. *Witness*, published in 1952, remains an important contribution to the conservative canon. But he also became suspicious of what he called the "crackpotism"[20] of the Right. In 1957, Chambers's harsh review of Ayn Rand's *Atlas Shrugged* in *National Review* essentially wrote her out of the conservative movement (Rand would never forgive *NR* founder Bill Buckley). "Out of a lifetime of reading," Chambers declared of Rand's classic, "I can recall no other book in which a tone of overriding arrogance was so implacably sustained. Its shrillness is without reprieve. Its dogmatism is without appeal." (If only he were still around to review Ann Coulter's latest book.) Conservative publisher Alfred S. Regnery enshrined Chambers's place in the conservative movement in his book, *Upstream*, noting, "Chambers planted the intellectual moorings for American conservatives that would last into the twenty-first century."

"More than the intrigue, more than the spy case, more than the vivid confrontation between the traitor and the patriot, the philosophical difference between East and West, between freedom and Communism, between God and godlessness, inspired the conservative movement," Regnery wrote. Chambers ultimately came to view the Cold War as a clash of two faiths—Godless Communism versus Christendom, which might also qualify him as a member of the third wing of the conservative movement: the traditionalists.

Thanks in part to Chambers, the conservative coalition was well equipped to criticize nearly every aspect of Communism. But if conservatism was to mean anything, it must also have a positive message. Fortunately, that was in the works.

The Rise of the Traditionalists

Today, it is fashionable for "thoughtful" conservatives to hearken back to Edmund Burke, even if they don't spend much time dwelling on why he's so important. In fact, it is somewhat of a cliché to suggest it's been all downhill since Burke. As policy analyst and *First Things* blogger Helen Rittelmeyer wrote in a 2013 *American Spectator* column, "The chart of that supposed decline, if you were to draw it *Ascent of Man* style, would start with Edmund Burke looking intelligent and walking upright, followed by William F. Buckley as Australopithecus, slouching. The present age would be represented by some knuckle-dragging, prognathous creature like Rush Limbaugh or Sean Hannity." That's not exactly fair to modern conservatives, but if Burke has become the hero of conservatism, it's at least partly because he had a great twentieth-century Boswell.

It was a young Michigan State professor named Russell Kirk who made the greatest contribution to presenting this positive definition of conservatism, helping give the cause its name, defining its positive attributes, and destigmatizing the term *conservative*. Published in 1953, Kirk's *The Conservative Mind* would become one of the most important works of the conservative canon, tracing the conservative tradition from Edmund Burke through to Kirk's time (including chapters on such diverse figures as John Adams and poet T. S. Eliot, who advocated reverence for what he called "the permanent things"). Had it done nothing else, Kirk's "fat book," as he called it, greatly contributed to reintroducing America to Burke, often thought of as the father of modern conservatism. (There's a fine line between brilliance and insanity, and Kirk was clearly an eccentric. He refused to drive, wore a cape, and apparently carried a sword cane. It's nice to know liberals aren't the only ones who know how to party.)

Traditionalism is in the spirit of Aristotle and Burke, in that it values an adherence to tradition and a sense that there is a transcendent moral order that must be preserved. For most of America's history, these were commonly held ideas. But in the post-World War II era—and especially with the rise of the hippie counterculture in the 1960s—these ideas would come under assault and eventually lose their standing as the default consensus opinions of Americans. In this environment, other conservative leaders arose who would sound the alarm[21]—but Kirk's contribution was unrivaled.

William F. Buckley

With Burke firmly ensconced as the historical model for conservatism, William F. Buckley Jr.—an upper-crust Catholic conservative with an Ivy League pedigree, a huge vocabulary, and a patrician accent—probably did more than anyone to fuse the various strands of conservative intellectual thought into a politically potent, and mostly coherent, force. The son of the former Aloïse Steiner of New Orleans and William F. Buckley Sr.—a self-made oil man who learned his lesson about governmental overreach when he was expelled from Mexico for opposing restrictions on American ownership of oil rights—the younger Buckley was adventurous and eccentric his entire life. In his younger years, Buckley did a two-year stint with the CIA in Mexico. In later years, legend has it that he sailed his yacht outside US territorial limits so he could smoke pot without breaking the law. He also ran for mayor of New York City in 1965, helping spread the conservative gospel in a decidedly urban environment. When asked what he would do should he actually win, Buckley famously quipped, "Demand a recount."

Buckley first bounded onto the scene while a student at Yale, when he published *God and Man at Yale* in 1951, alerting the school's alumni that their alma mater had degenerated into a breeding ground for anti-Christian, anticapitalism professors. To prove it, he named names. Reviews were mixed, and in some cases, brutal. Writing at the *Atlantic*, a Yale graduate named McGeorge Bundy (later national security adviser to Presidents Kennedy and Johnson) derided it as "a savage attack on that institution as a hotbed of 'atheism' and 'collectivism,'" dismissing it as "dishonest" and "false in its theory, and a discredit to its author." Others seemed to resent Buckley's aristocratic, charmed life. Writing at the *New York Times*, Peter Viereck observed, "Great conservatives—immortals like Burke, Alexander Hamilton, Disraeli, Churchill, Pope, and Swift—earned the right to be sunnily conservative by their long dark nights....You do not earn a heartfelt and conviction carrying conservatism by the shortcut of a popular campus clubman without the inspiring agony of lonely, unrespectable soul-searching."

Buckley proved a hardscrabble biography was not necessary to transform a movement. The creation of *National Review* in 1955—a magazine whose goal was to stand "athwart history, yelling Stop"— was among his greatest contributions. Prior to that, the Left had many notable periodicals, but the Right (save for a few outlets like the weekly newspaper *Human Events* and the fallen angel, the *American Mercury*) was essentially unarmed. So Buckley's magazine provided a source for like-minded conservatives around the nation seeking intellectual stimulation and ideas. It also provided—and this is not to be underestimated—a place for conservative opinion leaders to earn a living. Thanks to Buckley's bold vision, sharp pen, and impeccable intellectual credentials, the magazine forced the ideas espoused by conservatives like Whittaker Chambers, Richard Weaver, James Burnham, and Russell Kirk into the discourse of the intelligentsia.

Additionally, *National Review* provided a platform for uniting the disparate, and in the minds of some, mutually exclusive, elements of conservatism—an idea known as "fusionism," hatched and promoted by Buckley confidante Frank Meyer. In this important cause—a prerequisite to Reagan's election—Buckley and Meyer would mostly succeed in declaring a truce and a temporary alliance on the Right. What is more, in assuming the role as head of the de facto conservative "establishment," Buckley unilaterally assumed the moral authority to bestow a sort of seal of approval on those who qualified as mainstream conservatives and to revoke such status from fringe elements. Today, the world has changed, and leadership is more diffuse. In an increasingly democratized world where anyone can pontificate from a laptop at Starbucks, nobody needs the imprimatur of establishment-approved gatekeepers. And that means that nobody can uphold standards. In today's conservative movement, one would be hard-pressed to find any universally respected figure with the moral authority to write someone out of the movement.[22] Buckley, and by extension, *NR*, did exactly that to Ayn Rand *and* the conspiracy theory–laden John Birch Society,[23] the latter of which famously accused Republican president Dwight D. Eisenhower of Communist sympathies. ("Ike's not a communist, he's a golfer," quipped Russell Kirk—a quote Buckley widely disseminated.) Though Buckley did much to excommunicate the Right of its unseemly elements, he was not without blemish. It's fair to say that Buckley's early opposition to the civil rights movement stands as a mark of shame on an otherwise sterling legacy.

Aside from purging the movement of its cranks, Buckley was also instrumental in helping boost young conservative activists into the fold. (After all, politics is a game of addition, not subtraction.)

The founding statement of principles of the group Young Americans for Freedom (YAF), called the "Sharon Statement," was written at Buckley's Sharon, Connecticut, family compound.[24] It was another confidante, *National Review* publisher Bill Rusher, who deserves some credit for focusing Buckley on activism, political dynamics, and movement building. "Without William A. Rusher," conservative leader Morton Blackwell told me,[25] "William F. Buckley would have thought and acted as if being right [by this, he means being philosophically correct] is sufficient to win."

And if policing the conservative movement and helping a new generation of conservatives—or creating a magazine for intellectually minded conservatives—wasn't enough, Buckley also hosted a highbrow PBS TV show called *Firing Line* for *thirty-three years*. It would be nearly impossible for a young person (accustomed to YouTube clips or today's cable news "shout fest" format) to conceive of a show where an aristocratic conservative interviewed such diverse luminaries as economist Friedrich Hayek, liberal author Norman Mailer, beat writer Jack Kerouac, Ronald Reagan, Hugh Hefner, or Mother Teresa (all of whom appeared on his program). Buckley's show was renowned enough to warrant parody by Robin Williams on *Saturday Night Live*. Whether it was his unlikely friendship with Mailer or his famous feuds with Gore Vidal, Buckley proved that conservatives were intellectually equipped to go toe-to-toe against any liberal intellectual of the twentieth century.

Buckley was so significant that during a 2005 interview with conservative columnist George Will (marking the fiftieth anniversary of *NR*'s founding),[26] the latter told the former, "Let me invite you to take credit for winning the Cold War. The argument goes like this: Without Bill Buckley, no *National Review*. Without the *National Review*, no Goldwater nomination. Without the Goldwater nomination, no conservative takeover of the Republican Party. Without that, no Reagan. Without Reagan, no victory in the Cold War. Therefore, Bill Buckley won the Cold War."

Barry Goldwater's 1964 Campaign

If Buckley embodied twentieth-century conservative intellectualism, Barry Goldwater ignited today's debilitating conservative anti-intellectualism. Not that Goldwater *wanted* it that way. Had President John F. Kennedy not been gunned down that fateful November day in 1963, it is very possible the 1964 presidential campaign would have been a much different affair. As good friends, Kennedy and Goldwater had even discussed campaigning jointly—imagine an alternative history where the two opponents had conducted a series of "Lincoln-Douglas"-style debates. The whole race might have been high-minded and philosophical. But Kennedy's assassination changed everything. President Lyndon Johnson and his team would essentially invent the negative TV commercial—one of which, the infamous "Daisy" ad, suggested that a Goldwater presidency would trigger nuclear annihilation. It was the most cynical sort of politics. And sadly, it worked.

Before he was caricatured by the Johnson campaign, Goldwater rocketed to the Republican nomination, in part because of his 1960 best seller, *The Conscience of a Conservative* (ghostwritten by William F. Buckley's brother-in-law L. Brent Bozell). When one thinks of the poll-tested, talking point–laden pre-campaign books by recent presidential hopefuls like Mitt Romney or Scott Walker, it's hard to even conceive of a nascent presidential candidate releasing a philosophical treatise like Goldwater's.

But Goldwater had a fatal flaw: an inability to balance his intelligence and philosophical commitments with wisdom and prudence. His famous line, delivered during his 1964 Republican National Convention acceptance speech, is a prime example. "I would remind you," he roared, "that extremism in the defense of liberty is no vice. And let me remind you also that moderation in the pursuit of justice is no virtue."[27] This was an utterly coherent and defensible statement. It was also politically stupid, inasmuch as it reinforced Johnson's narrative that Goldwater was a crazy fringe candidate.[28] And it wasn't the only time Goldwater played to type. Regarding nukes, Goldwater gibed, "Let's lob one into the men's room at the Kremlin." Even without Goldwater's help, Johnson's team found ways to reinforce their narrative. The Johnson team parodied Goldwater's slogan, "In your heart you know he's right," as "In your guts you know he's nuts."

Goldwater got crushed, winning only six states, and garnering just 38 percent of the vote. But, as previously discussed, his candidacy also launched Ronald Reagan's long march to the presidency, and Goldwater's breakthrough in the previously Democratic South also helped shape future Republican electoral strategy. (In a later chapter, we will discuss how this influence was a double-edged sword.) And something else happened: many of Goldwater's young supporters and activists began studying how to win. In doing so, they coupled political philosophy with campaign know-how and political technology, based on the assumption that (as conservative leader Morton Blackwell[29] teaches) "you owe it to your philosophy to study how to win." The next phase of the conservative movement was upon us.

Another tragic and significant effect of the Kennedy assassination was the radicalization of the Left. JFK was a tax-cutting anti-Communist. Within a few years of his death, the Left would radicalize, and JFK's hawkish brand of politics would become a rarity in the Democratic Party.

The Real Nature of Politics and Elections

From Goldwater's drubbing at the hands of Johnson's scurrilous campaign, conservatives learned to fight fire with fire—politics wasn't merely about a battle of ideas; it turned out to be also about a contest of technology and fund-raising and organizing and campaigning and, yes, going negative.

In 1964, liberalism was considered the de facto philosophy of America. Literary critic Lionel Trilling had already written that "in the United States at this time liberalism is not only the dominant but even the sole intellectual tradition."[30] That would quickly change, and not entirely by accident. While some Goldwater supporters grew disenchanted with politics, others decided to document the lessons learned and apply them to future races. The youngest elected Goldwater delegate was Morton Blackwell, who went on to found the Leadership Institute.[31] In a lecture called "The Real Nature of Politics," Blackwell draws on the lessons of Goldwater's loss and juxtaposes them with Reagan's landslide victory just sixteen years later. Although conceding numerous variables, Blackwell argues that "the difference was that we Goldwater supporters tended to believe that being right, in the sense of being correct, was sufficient to win.... That's not the real nature of politics." He then reminds students of Goldwater's slogan, "In your heart, you know he's right." "Unfortunately the real world doesn't work that way," he adds, "as we who supported Goldwater found out when Lyndon Johnson trounced us."

Johnson's strategic decision to "nuke" Goldwater lifted the scales from quixotic conservative eyes. No longer believing you could win simply *with* your ideas, conservatives came to accept the reality that you must study how to win *because* of your ideas. To some, such as Blackwell, this simply meant learning how to more effectively participate in democracy. To others, it meant that the ends justified the means—that politics was a form of war.

Though many of these ex-Goldwater activists were intellectuals in their own right—a stark contrast to some of today's activists— movement leaders like Paul Weyrich, Morton Blackwell, Richard Viguerie, and Phyllis Schlafly would devote much of their lives to mastering the machinery of politics, such as how to win elections, build coalitions, and create an infrastructure of think tanks and nonprofits. The primary beneficiary of this devotion would be Ronald Reagan. In this light, Goldwater's candidacy proved a sort of trial run, and Goldwater would be a forerunner—a John the Baptist who came out of the Sonoran Desert, eating locusts and wild honey, basically doing campaign advance work for the future conservative savior, Ronald Reagan. (Ironically, this John the Baptist would later turn Judas, supporting Richard Nixon over Reagan in 1968, Nixon over John Ashbrook in 1972, and Gerald Ford over Reagan in 1976— but that's another story.)

Conservatism Was Smart

In the beginning, conservatism was smart. It can be again. Part of the problem is that conservatism today is too often defined by what it is *not*. It's anti-tax, anti-big government, or anti-abortion. This framing, unfortunately, fails to capture the positive attributes of conservatism or its fundamental worldview. You might not agree with conservative philosophy, but it's undeniable that the story of the rise of the conservative movement—from Burke to Buckley—is one of big, thoughtful ideas that address serious existential questions about human nature and the rise of civilization. Conservatism is about conserving the good things about Western civilization. It's about a rejection of utopian schemes and moral relativism—a humble acceptance that life is too complex for elites to plan. It's the belief that Western civilization didn't merely happen, but was instead the result of the accumulated wisdom of our ancestors. It's about a realization that Western civilization and its institutions evolved naturally, and that long-standing traditions must be preserved.

2

RONALD REAGAN:
A STUDENT AND A STAR

★ ★ ★

"Reagan was better read and better educated than we were."
—Robert Novak

More than a decade after his death and a quarter century after he left the White House, Ronald Reagan still looms large. Recent books about Reagan explore his leadership style, his faith, his days as spokesman for General Electric, his time in Hollywood—you name it. There are great biographies such as the trilogy from Lou Cannon, not-so-great ones like the oddly semi-fictional *Dutch* by Edmund Morris, and everything in between. You could fill a library with books about Reagan. *My* bookshelves are full of books about him. Why not? He was the greatest president of my lifetime and the only full-fledged modern "movement" conservative ever elected president. The Gipper managed to restore optimism in America after years of malaise. And he won the Cold War. Not bad for a graduate of tiny Eureka College whom former secretary of defense Clark Clifford once dismissed as an "amiable dunce."

But a largely untold story is that Reagan observers were mostly blind to his intelligence and scholarship, a factor that, along with his relentlessly sunny demeanor, allowed him to repeatedly mystify friends and foes alike and win campaigns and public policy battles. Between 1976—the year he lost the Republican primary to the incumbent president, Gerald Ford—and his successful presidential bid in 1980, Reagan delivered daily radio messages, which he personally wrote (you can find them in the book *Reagan, in His Own Hand*). "These are earnest policy sermons," David Brooks wrote in a *New York Times* book review. "Reagan covered everything from bilingual education to the Panama Canal to the political situation in Equatorial Guinea, engrossing himself in a level of detail that frankly surpasses that of almost all op-ed columnists today." Brooks then continued, "In 1978, for example, he came across a speech the Yale law professor Eugene Rostow gave on the proposed SALT II arms control agreement. Reagan couldn't do just one radio commentary summarizing and commenting on Rostow's views. He did six, going through the arcana about mobile launchers, MIRVs, Minutemen versus MX missiles and so on." This both dismantles the notion that Reagan was merely an "actor" reading a script and also serves to juxtapose his substantive commentary with the sort of "shock" radio format that came to define much of conservative talk radio in the twenty-first century.

The Education of a Would-Be President

Reagan's political accomplishments were the result of a man who, for decades, took ideas seriously. Long before being elected president, he was boning up on policy and philosophy. During his General Electric days, "Reagan needed to keep his material fresh, so he would load steamer trunks full of books and news articles and read them in the long hours traveling across the country, rather than going to the Club Car to knock back drinks with the other businessmen," says Reagan biographer Craig Shirley. "He traveled a long road from bleeding-heart liberal to populist conservative and an important part of that maturation process was his self-education—autodidact—on board those trains through all those years."[32] All that reading made a huge difference. And the good news is, he kept the books. Bearing witness to this fact, Lee Edwards, an unofficial historian of the American conservative movement, has recounted a 1965 visit he made to the Reagan home when Reagan was contemplating running for governor of California. At one point during the visit, Edwards availed himself of an opportunity to secretly peruse Reagan's bookshelves.

"I went over and began looking at the titles,"[33] he said. "They were history, biography, economics, politics. All serious stuff. I began pulling the books out of the shelves and looking at them," Edwards attested. "They were dog-eared. They were annotated. They were smudged by his fingers, and so forth. This was a man who had read hundreds of books. It was clear that he had read them, had digested them, and had studied them," he continued. "I knew right away, this was a thinking conservative. This was a man who loved ideas. He was comfortable with ideas and was able to take ideas and translate them into a common idiom."

Indeed, Reagan not only consumed the ideas of great conservative thinkers but also adapted them for his authentically American worldview. What is more, it's equally impressive that he never stopped welcoming such counsel from smart conservatives. One of the most significant turned out to be Representative Jack Kemp, then a back-bench Buffalo congressman and a former NFL star quarterback who was the antithesis of a dumb jock. Shaped by a wealth of diverse life experiences, Kemp advocated an uplifting conservative philosophy that was at least partly the product of his experience with diverse Americans. Newt Gingrich once quipped that "Jack Kemp has showered with more black Americans than most Republicans have ever met." And it was during the interregnum between Reagan's failed 1976 bid and his successful 1980 run that Kemp introduced Reagan to an innovative policy idea called supply-side economics, a school of thought that argues that lower taxes broaden the tax base, sometimes resulting in more revenue, which clicked with Reagan's innate optimism. Previously, Reagan, like the entire GOP, had been a "green eyeshade party"—pessimistic bean counters worried about deficits and balanced budgets. Those were fine things to be concerned with, but it also implied a zero-sum world where we were all fighting over limited resources. Thanks to Kemp, Reagan changed that paradigm, and the implications were huge. Who would have thought an ex-quarterback and a former actor would be among the GOP's most significant politicians?

And Reagan's interest in conservative philosophy and economics didn't end once he became president, either. In his terrific memoir, *The Prince of Darkness*, reporter and columnist Robert Novak recalled how he and his partner, Rowland Evans, were taken aback during a meeting with Reagan in which the president dazzled them with his knowledge of relatively obscure economic philosophers:

> Describing himself as a "voracious reader," Reagan cited nineteenth-century British free trade advocates John Bright and Richard Cobden and twentieth-century Austrian free market economists Ludwig von Mises and Fredrick von Hayek. He also said, "Bastiat has dominated my thinking so much." Bastiat? Rowly and I had to look him up. Claude Frédéric Bastiat (1801–1850) was a French political economist who preached against protectionism and socialism.... Reagan was better read and better educated than we were.

Reagan as an "Amiable Dunce"?

"Stupid is as stupid does," the title character of the film *Forrest Gump* famously averred. This means worldly intelligence isn't about the trappings of intellect, but instead, the proof's in the pudding. If

Ronald Reagan was stupid, then perhaps we should elect more like him?

This sentiment was captured well in a 2004 *Washington Post* column by journalist Howell Raines. "In 1981 Clark Clifford, the Democratic 'wise man,' entertained Georgetown dinner parties with the killer line that Reagan was 'an amiable dunce,' " recalled Raines. "Twenty years later we know that Clark Clifford was charged in a banking scandal and the dunce ended the Cold War."

Ultimately, Reagan's *accomplishments* are why we even know about his brand of conservatism. Had he simply faded into that good night after his primary loss to incumbent president Gerald Ford in 1976—or had an assassin's bullet strangled the conservative movement's baby in the crib—history would have been completely different, and Reagan's rhetoric, optimism, and intellect would have been largely lost to history. Or had Reagan's tenure not been marked by peace and prosperity, he might have served as a warning, not a role model, for aspiring conservative thinkers and leaders.

This raises an interesting question: Although it is widely understood today that Reagan was a great or near-great president, why was he continually derided as an "amiable dunce" during his tenure? To be sure, diminishing the intellect of a powerful Republican was and still is standard operating procedure for Democrats. That explains part of it, but the other reason is that Reagan benefited politically from being underestimated. I'm not suggesting he was faking his everyman persona—although there is reason to believe he certainly magnified it.[34]

Even some members of his own administration grappled with understanding the man. For example Bud McFarlane, the national security adviser, once said of Reagan, "He knows so little and accomplishes so much."[35] Likewise, even friendly journalists (the few who weren't inherently hostile to a Republican) were befuddled by Reagan. After a meeting with the president that yielded little news or insight, columnist Charles Krauthammer complained. "I don't get it," he told a *Washington Post* colleague as they left a White House lunch meeting together. "This is the most successful president of my lifetime, but he presents himself as a very simple man who's sort of out of it. What's going on?"

It's worth noting that Reagan's ability to feign this everyman persona was so effective that it confounded even those considered brilliant political observers. "It took me years to realize that that's how he preferred to present himself," Krauthammer, by then a conservative columnist, recalled.[36] "And it was really a function of his strength. He had no need to show himself to be smart...and he just wanted to tell stories, deflect me, and charm me. And it was part of his persona.... He never had to show himself to be the smartest guy in the room." Then, citing a famous *Saturday Night Live* skit that portrayed a shrewd and Machiavellian Reagan posing as a simpleton in front of the press, Krauthammer continued: "It's wise to be underestimated. That was part of Reagan's great political talent."

So where did this talent come from? "Reagan, when he was in elementary or junior high school, figured out that the smartest guy in class is not the most popular guy in class," explained journalist Fred Barnes, recalling a theory that had been bandied about by Reagan intimates.[37] "Reagan realized he wanted to be the most popular guy...and Reagan fashioned this person who doesn't appear that smart—but really a common man who fit in with the American people.... It worked marvelously, and got him elected."

Much has been made about the fact that Reagan, being the son of an alcoholic, fell into the role of family peacemaker. And from his time as a lifeguard, to his days in Hollywood—where he was almost always cast as a hero—Reagan, unlike Barry Goldwater, clearly had a deep need to be liked. To some degree, he seems to have made a conscious choice to accentuate his likability at the expense of stressing his intellectual side. Electorally speaking, it was a brilliant decision.

Reagan's Brand of Cosmopolitan Conservatism

Possessing an intentionally underrated intellect wasn't the Gipper's only secret weapon for political success. Reagan came to politics from Hollywood, which provided a cosmopolitan sheen that balanced his Midwestern upbringing and the Western cowboy image he assiduously cultivated. (In fact, the aforementioned nickname comes from Reagan's portrayal of Notre Dame football player George "the Gipper" Gipp in *Knute Rockney, All American*.)

His days hosting a TV show called *General Electric Theater* were vital to his evolution from Democrat to Republican. Reagan toured GE's 139 plants, where he met more than 250,000 employees, delivered speeches, and engaged in Q&A sessions with factory workers. His visits buttressed his populist appeal and served as a sort of extended focus group for understanding the plight of the average man. *That* is widely understood. Less understood—and perhaps more interesting for our purposes—is that Reagan's time hobnobbing with Hollywood elites, starlets, liberals, artists, and even gays (Reagan was publicly opposed to the Briggs Initiative, also known as Proposition 6—which would have banned gays and lesbians from working in California public schools) contributed to his ability to talk intelligently and comfortably to a certain type of American cognoscenti with whom many conservatives would feel out of place.

In public, though, Reagan diligently downplayed his urbane side in favor of cultivating the "everyman" image. He campaigned for president by running *against* Washington, but once he became president, at least some of his success in office can be traced to his efforts to woo elected officials, as well as some of Washington's upper crust. Chris Matthews recalled Reagan's whirlwind courting of DC elites in his book *Hardball*:

> The first thing Reagan did after being elected was attend a
> series of well-planned gatherings in the homes of the capital's

most prominent journalists, lawyers, and business people. The initial event was a party for the president-elect and his wife, Nancy, given at the F Street Club. The guests were the "usual suspects" of Washington political society; in other words, they were mostly Democrats. "I decided it was time to serve notice that we're residents," Reagan told the *Washington Post*'s Elisabeth Bumiller. "We wanted to get to know some people in Washington." They went to dinner at the home of conservative columnist George Will, where they met Katharine Graham, publisher of the *Post* and bête noire of recent Republican administrations. Next, they attended a party thrown by Mrs. Graham at her home in Georgetown. All this sent a clear signal: the Reagans and their people had come to join Washington society, not scorn it.

Matthews, who worked for Reagan foes such as Jimmy Carter and Tip O'Neill before becoming a liberal MSNBC host, notes that Reagan's "social courtship paid lasting dividends" for Reagan. And in what now sounds prophetic considering the obstructionism and gridlock in Washington (*Hardball* was written in 1988), Matthews laments, "The problem with new-breed pols is that in learning the skills of broadcasting they have forgotten the skills of schmoozing." Schmoozing, of course, has a negative connotation—like the word *networking*—and evokes images of smoke-filled backrooms and back-slapping politicians who don't stand for anything. But one man's schmoozing is another man's fellowshipping. And at least one cause of Washington's current dysfunction is that politicians no longer build strong friendships and relationships with colleagues on both sides of the aisle—or the people who cover them.

Reagan wasn't alone in using elite social currency to advance his conservative cause. From Austrian immigrants like Hayek to swashbuckling aristocrats like Bill Buckley, cosmopolitan conservatives have probably done as much to advance the cause as their more provincial counterparts, such as Tom DeLay, Jesse Helms, Robert Taft, et al. But just as Reagan intentionally downplayed his intelligence, he also downplayed his cosmopolitan background in favor of a more rustic image. For example, while there is little doubt Reagan liked to ride horses and cut brush at the Western White House, he and his team assiduously cultivated his rugged cowboy image. In 1966, a San Francisco reporter wanted to interview Reagan, then a candidate for governor of California. The idea was to get a glimpse of him at his ranch. But prior to the journalist's arrival, Reagan aide Lyn Nofziger—who himself had been a reporter—noticed the future president was wearing English riding boots. Sensing this would make the candidate look effete, Nofziger sent Reagan back inside to put on some Western riding clothes. Thus the image of Reagan as cowboy was born.[38] Nofziger's gut was right. He was simply recognizing a deep-seated American affinity for the cowboy. Writing about Theodore Roosevelt in 1899, *Harper's Weekly*[39] declared, "[The American public] are fond of the picture of the man on horseback—whether he is riding after Spaniards or grizzlies or steers, whether he is a soldier, hunter, or ranchman." Some things never change.

This penchant for playing up his cowboy image followed Reagan into the White House. For example, White House press secretary Marlin Fitzwater wanted to release the list of nonfiction books he was devouring, in order to undermine the notion that all the president read was Louis L'Amour Westerns. Reagan wouldn't allow it. "Reagan did not want to change and have people think that he's some highfalutin guy reading books with a lot of footnotes," Fred Barnes later speculated. The public kept on imagining Reagan was reading cowboy books.

The Great Communicator

It has become conventional wisdom that Reagan was a great communicator, but those who recall him as a folksy grandfather seem to forget that he earned the title of "the Great Communicator" not just with middlebrow relatability, but also with soaring poetic oratory. This thoroughly literate man used the full power of words to summon big ideas, transform the nation, inspire the world, challenge us and our enemies, and comfort a nation during some trying times.

Reagan's rhetoric was not the sort of intellectual talk that lacks moral clarity. The man who averred, "Tear down this wall!" and called the Soviet Union an "evil empire" could hardly be accused of such a thing. By the same token, though, it wasn't the sort of dumbed-down, red meat rhetoric that assumes we are a nation of rubes, either. Today, even the best politicians are usually skilled in displaying only one style of temperament. Some are masters at communicating indignation (Ted Cruz) *or* inspiration (Marco Rubio), but few can switch hit for a high batting average. Reagan was a master at both. He had Midwestern bona fides as a boy from Dixon, Illinois, who had worked in Iowa and toured GE factories—but who was simultaneously a movie star. He could play the populist card, and also appeal to our better angels. He could tell jokes and parables about average folks, but also quote poetry.

Some critics dismiss Reagan's rhetorical skills by suggesting he was just an actor reciting lines—or by assigning much of the credit to his speechwriters, most notably the terrific Peggy Noonan. But all modern presidents have writers, and once a president delivers a speech, it is *his* speech. (One deserves credit for having the good sense to surround oneself with topflight writers who can capture his vision.) Reagan alone deserves credit for having put in the intellectual work required to develop a coherent political worldview. If writers could help fine-tune this philosophy to fit a specific occasion in eloquent fashion, so much the better. Nobody begrudged John F. Kennedy for surrounding himself with some of the best and brightest speechwriters.

One could write an entire book simply by culling Reagan's oeuvre for greatest hits, but I'll focus on two of my favorite speeches, each aimed at important occasions: the fortieth anniversary of D-day, and the *Challenger* disaster.

Let's start with the D-day anniversary speech on June 6, 1984:

We stand on a lonely, windswept point on the northern shore of France. The air is soft, but forty years ago at this moment, the air was dense with smoke and the cries of men, and the air was filled with the crack of rifle fire and the roar of cannon. At dawn, on the morning of the 6th of June, 1944, 225 Rangers jumped off the British landing craft and ran to the bottom of these cliffs. Their mission was one of the most difficult and daring of the invasion: to climb these sheer and desolate cliffs and take out the enemy guns. The Allies had been told that some of the mightiest of these guns were here and they would be trained on the beaches to stop the Allied advance.... These are the boys of Pointe du Hoc. These are the men who took the cliffs. These are the champions who helped free a continent. These are the heroes who helped end a war.

Gentlemen, I look at you and I think of the words of Stephen Spender's poem. You are men who in your "lives fought for life…and left the vivid air signed with your honor."

Note the vivid imagery: the "lonely, windswept point" and the "cries of men" and the "crack of rifle fire." And note the use of poetry, in this case Stephen Spender's words—something missing in most of today's soulless, utilitarian, or technocratic political rhetoric. And note the original poetic flourishes: "These are the boys of Pointe du Hoc." At another event commemorating the anniversary, Reagan would share the story of a soldier who fought at D-day, and of his surviving daughter who was there in the soldier's stead:

> "Someday, Lis, I'll go back," said Private First Class Peter Robert Zanatta, of the Thirty-Seventh Engineer Combat Battalion, and first assault wave to hit Omaha Beach. "I'll go back, and I'll see it all again. I'll see the beach, the barricades, and the graves."
>
> Those words of Private Zanatta come to us from his daughter, Lisa Zanatta Henn, in a heart-rending story about the event her father spoke of so often. "In his words, the Normandy invasion would change his life forever," she said. She tells some of his stories of World War II but says of her father, "The story to end all stories was D-day."
>
> "He made me feel the fear of being on that boat waiting to land. I can smell the ocean and feel the seasickness. I can see the looks on his fellow soldiers' faces—the fear, the anguish, the uncertainty of what lay ahead. And when they landed, I can feel the strength and courage of the men who took those first steps through the tide to what must have surely looked like instant death."
>
> Private Zanatta's daughter wrote to me, "I don't know how or why I can feel this emptiness, this fear, or this determination, but I do. Maybe it's the bond I had with my father. All I know is that it brings tears to my eyes to think about my father as a twenty-year-old boy having to face that beach."

Here we have the blending of emotion with intelligence, of sincere appreciation that inspires but doesn't pander. The unattained dream, "Someday, Lis, I'll go back," captures the human desire to return to the spot of our greatest sacrifice and our finest hour—and to pay homage to fallen comrades. These words mean so much more than the trite patriotic pablum that so often passes for political rhetoric. They genuinely inspire awe and respect for the solemn sacrifices required to maintain a free civilization.

I am reminded of a speech then candidate Barack Obama gave in 2008 about the power of rhetoric: "Don't tell me words don't matter. 'I have a dream.' Just words? 'We hold these truths to be self-evident, that all men are created equal.' Just words? 'We have nothing to fear but fear itself'—just words? Just speeches?" Putting aside the fact that Obama heavily borrowed the lines from Massachusetts governor Deval Patrick, he was right. Words do matter. They inspire and instruct. It's easy to dismiss words as superficial, but part of the job of a leader is to use words to inspire and teach and persuade.

Now let's look at Reagan's speech in 1986 on the day the *Challenger* exploded. It's short, so I'm going to include the whole thing.

Ladies and Gentlemen, I'd planned to speak to you tonight to report on the state of the Union, but the events of earlier today have led me to change those plans. Today is a day for mourning and remembering. Nancy and I are pained to the core by the tragedy of the shuttle *Challenger*. We know we share this pain with all of the people of our country. This is truly a national loss.

Nineteen years ago, almost to the day, we lost three astronauts in a terrible accident on the ground. But, we've never lost an astronaut in flight; we've never had a tragedy like this. And perhaps we've forgotten the courage it took for the crew of the shuttle; but they, the *Challenger* Seven, were aware of the dangers, but overcame them and did their jobs brilliantly. We mourn seven heroes: Michael Smith, Dick Scobee, Judith Resnik, Ronald McNair, Ellison Onizuka, Gregory Jarvis, and Christa McAuliffe. We mourn their loss as a nation together.

For the families of the seven, we cannot bear, as you do, the full impact of this tragedy. But we feel the loss, and we're thinking about you so very much. Your loved ones were

daring and brave, and they had that special grace, that special spirit that says, "Give me a challenge and I'll meet it with
joy." They had a hunger to explore the universe and discover
its truths. They wished to serve, and they did. They served all
of us.

We've grown used to wonders in this century. It's hard to
dazzle us. But for twenty-five years the United States space
program has been doing just that. We've grown used to the
idea of space, and perhaps we forget that we've only just
begun. We're still pioneers. They, the members of the *Challenger* crew, were pioneers.

And I want to say something to the schoolchildren of
America who were watching the live coverage of the shuttle's
takeoff. I know it is hard to understand, but sometimes
painful things like this happen. It's all part of the process
of exploration and discovery. It's all part of taking a chance
and expanding man's horizons. The future doesn't belong to
the fainthearted; it belongs to the brave. The *Challenger* crew
was pulling us into the future, and we'll continue to follow
them.

I've always had great faith in and respect for our space program, and what happened today does nothing to diminish it.
We don't hide our space program. We don't keep secrets and
cover things up. We do it all up front and in public. That's the
way freedom is, and we wouldn't change it for a minute. We'll
continue our quest in space. There will be more shuttle flights
and more shuttle crews and, yes, more volunteers, more civilians, more teachers in space. Nothing ends here; our hopes
and our journeys continue. I want to add that I wish I could
talk to every man and woman who works for NASA or who
worked on this mission and tell them, "Your dedication and
professionalism have moved and impressed us for decades.
And we know of your anguish. We share it."

There's a coincidence today. On this day 390 years ago, the great explorer Sir Francis Drake died aboard ship off the coast of Panama. In his lifetime the great frontiers were the oceans, and a historian later said, "He lived by the sea, died on it, and was buried in it." Well, today we can say of the *Challenger* crew: Their dedication was, like Drake's, complete.

The crew of the space shuttle *Challenger* honored us by the manner in which they lived their lives. We will never forget them, nor the last time we saw them, this morning, as they prepared for the journey and waved good-bye and "slipped the surly bonds of earth" to "touch the face of God."

The last line of the speech was surrounded by quotation marks because it comes from the first and last lines of John Gillespie Magee Jr.'s poem "High Flight," a wonderful reference demonstrating both an interest in cultural literacy, and a respect for the audience's intelligence.

To give you an idea of how far we've sunk since that speech, compare Reagan's grand talk about the space exploration to the mockery that ensued when former Speaker and 2012 presidential candidate Newt Gingrich declared, "By the end of my second term, we need to have the first permanent base on the moon, and it will be American."

"I am sick of being told we have to be timid, and I'm sick of being told we have to be limited to technologies that are fifty years old," Gingrich said. And, for this, Gingrich was mocked. "If I had a business executive come to me and say I want to spend a few hundred billion dollars to put a colony on the moon, I'd say, 'You're fired,'" Mitt Romney snarled in response during a debate in Jacksonville, Florida. *Saturday Night Live* made fun of Gingrich, too. Gingrich was encountering a phenomenon all too common in America today—a pessimism about reaching for the stars. What is more, this negativity might have been even more acute within the GOP, where doubts about our capacity to do great things were reinforced by concerns about budgets and a growing sense that we had to worry about keeping what we have—doing "nation building at home."

Always optimistic, Reagan encouraged us to preserve our pioneer spirit. And during that moment of crisis, Reagan did about the only thing a political leader could do. He comforted us. He inspired us to believe that these lives were not lost for nothing—that they had purpose. He embraced the ongoing work of science and, invoking the explorer Sir Francis Drake, he reminded us of the thrill and romance of science—that the men and women who perished were modern-day explorers seeking to discover "the final frontier."

The Reagan Legacy

"[Reagan] did not dislike intellectuals," wrote Peggy Noonan (who crafted some of Reagan's most poetic speeches) in a *Wall Street Journal* column that ran after his 2004 death.[40] "His heroes often were intellectuals, from the Founders straight through Milton Friedman and Hayek and Solzhenitsyn. But he did not favor the intellectuals of his own day, because he thought they were in general thick-headed." They weren't the only ones. Sadly, the conservatives who followed could not duplicate Reagan's delicate balance of intellectual and everyman optimism—or of populism and cosmopolitanism. Republicans have won some elections since, but the Reagan era marked the apogee of conservative governance. Reagan, in downplaying his intellectual side for political gain, might even have created some long-term unintended consequences, reinforcing the notion that conservatism—and its greatest champion—was unsophisticated.

Not to knock common sense, but it took Reagan more than good old-fashioned horse sense to fix America. And fix it he did. As Peggy Noonan noted in that same *Wall Street Journal* column, by the end of his presidency, "the Berlin Wall had been turned into a million concrete souvenirs, and Soviet communism had fallen. But of course it didn't fall. It was pushed. By Mr. Know Nothing Cowboy Gunslinger

Dimwit. All presidents should be so stupid." Not bad for a graduate from Eureka College. Still, not everyone was satisfied.

In R. Emmett Tyrrell Jr.'s 1992 book, *The Conservative Crack-Up*, the author laments that Reagan's tenure didn't leave the lasting mark that FDR's presidency did. Whereas FDR's presidency transcended politics and entered into nearly every institution of the culture—entertainment, academia, literature—Reagan's presidency existed on an almost solely political plane. This, Tyrrell argues, is because the conservative intellectuals surrounding Reagan "were neither literary nor artistic" and thus, were not as interested in "affecting culture." It's hard to blame a guy who was busy winning the Cold War, but in the years since Tyrrell wrote that book, his criticism only looks truer. If we are to judge one's performance—not merely based on what he did while he was in office, but also based on what happens after he leaves office (a high bar, indeed)—conservatives might rightly see Reagan's presidency as the high-water mark for conservatism. But at the same time, at least some of what has followed can be attributed to the failure of Reagan-era conservatives to address the long-term cultural decay.

3

TEAR DOWN THIS PARTY!

"There's an old saying... that says, fool me once, shame on—
shame on you. Fool me... you can't get fooled again."
—George W. Bush

As in most tragedies, the seeds for the decline of thoughtful conservatism were sown long before its decline manifested. And as is almost always the case, that drop didn't proceed in a straight trajectory. The rise of conservatism was checkered with fits and starts; likewise, its intellectual diminution has not been a precipitous line. There have been good men and women—thoughtful conservatives—who have made a major impact, despite an unaccommodating political and media milieu. And, as later chapters will detail, I believe there is great hope for a renaissance of thoughtful conservatism.

The presidency of Ronald Reagan constitutes the apex of modern conservatism. After the Gipper rode off into the sunset, Republicans were rewarded with his third term, in the person of George Herbert Walker Bush. Despite being a prudent statesman who helped oversee the collapse of the Soviet Union and the fall of the Berlin Wall (and who enjoyed sky-high approval ratings after the first Gulf War), Bush is best remembered for breaking his "Read My Lips, No New

Taxes!" pledge, and for losing his 1992 reelection to a slick Arkansas governor named William Jefferson Clinton. It has been said, "Without a successor, there is no success," and if that's the case, it's fair to question whether the Reagan Revolution was doomed when Bush, Reagan's moderate rival in the 1980 primaries, was selected to balance the ticket as his running mate—despite having disparaged Reagan's economic theories as "voodoo economics." (One wonders what might have been had Vice President Jack Kemp been given the same opportunity.)

The Clinton Era

Bill Clinton, whose political skills are legendary, deserves credit for winning in what was, at the time, a hostile environment for any Democrat. Despite his own electoral success, Clinton's victory did not usher in a liberal renaissance. His early attempts—such as lifting a ban on gays in the military (which turned into a compromise dubbed "Don't Ask, Don't Tell") and health care reform (dubbed "HillaryCare" after then First Lady Hillary Clinton, who headed the task force to sell the plan)—were rebuffed. In fact, it's fair to say the market corrected itself and that the early years of Bill Clinton led to a backlash that, in the short term at least, made the conservative movement even stronger. On his watch (or, perhaps, in response to his election and policies), Rush Limbaugh became a rock star, Fox News was launched, and Matt Drudge's rudimentary website became a behemoth and submerged the Clinton White House in scandal after scandal. After two years of attempting to push a liberal agenda, Clinton 'ɔst both houses of Congress. And, unlike President Obama, he responded by pivoting to the center, "ending welfare as we know it," and declaring, "The era of big government is over."

The 1994 midterm congressional election (known as the Republican Revolution) deserves mention as a high point of the post-Reagan era for conservatives. Previously, Tip O'Neill's maxim that "all politics is local" suggested that increasingly conservative voters—the so-called Reagan Democrats—would continue to pull the lever for their local Democratic congressman, who, after all, they knew personally and who (they also understood) would make sure to "bring home the bacon" in the form of allocating federal dollars to pay for projects like bridges and roads. But in taking the House for the first time in forty years, Republicans defied this theory, effectively nationalizing the midterm elections by running aggressively on an ideologically conservative platform dubbed the "Contract with America." Two of the revolution's leaders, Speaker Newt Gingrich and Majority Leader Dick Armey, were professors, and it showed. Few would accuse Gingrich of lacking intelligence. (Judgment and wisdom, yes. But intelligence he had in spades.) Ditto a joie de vivre. Gingrich was charismatic, but grandiose. He was a leading example of a new breed of politician who understood public relations and marketing far better than the old bulls who had been running Congress for decades. Some of Gingrich's innovations, such as the theatrical, made-for-TV speech on the House floor, still plague us today. As Katharine Seelye reported in the *New York Times* in 1994, "Mr. Gingrich made his name in the House...by denouncing the Democrats on the floor while the cameras rolled. What they did not show, because they were locked into a narrow field of vision, was that Mr. Gingrich was hurling his barbs at an empty chamber, when his victims could not respond."

Thankfully for conservatives, the Reagan era did not end with Reagan. Bill Clinton figured out he was still operating under a conservative paradigm. The downside for Republicans, however, was that Clinton was ideologically flexible and strategically sophisticated enough to simply co-opt their ideas, including balanced budgets and welfare reform, while snookering them into major missteps like shutting down the government. The end of the Clinton years was marked by his impeachment over the Monica Lewinsky affair, which ironically turned out to be another political misfire by congressional

Republicans. It's hard to blame them. Clinton was impeached by the House of Representatives on charges of perjury and obstruction of justice, no small thing. Republicans probably assumed impeaching Clinton would turn him into Richard Nixon—a disgraced shell of a man. Instead, he only seemed to grow more popular. Ironically, the politicians taken down by the scandal were Gingrich, who was carrying on his own affair, but was pushed out after Republicans had a disappointing midterm in the 1998 run-up to impeachment, and the man who was set to replace him as Speaker, Representative Bob Livingston, who quickly acknowledged his own adultery.[41] Clinton would leave office in 2000 with high approval numbers. By then, conservatism seemed to be struggling or at least in need of reinvention. George W. Bush provided that during the 2000 election, albeit without winning the popular vote.

A Permanent Governing Majority?

For a while, it seemed like we had it all figured out. Just stick to the tried and true conservative doctrine that had worked since 1980, and then soften it up a tad. That was essentially the winning formula that George W. Bush used in 2000. He called it "compassionate conservatism." The theory was to keep everyone in the conservative coalition happy and then inoculate himself against the predictable charges that Republicans are uncompassionate and mean-spirited. By following this strategy, Bush hoped to do better with Hispanics ("Family values do not stop at the Rio Grande River"), African Americans (some of whom Bush thought might like his proposal on faith-based initiatives, or the fact that Colin Powell and Condi Rice were key players in his administration), and soccer moms (who might share some conservative values, but would be turned off by the harsh conservative rhetoric that had emerged during the Clinton years).

September 11, however, changed everything. It's worth pausing to consider what would have happened had the 9/11 attacks not occurred. The magnitude of that day was so great that without it, much of the American political landscape—and certainly the conservative movement—would be different today. Might George Bush have been remembered for compassionate conservatism, instead of the Iraq War and waterboarding? Absent the Iraq War that followed, does Barack Obama get elected? (Does he even speak at the 2004 Democratic Convention, where he first made a major national splash? Unlikely, since John Kerry probably isn't the nominee.) Does Hillary Clinton win the 2008 nomination that year because she wasn't forced to take a tough vote authorizing military force in Iraq? (As I type these words, perhaps in some alternate universe, Republican president Colin Powell is wrapping up his second term and Vice President Condi Rice is already the front-runner for the 2016 Republican nomination.)

Instead, 9/11 caused millions of formerly apolitical or apathetic people to suddenly discover their country was in trouble and they sought to make up for lost time. Some of these new conservatives were very smart, but few were full-spectrum conservatives, and even fewer had a Burkean conservative temperament. Nevertheless, the zealotry of the convert is a powerful thing, and many of these folks took to blogs and emerging media outlets and, in some cases, advanced fringe theories. Take, for example, the case of Pamela Geller, a blogger the *New York Times* described in 2010 as waging "a form of holy war through 'Atlas Shrugs,' a Web site that attacks Islam with a rhetoric venomous enough that PayPal at one point branded it a hate site." September 11 "drove Ms. Geller to her keyboard. She had barely heard of Osama bin Laden, she said, and 'felt guilty that I didn't know who had attacked my country.'" In 2009, Geller helped lead the movement against building a mosque in Manhattan. And in 2015, Geller organized a cartoon contest where participants competed by drawing the Prophet Mohammad. Two gunmen opened fire outside the Garland, Texas, event before being shot and killed by police. A debate ensued. Was Geller a hero of free speech, or someone who was engaging needlessly in offensive and provocative activities? Maybe *both*.

One could argue that defending Western civilization from radical Islam is a noble and conservative thing to do, even if Geller does it in a radical and *un*conservative manner. The point, though, is that events are changing what—and who—qualifies as "conservative." As the *Washington Post* noted in 2015, "Geller portrays herself as emerging straight from Ground Zero." Should the definition of conservatism simply be "One who takes a hard-line stance against radical Islam?" Some would suggest that in an existential war, you focus solely on survival and embrace strange bedfellows. Others say that in welcoming our new allies into the fold for the sake of convenience, we may win the battle only to one day realize that the conservative movement is now simply a cause for erstwhile liberals who fetishize free expression and radical individualism and simply believe the Left has gotten too soft and politically correct.

It's difficult to tell activists who had awoken from a decades-long slumber that they should go read about conservative philosophy and strategy before diving into political debates. Yet, there is little doubt that the involvement of this new breed of conservative activist in the wake of 9/11 contributed to some of the harsh rhetoric and unsophisticated political calculations that only accelerated after President Obama's election and the rise of the Tea Party. I like to refer to these converts as conservative "immigrants"—a term I'm sure they would despise. My point is simply this: Like a nation, a movement needs an influx of new people and ideas. But if this influx comes too quickly, and if the new "immigrants" fail to be assimilated, then you wake up one day and your movement (or country) has suddenly become something you don't recognize.

There were many, many consequences of the 9/11 attacks, and one of them was that the conservative movement began to attract people who weren't all that conservative. It also took people who had long been conservative and inflamed their passions. If George W. Bush's "compassionate conservatism" was aimed at growing the GOP, then 9/11 would make that kind of rhetoric sound naive and weak. Though Bush would be careful to continue parsing his rhetoric, conservative commentators weren't always so specific or delicate. "We should invade their countries, kill their leaders, and convert them to Christianity," declared conservative commentator Ann Coulter.

Contributing to the conservative angst was the fact that conservatives had little to show for the Bush years. Republican majority leader Tom DeLay took the practice of using earmarks (a legislative provision that designates funds to be spent on a specific project and was traditionally used as leverage to win the support of wavering congressmen by promising to fund an infrastructure project in their home districts) as an incentive to entice party discipline to the extreme. Today's Republican leadership, who find themselves without many sticks or carrots to get anything done, can probably thank him for removing that arrow from their quiver. There was a backlash due to DeLay's aggressive use of earmarks, leading to their banishment in 2010. The (unintended?) consequence has been Republican leadership can't get members to follow the party line.

Another tactic that cannot be blamed on DeLay, but certainly thrived during his tenure, was the practice of gerrymandering—the drawing of congressional lines in a way to increase "safe" districts. The result has been the proliferation of members of Congress who must go hard-Right or hard-Left in order to win, and maintain, a congressional seat. Many of the structural changes that empower today's Freedom Caucus (the congressional caucus made up of the House's most conservative members), and gave rise to our polarized political environment, can trace their origins to this era.

It might sound like an oxymoron, but this was also a time of big government conservatism—an era marked by spending increases, unfunded programs like the Medicare Part D prescription drug program, and few presidential vetoes. Major reform efforts, such as fixing Social Security, were put off until the second term and eventually abandoned. There was also a larger sense that the president prized loyalty to old friends and Texas pals over competence ("You're doing a heckuva job, Brownie"). Republicans could console themselves with election wins until Bush's presidency ended with the collapse of the housing market and the Great Recession. By the time Bush left office in January 2009, the conservative movement looked very different, and, in fact, conservatives were undergoing what might be described as an identity crisis.

Obama's Election and Its Impact on Conservatism

Much has been made of the fact that Barack Obama is the first African American president, and surely there is some percentage of racists out there for which this is greatly troubling. But I think we have largely downplayed the cultural aspects of Obama, which are incidental to his skin color. Though there is little doubt that "urban" is sometimes used as racial code language, that doesn't mean it's not fair game for discussion. For one thing, he is, to put it plainly, *citified*. And this descriptor is unusual for a president. On the 2008 campaign trail, he provoked the ire of small-town folk with this statement about "small towns in Pennsylvania" and "the Midwest" that have been losing jobs for the last twenty-five years: "They get bitter, they cling to guns or religion or antipathy toward people who aren't like them or anti-immigrant sentiment or anti-trade sentiment as a way to explain their frustrations."

Obama is a professorial liberal, and this sort of intellectualism has traditionally been damaging to Democrats because it reinforces preexisting narratives about the pretentious, elite Left. It's probably fair to say that you can get away with being more intellectual than you could even a few years ago. But the best politicians represent a balance of down-to-earth, rural America and urban savvy. Both sides of the political aisle must worry about getting the balance wrong. But liberals are usually in danger of coming across as too wonky. So how is it that a citified professor managed to win *twice*?

How did Obama successfully balance intelligence and populism? Republicans, it seems, misunderstood his success, either thinking he was easy pickings because of his urban liberalism, or that he won only because of America's white guilt. This led them right off the deep end when they should have been mining Obama's communications strategy for applicable lessons they could themselves co-opt. Obama's election victories, coupled with the bailouts and stimulus, and his liberal policies like Obamacare (and the fact that Republicans performed well in 2010 and 2014 midterms) pushed Republicans further to the extremes.

During the conservative Reagan years, Democrats responded to Reagan's popularity by doubling down on their elite brand of liberalism. This led to historic defeats, including Walter Mondale losing forty-nine states in 1984. Eventually, Democrats wised up and went for a centrist named Bill Clinton. Now, during Obama's aggressively liberal presidency, Republicans have responded by doubling down on populist conservatism. Every action has an equal and opposite reaction. Why was the Republican backlash to Obama even harsher than the reaction to Clinton? I suspect part of the reason is that Obama was more liberal, and less pragmatic, than Clinton.

In a 2015 *New York Times* article, Jonathan Martin captured the degree to which Obama's presidency had transformed the GOP, by noting the interesting evolution of former Arkansas governor and Fox News host Mike Huckabee's book titles. "Three years before he ran for president in 2008, a newly slim Huckabee peddled a book with a title that doubled as a lecture: *Quit Digging Your Grave with a Knife and Fork*. Now, as he considers a second White House run, he has written another book with a decidedly different but equally direct title: *God, Guns, Grits, and Gravy*." Martin further observed:

> Huckabee's march from author of a self-help and clean-living guide to cheerleader of artery-clogging calories and conservative traditionalism highlights the Republican shift during

the Obama era. The party is different in tone and substance, moving toward a stricter, limited-government brand of conservatism in response to President Obama's liberalism, a change that has generational and ideological dimensions.

Now, deviations from orthodoxy on education, health care, immigration, and the environment that some Republicans flirted with or embraced during George W. Bush's presidency are as out of vogue on the Right as flip phones.

This is a really unfortunate development, but Huckabee is hardly alone. Early in the presidential primaries for 2016, Wisconsin governor Scott Walker, whose candidacy unwisely rested on the notion that he had to win the Iowa caucuses, suddenly discovered that he no longer favored a pathway to citizenship for undocumented immigrants. The change of tone and substance made perfect sense in a short-term Machiavellian sense. But the danger (and Walker tripped over such dangers more quickly than anyone imagined) is that we have created a system whereby all our rising stars are essentially forced to adopt positions that tarnish their chances of ever being able to appeal later to a more diverse, cosmopolitan audience. It's hard to sell conservatism to non-Republican primary voters when the messenger has a paper trail of questionable and controversial past statements. It would take a superb leader to be able to simultaneously refuse to pander to the Republican base and still win them over. But most politicians take the path of least resistance, choosing short-term survival at the expense of preserving long-term integrity. This is a vicious cycle.

Christine O'Donnell and the Rise of No-Qualification Candidates

The rise of the Tea Party certainly had some salutary benefits, such as the election of rising star conservatives like Senators Marco Rubio, Rand Paul, and Pat Toomey. But election waves also bring in the rickety boats, and who could forget the candidacy of Christine "I'm not a witch" O'Donnell of Delaware? O'Donnell has become an easy target, as the Left hates her and the Right has now mostly abandoned her. But her candidacy was highly instructive as an example of how conservatism had metastasized into a movement that preached populism and how a conservative could thrive as a professional victim.

A 2010 speech by O'Donnell highlights how her message was aimed, not simply at liberals, but at *elites*.[42]

"The small elite don't get us. They call us wacky. They call us wingnuts. We call us, 'We the people,'" she said to applause. "We're loud, we're rowdy, we're passionate.... It isn't tame, but boy, it sure is good.... I never had the high-paying job or the company car. It took me over a decade to pay off my student loans. I never had to worry about where to dock my yacht to reduce my taxes," she said, taking a swipe at Senator John Kerry for avoiding a six-figure yacht tax in Massachusetts by docking it in Rhode Island. "And I'll bet most of you didn't, either."

O'Donnell was essentially arguing that her lack of sophistication wasn't merely something to be overlooked; it was actually a *qualification* for the job of US senator.

While this message ultimately failed to resonate with Delaware voters—she lost the general election by a 17 percent margin in favor of Democrat Chris Coons—for a moment, at least, it turned O'Donnell into a national conservative star. Hers was a message all those Tea Party–going grassroots conservatives wanted to hear. Meanwhile, skeptical conservatives who saw O'Donnell as both sloppy and opportunistic were branded apostates. Some center-right journalists mustered the courage to push back at this. For example, *National Review*'s Jim Geraghty wrote that "she told blatant, easy-to-check lies on the campaign trail," and raised questions about her financial disclosures, noting that she "somehow managed to pay $11,744.59 in back taxes in a year she reportedly earned about half that." But O'Donnell had cast herself as a victim—our victim—and anything less than defending this conservative darling was considered not just unchivalrous, but downright heresy.

To be fair, every family has that aunt or uncle that they'd prefer be kept in the attic; and similarly, both sides of the political aisle have their share of laughable candidates. In this regard, it feels petty to pick on Republicans. The liberal media tends to give their embarrassing figures a pass while demonizing conservatives who either mess up, or (in the case of O'Donnell) aren't ready for prime time in the first place. While O'Donnell was merely a failed Senate candidate, her fellow Delaware pol, Vice President Joe Biden, was *literally* (a word he likes to use) a heartbeat away from the presidency. But one would be hard-pressed to find a politician who has said more stupid things, or committed more gaffes, than "Uncle" Joe Biden.

Failing Forward

The early Obama years were marked by outrage and disillusionment among conservatives. Rush Limbaugh declared of Obama, "I hope he fails," Fox News host Glenn Beck suggested Obama was "a racist," and Sarah Palin—John McCain's 2008 running mate—resigned her job as governor of Alaska and turned her attention toward reality TV and fighting the Left.

In 2010, Republicans had a very good midterm, taking back the House of Representatives. But midterm elections are different than presidential elections. For one thing, the universe of voters is much smaller and less demographically diverse. As such, success in 2010 masked some larger problems. But winning covers a multitude of sins, and a party that has just won an election isn't in much of a mood to make any changes—or to soften any rhetoric. Steps that could have been taken to preemptively address the coming demographic.time bomb—or the fact that cultural attitudes were rapidly changing—got kicked down the road. In 2012, Obama was reelected, and new Republican controversies erupted: Missouri Republican

Senate candidate, Todd Akin, used the term "legitimate rape," Indiana Senate hopeful Richard Mourdock said that when a rape happens, "it is something that God intended," and Rush Limbaugh poured gasoline on the whole mess by calling feminist activist Sandra Fluke a "slut." Democrats would effectively use the so-called war on women card to damage Republicans.

The next year, Republicans would attempt to defund Obamacare, a fool's errand championed by Senator Ted Cruz and Heritage Action, the activist arm of the Heritage Foundation. Dubbed the gospel of "defundamentalism" by John Hart, a former communications director for Senator Tom Coburn, Republicans' effort to defund Obama's signature legislation was destined to fail—and fail it did.

Or did it? This book is called *Too Dumb to Fail* for a reason. And the defund effort is an example of how some conservatives manage to fail forward. To many, Cruz and others are not viewed as losers who misled the public into a quixotic adventure, but instead as champions who at least had the guts to try. Rather than owning up to the fact that the defund effort was a fool's errand, the people responsible for it actually claimed credit. The term *gaslighting* means "to cause (a person) to doubt his or her sanity through the use of psychological manipulation." The people who were pushing the defund movement will argue till they're blue in the face that—surprise!—it worked. (Who are you going to believe—them or your lying eyes?)

The truth is that the defund fiasco arguably helped Republicans in the long run, by teaching them this was a stupid attempt they shouldn't replicate before the next election. Chastened by the defund experience, Republicans ran a much smarter campaign in 2014 and won the midterm election. So, ironically, I guess you *can* thank the defund effort for helping Republicans win the 2014 midterms (just not for the reasons the "too dumb to fail" crowd thinks).

Still, conservatives lost a lot of winnable seats in 2010 and 2012 because of bad candidates and flawed strategy. In 2010, they should have won in Delaware, Nevada, and Colorado, but Tea Party candidates

Christine O'Donnell, Sharron Angle, and Ken Buck each committed costly errors. In 2012, Republicans again missed an opportunity to take the Senate when they blew races in Missouri (Todd Akin's gaffe), Indiana (Richard Mourdock's gaffe), North Dakota (establishment representative Rick Berg couldn't win an open seat), and Montana (establishment Republican Denny Rehberg failed to oust an incumbent). On their third try—having learned the lessons of their previous two failures—Republicans finally captured the Senate in 2014, partly thanks to having run better candidates and better campaigns in blue or purple states. In the senate, this meant electing Joni Ernst in Iowa and Cory Gardner in Colorado. In the state houses, this meant electing Republicans like Larry Hogan in my birth state of Maryland.

But all victories are short-lived, and although it's nice to control Congress, conservatives won't be able to fully achieve public policy victories without the White House. Without restoring conservatism's once proud intellectual tradition and returning to the delicate balance between populism and intellectual optimism, the White House will remain elusive. Republicans have occasionally demonstrated that if they can avoid strategically unwise gambits like government shutdowns, they can win midterm elections, but winning the White House will require some more intensive brand management. And here, some of the stereotypes about "the stupid party" continue to plague the GOP. When NBC's *The West Wing*'s fictional president Jeb Bartlet's equally fictional Republican opponent complains that Bartlet is calling him "dumb," Bartlet replies, "I wasn't, Rob. But you've turned being unengaged into a Zen-like thing, and you shouldn't enjoy it so much is all." Bartlet's GOP foe, Governor Robert Ritchie, is a tough-talking Southerner who gloried in his everyman qualities by going to baseball games and scoffing at "big words." Sound familiar? Even if George W. Bush had never entered the universe of American politics, this would still be a pretty accurate portrayal of the typical "red state," cowboy boots–wearin' Republican candidate. Of course, there's nothing wrong with conservatives who wear cowboy boots (I own a pair), but the problem comes when this caricature comes to define an entire philosophy.

Winning elections means having a tent big enough to attract a majority. So if you want to understand why today's GOP is the way it is, the easiest way is to take a look at who constitutes Republican *voters*. The next several chapters describe how, in building an electoral coalition big enough to win national elections, Republicans have inexorably sown the seeds that have blossomed into their current identity crisis.

PART TWO

THE GREAT BETRAYAL

4

HOW THE GOP WENT SOUTH

"In Birmingham they love the governor."[43]
—*Lynyrd Skynyrd*

By joining the Republican Party, once hated in Dixie for being the party of Lincoln and subsequent carpetbaggers, the South helped transform the GOP into the dominant national party for decades. It also guaranteed a book like this one would be necessary. The conservative movement's founders might have been intellectuals and the GOP establishment once might have been Northeastern elites, but that arrangement was always tenuous. When Willie Sutton was asked why he robbed banks, the infamous outlaw supposedly replied, "Because that's where the money is." Likewise, anyone who seeks to understand why conservatism became what it is can only expect this answer: "Because that's where the votes were." Indeed, after the 2014 midterms, almost half of the Republican congressional delegation represented Southern districts.[44] But what happens when you build your political coalition around a constituency that is no longer sufficient? What is more, what happens when appeasing your base and growing your coalition become mutually exclusive goals?

Times change, and yesterday's solution becomes tomorrow's challenge. Such is the case with today's GOP and the South. The South helped fuel Richard Nixon's romp over George McGovern and Ronald Reagan's 49–1 rout of Walter Mondale. It did its part in saving us from a President Dukakis or Kerry. It would be hard to overestimate the importance of the GOP aligning with Southern values. Redskins coach George Allen was famous for saying, "The future is now."[45] Sometimes, to borrow a phrase from Donald Rumsfeld, you go to war with the army you have. That's the tradeoff Republicans made, and it was perfectly rational. But there were also unintended consequences. A political party inevitably reflects its constituents' attitudes and biases. The notion that any party can change its voter base without changing its philosophy and its politicians is naive; pandering inevitably becomes a self-fulfilling prophecy. Republicans captured the South, yes, but the South also captured the GOP.

The addition of the South and rural communities in states like South Carolina, Alabama, and Mississippi as a reliable bloc of the Republican coalition was one of the many factors leading to the GOP's image as both the stupid party and the party of white men with Confederate flag stickers on the backs of their trucks. This may not be fair—it certainly plays to stereotypes. But that hardly matters. Today, this is increasingly seen as a liability.

The Southern Strategy

You've probably heard of the Southern strategy, but you might not know exactly what it means or how the Republican Party allegedly employed it. The Southern strategy, as Mike Allen defined it in the *Washington Post*, "described Republican efforts to use race as a wedge issue—on matters such as desegregation and busing—to appeal to white Southern voters."

Whether you believe this was an overt scheme or just how things shook out, this much is true: at some point around 1972,[46] the once reliably solid Democratic South became a Republican stronghold. We may differ about what this means and about whether the GOP deserves culpability for stirring up racial animus to achieve it. But the key takeaway is that the addition of the South to the Republican fold, followed by the party's abandonment of urban areas, the northeast, and then the Pacific Coast dramatically changed the face of conservatism—and not just because it fairly or not associated the GOP with segregationists—an ironic turn of events for the party of Lincoln.

It helps to consider just who the Southerners who joined the GOP in the sixties were. Viewed in the most negative light, they were segregationists who felt betrayed when Democrats like Lyndon Johnson pursued the Civil Rights Act of 1964 (which Barry Goldwater opposed).[47] It would also be fair to say that, putting aside the race issue, these Southern Democrats also saw the degree to which the American Left was lurching in a radical cultural direction and jumped ship. "Nixon won the South," wrote his former aide Pat Buchanan, "not because he agreed with them on civil rights—he never did—but because he shared the patriotic values of the South and its antipathy to liberal hypocrisy."

While some on the Right want to downplay the race angle, others on the Left suggest that the entire success of the modern GOP was premised on exploiting Southern racism. Interestingly, though, much of what both sides *think* we know about this trend appears to be wrong. Elections analyst Sean Trende recently argued that "while the dominant narrative continues to insist that the South began to realign toward the Republicans in the wake of the passage of the Civil Rights Act of 1964, in fact, Southern loyalties had begun to weaken during the presidency of Franklin Roosevelt." As evidence, Trende notes that the South voted increasingly Republican every year of FDR's presidency, and that although Eisenhower lost Dixie, he did so by only *three* points.[48] What is more, while Eisenhower was gaining support in the South, he was simultaneously pushing civil rights legislation. So why did the South become increasingly Republican starting in the 1940s? According to Trende, "Southern whites simply became wealthy enough to start voting Republican." This, of course, flies in the face

of everything we think we know about why the South became sol-
idly Republican. This is not to suggest that race wasn't involved in the
shift that really began to reach a tipping point after the 1960s, but it
does suggest that history is more complex than the *Reader's Digest* (or,
rather, the *Mother Jones*) version many of us are taught in school.

Southern Domination

After the post–Civil Rights Act "Dixiecrat" shift, economics and
air-conditioning conspired to send American voters fleeing the Rust
Belt for the Sun Belt,[49] further eroding the power of the Northeast
Republican establishment, personified by the New York governors
and presidential aspirants Thomas Dewey and Nelson Rockefeller.
(This is a trend that is still under way; according to the US census, the
city of Austin, Texas—the liberal enclave in a deeply red state—was,
by far, the fastest growing city in America from 2010 to 2013.) It's
unwise to write off an entire swath of the nation, but that's just what
Barry Goldwater, who represented Arizona in the US Senate, seemed
to do when he declared that "sometimes I think the country would
be better off if we could just saw off the Eastern seaboard and let it
float out to sea." The Johnson campaign turned that line into a dev-
astating ad in which the eastern side of a US map, floating in water, is
literally sawed off.

   Truth be told, the South's influence came to dominate both parties. Democrats soon saw that the only way they could win would be
to cut into the GOP's base. For a while, it looked like the only path
to Democratic victory was through nominating a son of the South.
From Texan Lyndon Johnson to Georgia peanut farmer Jimmy
Carter to Arkansas's Bill Clinton (and even to, yes, Al Gore), seemingly only Southern Democrats could win the White House—and
even that trend was not very recent; consider Georgia-born segre-
gationist Woodrow Wilson or Harry Truman, the descendants of
slaveholders and Confederate sympathizers, or even Warm Springs,

Georgia, resident FDR. In the post-Reagan years, Southerners so dominated both parties[50] that at one point, we had a president from Arkansas (Clinton) a vice president from Tennessee (Gore), a Majority Leader from Mississippi (Trent Lott), and a House Speaker from Georgia (Newt Gingrich). The chairman of the GOP was Haley Barbour, from Mississippi. President George W. Bush of Texas,[51] Senate Majority Leader Bill Frist of Tennessee, and House Majority Leaders Dick Armey and Tom DeLay (Texans) soon followed in what was, perhaps, the apex of Southern domination of the GOP, and simultaneously, of Republican triumphalism. Talk circulated that the GOP had achieved a "permanent governing majority."

All the while, Southern Republicanism, having descended from Southern Democrats, churned out culturally conservative, yet big-spending, governmental policies. In the 2000s, deficits ballooned and unfunded entitlements like Medicare Part D were enacted. Meanwhile, some of the GOP's most prominent Southern governors also played to type. In 2008, the fiscally conservative Club for Growth issued a white paper slamming then Arkansas governor Mike Huckabee for having raised sales taxes, state spending, and the minimum wage. And then it all came crashing down. Republicans forfeited their congressional majority in 2006, victims of a faltering war in Iraq, incompetent handling of Hurricane Katrina, mounting debt, and a slew of corruption and sex scandals that exploded just in time for the midterms. Presidents almost always suffer bad second-term midterms, but George W. Bush's mishandling of so many high-profile issues undoubtedly exacerbated voters' "Bush fatigue." Simply put, the Bush shtick had worn thin.

A "Stupid" Stereotype

In Chapter Two, I discussed how Ronald Reagan downplayed his intellectual and cosmopolitan credentials to accentuate his everyman persona. In similar fashion, Dwight Eisenhower, the former supreme commander of Allied forces in Europe and president of Columbia University, dodged questions by employing bumbling answers at press conferences. "In public he wore a costume of affability, optimism, and farm-boy charm," wrote David Brooks in *The Road to Character*. "As president, he was perfectly willing to appear stupider than he really was if it would help him perform his assigned role. He was willing to appear tongue-tied if it would help him conceal his true designs." Biographer Andrew Sinclair said much the same thing about the much-maligned Warren Harding's "mute your own horn" leadership style. In this regard, George W. Bush simply followed a long-standing tradition—albeit with a Texas twang. Tevi Troy, the former Bush aide who authored *What Jefferson Read, Ike Watched, and Obama Tweeted*, believes that "Bush probably read more history than [Jack] Kennedy."[52] If that sounds absurd, it's partly because Kennedy highlighted his intellectual credentials, while the Yale-educated Bush downplayed his. As a result, we consider Kennedy (no dummy, but no genius, either) smarter. Is this only the result of a liberal media painting Republicans as illiterate Babbitts? Hardly. "To be fair," Troy writes, "Bush was not blameless in acquiring a reputation for not reading."

Here's the backstory, according to Troy's book:

> In 1978, [Bush] ran for Congress in West Texas against Kent Hance, the conservative Democratic incumbent. Degrees from Yale and Harvard might help a politician in some parts of the country, but not where Bush was running. After he lost, he vowed "never to get out-countried again." "He plays up being a good ol' boy from Midland, Texas," says [Karl] Rove, "but he was a history major at Yale and graduated from Harvard Business School." Playing down the Ivy League credentials helped him get elected governor of Texas and president of the United States—two times each—but the cost was being treated like a bumpkin by the media.

The "out-countried" line has always struck me as noteworthy. After losing a Democratic primary for Alabama governor, George Wallace had declared that no one "will ever out-nigger me again." Bush, I suspect, would have been familiar with that line. Was it a play on words or a mere coincidence? Either way, Bush honored the pledge. In 2000, the *New York Times*' Nicholas Kristoff wrote that Kent Hance believes he "helped teach Mr. Bush the need to be more folksy." As Mr. Hance put it, "He wasn't going to be out-Christianed or out-good-old-boyed again." If this is true (and one suspects it is), then it's hard to fault Bush for doing what he *had to do* to win. And let's not forget that he wasn't just trying to forge his own comeback; he was also attempting to avenge his father's defeat at the hands of Bill Clinton in 1992. What is more, his father, former President George H. W. Bush, had been mocked as a tax-raiser and a preppy wimp. George W. Bush did everything possible to be the opposite of that. The adoption of the Texas persona helped, but the younger Bush overswaggered and overtwanged. But hey, he managed to win two elections,[53] and winning is everything, right?

The younger Bush might have benefited from being "misunder-estimated" by his adversaries, but the "bumpkin" label stuck to the rest of us. To the extent conservatives are now associated with this stereotype, one wonders to what degree this was self-inflicted by past *winning* Republican leaders who posed as the bumbling everyman, going all the way back to Ike.

The problem was, although this is a bipartisan phenomenon, it just happens to have disproportionately impacted the Right. Again, Republicans are thought of as the *stupid* party. Both sides of the political aisle occasionally genuflect at the altar of rural superiority, even if Republicans are decidedly better at it. Although President Obama's appeal to urbanites and minorities is obvious, as we've already noted, he is not above the affectation of droppin' his *g*s and prattlin' on about "folks." Likewise, prep school–bred John Kerry ("Can I get me a hunting license here?") experimented with some downright, down-home Forrest Gump elocution during his 2004 race. Hillary Clinton has been known to affect a Southern accent when convenient. Even less subtle was the over-the-top, twangy country music song "Stand With Hillary" released in late 2014—"Put your boots on and let's smash this ceilin'"—where all the *g*s were dropped. The producer of the "Stand With Hillary" song also produced a 2008 viral mariachi video, "Viva Obama." Nothing happens by accident in politics. Hillary's pandering is a transparent attempt to woo the "real America." Noting the dichotomy between Obama's pop-culture outreach—which featured the Will.I.Am song "Yes We Can" and Hillary's—Ben Domenech, publisher of *The Federalist* website, observed, "The attempt to pander to the white working class voters left out by the Democratic agenda for so many years is obvious and clumsy, but also revealing, signaling their perception of what's happened to the electorate in the course of the Obama era."

For all the GOP's problems, it is perhaps instructive to remember that Democrats also face their own challenges, which include struggles to win white votes—and their own gender gap with men. Putting aside politics, the notion that America should have one de facto white party and one de facto minority party strikes me as unhealthy. We should all resist this sort of racial balkanization. And, of course, just as Republicans confront regional geographic problems, the Democrats missed winning the White House in 2000, at least partly because Al Gore couldn't deliver his home state of Tennessee. Just a dozen years ago, former senator Zell Miller, a conservative Democrat, penned a book titled *A National Party No More*, lamenting the fact that his beloved party had written off the South, and would continue to pay an electoral price. "Today, our national Democratic leaders look south and say, 'I see one-third of a nation and it can go to hell,'" he wrote. This is a good example of how political fortunes can quickly change. Just as Miller's book hasn't aged well (electorally speaking, the Democrats seem to have made the right political moves), a dozen years from now *this* book might seem antiquated. I won't be at all upset if that happens. Still, almost all the long-term trends (including demographic shifts and shifts in public opinion) seem to suggest the GOP is in trouble if it doesn't adapt and overcome.

Rural Deification

The Republican electoral shift transcends the deep South. While the GOP became the Southern Party, it also became the Rural Party. That's a big part of this story, too.

In the introduction of this book, I wrote about my rural background in Western Maryland and the deep abiding respect I have for rural Americans who have done much to make this a great country. I don't want to see an America where everyone is huddled into cities. In the words of Hank Williams Jr., we need Americans who still know how to "skin a buck" and "run a trotline." But one of the many challenges confronting conservatives is that America has transitioned from the agrarian age to the industrial age to the information age. Unlike the industrial age, where the top-down assembly line model favored liberals, the tech revolution may favor the rugged individualism embraced by libertarian-leaning conservatives. Regardless, given these trends, it makes little sense for a movement or a party to allow the rural-versus-urban paradigm—and the many cultural issues tied up in that—to define and assign membership status. So long as Republicans could win this way, it made perfect sense to exploit the cleavage between city folks and "Real America." Not only was this smart politics, but it also tapped into deep-seated beliefs.

So where did this traditional deification of rural areas come from? Among other things, credit (or blame) the influence of religion (think the Garden of Eden versus the Tower of Babel), philosophy (Rousseau's notion about noble savages, and later, transcendentalists like Ralph Waldo Emerson—and Walden Woods–loving Henry David Thoreau), and various ideas conceived during the time of America's founding, such as Thomas Jefferson's agrarianism. "I think our governments will remain virtuous for many centuries," Jefferson wrote Madison, "as long as they are chiefly agricultural; and this will be as long as there shall be vacant lands in any part of America. When they get piled upon one another in large cities, as in Europe, they will become corrupt as in Europe." This was bipartisan. Believe it or not, in the run-up to his 1932 election, Groton- and Harvard-educated Franklin Roosevelt enjoyed far more support from rural and Southern voters than with big-city types—and painted himself not as a former Wall Street lawyer but rather as a simple "farmer."

It's hard to deny that Americans—particularly traditional or conservative Americans—internalized a worldview that lionizes rural areas and comes close to demonizing urban ones. Look no further than our national myths and heroes. Alan Crawford, author of the 1980 book *Thunder on the Right*, argued that it all goes back to the cowboy mythology. "The great cult figure of the New Right is John Wayne," he writes, "the swaggering, tough-talking loner motivated by duty, principle, and a deep sense of justice. Wayne feared no man, respected all women. He displayed the *macho* qualities that are admired and emulated in the political and cultural heroes of the New Right." Top that, *pilgrim*!

The entire concept of rural superiority is built on questionable premises. Sometimes the Bible holds up desolate areas as ideal (Jesus would often withdraw to the wilderness or desert), but as Tim Keller, pastor of New York City's Redeemer Presbyterian Church, notes, "When God sends the people of Israel from Egypt into Canaan, he will not let them be exclusively agrarian. He commands them to build cities in the book of Numbers."

"The reason [the Bible is] positive about cities," continues Keller, "is that when God made Adam and Eve creative...it was inevitable that they would build cities. Cities are places of creativity. Cities are places where culture is forged. That's the reason why culture does not begin to happen until there's a city."

For small government conservatives, even before the plague of inner-city crime in the 1960s, there were other inherent reasons to fear the city. As Steven Conn, author of *Americans Against the City: Anti-Urbanism in the Twentieth Century*, noted,[54] "The idea that in New York City now eight million people can turn on their tap and get drinkable water, that's a miracle. The efficiencies that government manages to deliver in cities become anathema to this kind of antigovernment tradition that I see as part and parcel of the anti-urban tradition."

Free Market Dynamists versus Populist Catastrophists

This brings us to a contradiction within conservatism. Much of conservatism—a belief in free markets, for instance—is premised on the dynamic notion that more people equal more ideas. But while optimistic free marketeers adhering to this Reagan and Kemp model subscribe to this theory, most populists do not. The more optimistic worldview made major strides when economists like Julian Simon and Ester Boserup took on the Malthusian catastrophe argument, which erroneously predicted that global overpopulation would lead to mass starvation, and demonstrated that more people equals more ideas, innovation, and prosperity. When you think about it, it makes sense. Rural societies tend to work on subsistence (you eat what you grow—be careful what you wish for, "local foods" advocates!), but cities, by their very nature, demand free market economic skills such as cooperation, specialization, and trade. These things make us rich. And cities are the areas where these things are appreciated and magnified. And let us not forget that great cities, after all, not only have fostered great hedge funds, but have also built great cathedrals stone by stone.

More people—constantly bumping into one another—lead to all sorts of entrepreneurial inventions and progress. Cities, it has been said, are where "ideas have sex."[55] Indeed, some optimistic cosmopolitan conservatives, such as the late Jack Kemp and his protégé Wisconsin representative and Speaker of the House Paul Ryan, have embraced a pro-urban philosophy in a consistent manner, which can be reflected in their support for policies like enterprise zones, which encourage growth and development with lower taxes and fewer regulations in urban communities. But since President Obama's election in 2008, these ideas have been on the outs with conservatives.

The greatest irony of the conservative adoption of an anticity worldview is that it is based largely on a philosophy advanced by the high priest of romanticism, Jean-Jacques Rousseau. As discussed in Chapter One, instead of following the Christian understanding of creation that views man as a fallen creature due to original sin, Rousseau envisioned early man as a sort of noble savage. It wasn't until man recognized the concept of property and ownership, Rousseau argued, that he became greedy and corrupted.

According to this way of thinking, a simple life is good and pure, while a modern urban life is dirty and unnatural. "Many scholars have pointed out the romanticists' idea that somehow cities are breeders of sinful behavior and people who live in the country are more virtuous is actually something that's been passed into the American psyche and actually into the American Christian psyche so that we have a tendency to have a very negative view of cities," says Pastor Tim Keller. When one looks at the meth epidemic that is springing up in many of our rural communities or considers the inherent temptations and boredom that arise from being a latchkey kid living in some sterile suburb, the city begins to look less dystopian.

The New South

Something horrible happened while I was writing this book. On June 17, 2015, a young white man shot and killed nine worshippers at Mother Emanuel, a storied African Methodist Episcopal church with one of the oldest black congregations, in Charleston, South Carolina. Among the dead lay Reverend Clementa Pinckney, who also had served in the South Carolina state senate. Pictures of the shooter flaunting a Confederate battle flag soon emerged, as did calls for rebel flags to come down from statehouses across the nation.

Leaders emerge during times of tragedy and crisis, and it was at this moment that Nikki Haley, the female, Indian American governor of South Carolina, who also happens to be a conservative Republican, seized the moment. "Today we are here in a moment of unity in our state without ill will to say it is time to remove the flag from our capitol grounds," Haley said at a press conference on June 22, 2015. "This flag, while an integral part of our past, does not represent the future of our great state." She was flanked by Republican senators Lindsey Graham and Tim Scott, who is one of only two African Americans in the US Senate. And, in a way, the South Carolina governor and these senators represent a changing Republican Party, as well as a changing South. Graham, the only white representative, is probably the least conservative of the three. But they bring diverse perspectives that not very long ago were absent from Republican politics in the South. "The biggest reason I asked for that flag to come down was I couldn't look my children in the face and justify it staying there," Haley later told CNN's Don Lemon. "What I realized now more than ever is people were driving by and they felt hurt and pain. No one should feel pain.... My father wears a turban. My mother, at the time, wore a sari. It was hard growing up in South Carolina."

Haley's leadership deservedly drew acclaim. "South Carolina Republican governor Nikki Haley stared down hate and history this summer, turning an impassioned debate over the Confederate flag into a political launching pad," wrote CNN's Nia-Malika Henderson. The governor provided crucial leadership at an important moment. But Haley couldn't unilaterally remove the flag; she could only sign a bill to do so after it passed the Republican-dominated state house and senate—which it did. On July 10, the flag was removed from state capitol grounds and placed in a museum.

Considering the stereotypes against Southern Republicans, it is equally notable that while controlling the senate, the house, and the governorship in the Palmetto State, Republicans did the right thing. The good news is that Haley and a generation of conservative Republican leaders like her are taking steps to bring their party into the twenty-first century, and they are resisting calls to hold on to baggage that was never theirs to begin with. In fact, it was an all-white, Democrat-controlled legislature that raised the flag in 1962. And it was Republican David Beasley who fought to have it removed from the capitol dome in the 1990s.

That's not to say that there weren't plenty of Republicans who supported flying the flag. But it is to say that there's absolutely nothing inherently Republican or *conservative* about the Confederate battle flag.

If conservatives are going to thrive in the New South, they will have to embrace an inclusive conservative message like Nikki Haley's—and they can't afford to be bogged down by carrying the offensive baggage that they, after all, had nothing to do with.

5

LIVING ON A PRAYER

*"Our government has no sense unless it is founded in a deeply
felt religious faith, and I don't care what it is."*
—Dwight Eisenhower

If modern conservatism "begins" with Edmund Burke, then the
tale of evangelicalism in politics may well begin with Burke's
contemporary and colleague, William Wilberforce. His story has
thankfully become more widely known in recent years, thanks to a
Walden Media film and an Eric Metaxas book—both called *Amazing Grace*, which is a reference to Wilberforce's mentor John Newton, an ex-slave ship captain who became a Christian, renounced his
past, and penned the famous hymn by the same name.

Born on August 24, 1759, Wilberforce dabbled with Christianity
as a child under the influence of his Christian aunt and uncle, who
helped raise him, but drifted away from their simplistic, if sincere,
version of Christianity in his youth. He attended Cambridge, experienced what pleasures the world offers, won election to Parliament,
and moved to London.

The seeds of faith planted by Wilberforce's aunt and uncle lay dormant for years, until he decided upon a road trip through the French
and Italian Riviera. When his first choice for a travel companion was

unable to accept, Wilberforce invited an old acquaintance named Isaac Milner on the all-expenses-paid journey. Milner was no ordinary man. He held the title of Lucasian Professor of Mathematics—a post that has since been occupied by such brilliant men as Stephen Hawking. Milner was also a devout Christian. And it was on this trip that Wilberforce came to discover that evangelicalism and intellectualism were not incompatible. In fact, being intellectually honest would require him to actually *live* the teachings of Christ in all spheres of his life—including his vocation.

Back in London, Wilberforce contemplated quitting Parliament altogether, fearing that politics would inexorably pollute his faith. First, however, he sought counsel from the aforementioned repented slave ship captain, John Newton, now a respected local church rector. Wilberforce had met Newton through his aunt (yet another example of his aunt and uncle's early influence planting seeds that would later sprout). Much to Wilberforce's surprise, rather than advising him to eschew politics, Newton advised him to use his perch for the glory of the Lord. But what would that look like? What great cause was he being called to champion?

Wilberforce later wrote in his diary that "God Almighty has set before me two Great Objects: The suppression of the Slave Trade and the Reformation of Manners." With the help of a motley crew of Christians known as the Clapham Sect, a network of social reformers named after a wealthy London suburb, he would dedicate his life to these great causes. (It also didn't hurt that he was a close personal friend of William Pitt the Younger, who at twenty-four, became the youngest prime minister in 1783.) Even with a little help from his friends, it still cost Wilberforce twenty-six years of constant struggle before Britain banned the slave trade in 1807, imposing fines on slave ship captains who transported slaves from Africa. Yet, Wilberforce continued the fight, until—just three days after hearing of passage of the Slavery Abolition Act of 1833 (effectively banning the institution of slavery in the majority of the British Empire)—he died.

This is not the story of an overlooked or underrated hero; Wilberforce was celebrated in his day and for years after. Abraham Lincoln once declared that even "schoolboys know" that Wilberforce helped end slavery in Great Britain. Today, Wilberforce has been adopted as a hero to many social conservatives—a prime example of faith and politics intersecting for a Godly cause. Many modern right-to-life activists equate their fight to abolish abortion with Wilberforce's uphill—but ultimately victorious—fight to abolish slavery. He fought the good fight, and one can think of worse men to emulate. Ultimately, William Wilberforce proved himself to be thoughtful, serious, devout, intelligent, and effective. He was also a happy warrior. British politician James Stephen recalled after Wilberforce's death, "His presence was as fatal to dullness as to immorality." If only we could say the same about many of today's culture warriors.

Rise of the Christian Right

I began with Wilberforce's story for several reasons: First and obviously, Christians are a key component of today's conservative movement, and any evaluation or analysis of the movement's strengths or weaknesses necessarily reflects their contribution. Wilberforce remains a prime example of how Christians can eloquently and effectively—and compassionately—contribute to public policy battles. This is not to suggest that Wilberforce (or Abraham Lincoln or Martin Luther King Jr.) was a conservative Republican. Though some comparisons can be made, the issue matrix has changed. Liberals may rightly claim ownership of some aspects of these men's legacies. For example, Wilberforce fought against cruelty to animals, an issue today more closely identified with the Left than the Right. The larger point remains that Christians constitute a large portion of the conservative base, and though this has pros and cons, don't discount the pros. I firmly believe that people of faith can and should make a positive contribution in politics. But I also believe that political involvement is seductive and fraught with danger. More and more young Christians are coming to the same conclusion. Decades after the Supreme Court's ruling on 1973's *Roe v. Wade* abortion decision, and as the culture has shifted Leftward on a variety of issues, Christians may fear that their involvement in modern politics has yielded little tangible results—except for, maybe, corrupting the faithful.

Additionally, a growing sense exists among an increasingly secular group of Americans that religion has done more harm than good in the world.[56] And here, I'm not just talking about the Crusades, fundamentalist cults, or today's radical Islamist movements like ISIS. Even libertarian-leaning conservatives sometimes argue that "do-gooder-ism" leads to a big-government "nanny state"—that "if we learned anything from Prohibition, it's that you can't legislate morality." Yet, Wilberforce's antislavery campaign stands as a shining example of why men and women of faith must involve themselves in the political process. And it wasn't the last time people of faith flexed their political muscles for the good of humanity. Would our politics have been better served without William Wilberforce or Reverend Dr. Martin Luther King Jr.? Certainly not.

Still, while some of today's evangelicals (a short definition of the term being "Protestant Christians who believe in a conversion experience and in sharing the Gospel as a mission") are doing good work and enriching the intellectual discussion, the sad truth is that in recent decades, the influx of Christian conservatives into the GOP has arguably left both groups worse off. Meanwhile, as some more cynical observers have declared, it made the party resemble something akin to the cantina scene in *Star Wars*. It has been said that Christianity would be great if it weren't for the Christians. I suspect this is a common lament of any group. As Sartre said, "Hell is other people."

The Moral Majority

How did we get from William Wilberforce to the Duggar Family (of *19 Kids and Counting* fame)? It was a process that began with the rise of the Christian Right in the late 1970s, which gave the GOP its foot soldiers and helped elect Ronald Reagan. And it didn't happen by accident. Leaders of the conservative movement specifically sought to bring Christians into the movement. "During one conversation, I said, 'Theologically conservative Americans are the largest tract of virgin timber on the political landscape,'" recalls Morton Blackwell, one of the leaders involved in courting the Religious Right.[57] These conservative leaders discussed which pastor they should recruit. But, at that time, most theologically conservative religious leaders believed politics to be outside the scope of their calling. "We agreed that Reverend Jerry Falwell should be approached," Blackwell continued. "He already had a popular, syndicated national TV program called *The Old Time Gospel Hour.*"

Among the delegation sent to Lynchburg, Virginia, to meet with Falwell was conservative leader Paul Weyrich, who observed, "There's a moral majority out there waiting to be organized." Falwell adopted the phrase as the name of his organization. As Falwell increasingly employed his TV program to encourage political participation, his viewing audience grew. Other religious leaders took note. They, too, started to urge their flocks to rise up and exercise their political rights. The news media dubbed the phenomenon the Religious Right. By 1980, millions of theologically conservative Americans were newly active in politics.

In many ways, the politicization of the church was a positive development. It certainly contributed to Ronald Reagan's election, as well as to 1994's Republican Revolution. New adherents brought numbers and zeal to the movement, but also an often less salutary "zealotry of the convert."

Ideological Immigrants

The influx of Christians into the political process changed the GOP. How could introducing a large number of Southern evangelicals *not* change things? The Republican Party has struggled to absorb ideological "immigrants" into its ranks. As previously noted about the activists who became politically active after 9/11, just as ethnic immigrants contribute to a nation, making it more diverse and dynamic, political immigrants can help grow a party. But the influx of outsiders also poses serious challenges to any existing culture. Over time newcomers usually assimilate and provide tremendous advantages, but they also bring new ideas and customs to the party—and, for better or worse, this ultimately leads to change within it.

In the 1960s and 1970s, for example, the conservative movement gained the support of neoconservatives; a relatively small group of New York intellectuals (often, but not always, Jewish) whom Irving Kristol described as former liberals who had been "mugged by reality." Just as many evangelicals departed the Democratic Party in the late 1970s and early 1980s, neoconservatives paved the way by abandoning the Left when the Democratic Party radicalized in the late 1960s. Whereas evangelicals provided ground troops, the neoconservatives infused the conservative movement with much-needed gravitas and intellectual firepower. Today, the neocon contribution is more controversial than ever. Because of the role played by some neoconservatives who served as the intellectual architects of the unpopular Iraq War, *neocon* has become an epithet meaning "warmonger," and sometimes, even, an anti-Semitic code word—a perversion of the term's original meaning. Some conservatives lament the neoconservatives' involvement within the GOP, even suggesting that Bush-era adventurism was a result of their influence. Regardless, the addition of neoconservatives clearly injected a dose of intellectualism into the Republican Party. Unfortunately, the same cannot be said for the rise of Christian conservatism.

The Scandal of the Evangelical Mind

Christian historian Mark Noll wrote in his book *The Scandal of the Evangelical Mind* that the scandal is that "there is not much of an evangelical mind." Anyone who has observed the stereotypical "dumb" Christian conservative (think Michele Bachmann) knows what I'm talking about. Things have improved since Noll wrote his book two decades ago, but evangelicalism still struggles intellectually. "Evangelicalism as an identity has lost its shape," Gregory A. Thornbury (now president of the King's College) said in a 2013 interview.[58] "When prominent thinkers convert to Roman Catholicism, they speak of returning 'home' to the Great Tradition—it's a *milieu*." Meanwhile, evangelicals wander diffused, theologically and culturally, all over the map. It's likely a predictable result of evangelicalism lacking the type of hierarchy and tradition that Catholicism, almost by definition, provides. Reinforcing this point, Thornburg quotes Paul Simon's "You Can Call Me Al," saying that the evangelical worldview has "gone soft in the middle now...now that our role model is gone."

Is Evangelicalism Destined to be Dumb?

So what's to blame? How did Christianity (preserver of literacy in a barbarian-ravaged world; protector of the weak; the most powerful advocate of mercy and forgiveness) become associated with ignorance and intolerance? Why are people of faith so often portrayed in the entertainment world as either rubes and/or hypocrites? And why is this portrayal not always exactly unfair? (Hint: original sin!)

Can evangelicals blame their poor reputation on the inevitable product of a theology that lacks a clear hierarchy to instill order and discipline? Is the problem too many denominations? Competition is a good thing, but when it comes to matters of faith, isn't it predictable that the denominations that prosper will be the ones preaching a gospel of emotion and prosperity—not of sacrifice or tradition? It hasn't always worked out that way, but there is always a temptation to tell people what they want to hear.

It's easy to gaze fondly back at the intellectual accomplishments of brilliant, saintly medieval philosophers such as the thirteenth century's Thomas Aquinas and juxtapose them with a modern televangelist like, say, Joel Osteen. And this might even lead us to fix blame on the Protestant Reformation. But this is a logical fallacy. One could just as easily suppose that the Protestant belief in the "priesthood of the believer"—the notion that each Christian is responsible for *his or her own salvation* and therefore doesn't need a priest to serve as an intermediary—is a powerful argument for taking charge of one's own intellectual development. It seems that both Protestants and Catholics once took education very seriously. Consider, for example, that universities such as Harvard and Yale (originally Puritan) and Princeton (originally Presbyterian) started as religious institutions, to say nothing of numerous Catholic schools like Georgetown and Notre Dame, let alone the medieval church's creation of the university system itself.

Moreover, early Protestants like Jonathan Edwards, one of the leaders of the Great Awakening, were clearly brilliant minds. But Edwards (and later, revivalists like Charles Finney) may bear some responsibility for the anti-intellectual urges that followed. Religious revivals, for example, were terrific at gaining converts and stirring emotion, but they were much less successful at imbuing believers with theological information. Even before television raised its first primitive antennae, intellectuals could lament how the spoken word was replacing the written word. Things we say extemporaneously tend to be less eloquent and more emotional. Demagoguery and sophistry are made easier. And while Edwards was a brilliant and intellectual writer, the era's other leading revivalists, such as the pioneering Methodist George Whitfield, were great showmen—great *orators*. And once public speaking (not written sermons) became the primary way converts were won and sermons were understood, the die was cast. New adherents to the faith would necessarily be less intellectual and more populist. Edwards inadvertently helped, as Noll writes, to "plant the seeds of individualism and immediatism that would eventually exert a profound effect on Christian thinking."

Another uniquely American element contributed to evangelism's emerging anti-intellectual strain. As Noll notes, because the American government didn't support any particular denomination, churches were "now compelled to compete for adherents," which, in some cases, resulted in a virtual race to the bottom. I doubt if anyone reading this book wants to live in a nation that doesn't support the free exercise of religion, and one supposes that competition and a free market have many positive effects, even for religions and places of worship. Because the stakes of eternal damnation are so huge, one can certainly appreciate the desire to place great emphasis on "fire and brimstone" salvation sermons meant to tug at emotional strings and win converts, and much less emphasis on discipleship or worldview—or how to actually follow the Christian walk—after the revivalist packs up his tent (think the very real Billy Sunday and Aimee Semple McPherson—or the very fictional Elmer Gantry) and heads off to the next town. Selling religion the way we sell used cars is, itself, a form of worldliness. A result is a large number of nominally Christian Americans who are neither spiritually committed nor intellectually equipped to live a Christian life. They have built their houses on the sand.

The Rise of Anti-intellectualism (and Its Notable Exceptions)

A famous moment that helped give evangelicalism its anti-intellectual reputation was the 1925 Scopes Monkey Trial, in which a substitute Tennessee high school biology teacher named John T. Scopes violated state law by teaching evolution.[59] As Richard Hofstadter notes in *Anti-intellectualism in American Life*, "The evolution controversy and the Scopes trial greatly quickened the pulse of anti-intellectualism. For the first time in the twentieth century, intellectuals and experts were denounced as enemies by leaders of a large segment of the public."

John Scopes was actually found guilty (and fined $100—a sum he never paid), but that hardly matters. In the world of public opinion, mainstream culture has long accepted his ideas, while those opposing teaching evolution have gone down in history as inbred Neanderthals. But it's worth asking why some Christians saw this as a hill to die on? Certainly, John T. Scopes, himself, did not present a serious danger. He was but a symbol. Moreover, the danger was not merely, or even *principally*, that people would start believing in evolution. No, like so many of our political battles today, the danger was that this would have a domino effect. People might begin to say, "If humans came from animals, then humanity isn't anything different or special." This opens a can of worms that might lead to all sorts of dangerous conclusions. In other words, the question wasn't even really about evolution, but instead about human dignity. But there were other implications. If people began doubting the validity of what they thought about creation, then the entire Christian weltanschauung might be one big house of cards about to come tumbling down.

It's worth noting that the Scopes trial happened in Tennessee, which is at least technically considered part of the South. The previous chapter discussed the South's impact on the GOP, and, of course, there is a huge continuing overlap between Southerners and evangelicals. Gallup's Frank Newport reported in 2014 that "residents in the South are more likely to believe in the creationist view of the origin of humans than are those living in other regions, making it clear why the fights to have creationism addressed in the public schools might be an important political issue in that region."

The Scopes trial damaged the cause of Christians even though William Jennings Bryan *actually won the case*. It was a Pyrrhic victory; the national media trashed Bryan and treated the verdict with the same respect as O. J. Simpson's acquittal. As John Maynard Keynes said, "Ideas are more powerful than is commonly understood. Indeed, the world is ruled by little else....Sooner or later, it is ideas, not vested interests, which are dangerous for good or evil." In the case of evolution, the introduction of this *idea* was more powerful than court defeats or electoral results. As Frederick Lewis Allen observed, "Legislators might go on passing anti-evolution laws and in the hinterlands the pious might still keep their religion locked in a science-proof compartment of their minds; but civilized opinion everywhere has regarded the...trial with amazement and amusement, and the slow drift away from Fundamentalist certainty continued."

The Scopes trial laid the groundwork for the culture war divide that we're still fighting today. As such, it is understandable why Bryan—a three-time Democratic nominee, a quintessential agrarian populist, and a foreign policy isolationist (to give you an idea of how much our politics has changed)—would take the stand during the trial, arguing for the prosecution and objecting to the notion that salt-of-the-earth taxpayers should fund a curriculum they find morally objectionable.[60] Instead of a faith that recognized the need to be *in* this world but not *of* this world, these culture war fights led to an unfortunate split within twentieth-century Protestantism. There were, of course, exceptions. But it's fair to say many believers were forced to make a binary choice between the devout, but dumb, fundamentalists on one hand, and the respected mainline Protestants, many of whom endorsed a sort of saccharine Christianity that in some cases rejected even the existence of a heaven and a hell, on the other. In the second half of the twentieth century, fundamentalists prospered numerically, while mainline churches withered.

In even what might be considered some of the darkest days, there were plenty of evangelicals interested in ideas. Billy Graham, for example, was the bridge between the grassroots and intellectual classes. Another notable example was Francis Schaeffer, who founded a Swiss commune called L'Abri that became a sort of Christian safe haven for 1960s expats trying to "find themselves." L'Abri's guests included hippies like Timothy Leary and Eric Clapton—all of whom were presumably subjected to Schaeffer's nightly talks about Christian worldview. Another voice in the wilderness was that of Carl F. H. Henry, the first editor of *Christianity Today*, and one of the twentieth century's most significant evangelical scholars. "Two of his works," writes *First Things*, "provide the bedrock for what we now know as Evangelicalism (contra 'Fundamentalism'), particularly as it intersects with Catholic thought." Ensuing generations included some terrific thinkers and theologians, including names like John Piper, Albert Mohler, R. C. Sproul, Russell Moore, Lee Strobel, William Lane Craig, James K. A. Smith, Tim Keller, and Gregory Thornbury—just to name a few. Today, there are probably more evangelicals doing scholarly work than ever before, laboring to fix the "scandal of the evangelical mind." But there's much to do, because for too long Christians got away with ignoring ideas—in large part, because they *could* get away with it.

The Moral Majority Meets Highly Educated Americans

During much of the twentieth century, the secular elite still constituted a small number, and the Moral Majority *could* simply turn inward and tune them out. They really *were* the majority. But more and more Americans starting to attend college (partly because of the GI Bill, etc.), coupled with the ubiquity of a secular and often anti-Christian mass media, immeasurably complicated the political challenge of winning the hearts, minds, and votes of urban and college-educated Americans. This "evolution" happened over the course of decades, if not centuries. In the 1963 book *The Lively Experiment*, Sidney E. Mead writes that since about 1800, Americans have been "given the hard choice between being intelligent according to the standards prevailing in their intellectual centers, and being religious according to the standards prevailing in their denominations." Granted, this is a *false* choice. But to the extent this was perceived to be true in 1800, imagine how true it is today.

Still, until World War I, most Americans could believe they were safely isolated from the outside world and, to a large extent, they were. And this didn't just mean that our two great oceans separated us from entangling international alliances. Except for the very elite, most Americans were shielded from the world's ideologies, philosophy, art, and literature. But just as we were eventually thrust into Europe's world wars, we were also eventually thrust into the culture wars. Isolationism failed. We would have to be in this world, if not *of* this world. Christian conservatives' failure to keep up intellectually—and even to acknowledge the necessity of doing so—had serious political implications that would eventually manifest. Is it a coincidence that, out of nine justices, not a single Protestant sits on the US Supreme Court? When they have gone looking for the most intellectually fit minds and temperaments for our nation's highest court, Republican and Democratic presidents alike don't tend to think of evangelicals.[61]

The Problem for Politicians

Today's Republican politicians confront these lingering problems, contradictions, and conundrums. The tension between a conservative base consisting largely of evangelicals and an American public who increasingly holds in contempt some Christian values (and some Christians) creates problems. Politicians can pander to their bases but alienate the larger electorate, or pander to the larger electorate but alienate their bases. A third option is perhaps even worse: adopt a weak-kneed tentativeness that seeks to nuance everything and be all things to all people. Neither the politicians, nor their Christian supporters, have developed a coherent worldview that allows them to square their beliefs with science or modernity and to explain them in ways true to their faith yet eloquent and compassionate.

As recently as a decade ago, conservatives counted on winning on hot-button social issues. Today, these issues drive a wedge between a Republican politician trying to win a general election and his base. Answering these questions is too often a lose-lose proposition. The mainstream media constantly seeks opportunities to put Republican presidential candidates with evangelical backgrounds on the spot. For example, in 2015, Wisconsin governor Scott Walker (son of a preacher man) visited London and local journalists felt compelled to ask him about...evolution. Walker punted, setting off a debate over whether he was prepared to be president. Yet, he got off easy. During an interview with *GQ* right after the 2012 presidential election, Florida senator Marco Rubio, normally one of the GOP's most eloquent spokespersons, was asked, "How old do you think the Earth is?" Rubio's hemming-and-hawing answer, which included lines like "I'm not a scientist, man," drew predictable scorn. (In between the Walker and Rubio question, Louisiana governor Bobby Jindal, a Rhodes scholar who majored in chemistry as an undergraduate, answered a similar question by declaring, "The reality is I was not an evolutionary biologist.") Rubio's dodge probably didn't hurt his standing in the "invisible primary" that much, but it played into a larger narrative that Christian conservatives are antiscience.

Are these legitimate queries "wedge issue" questions? Some questions, even if they are "gotcha" questions ("Is it lawful to give tribute to Caesar; or shall we not give it?"), need to be answered head-on. Is such questioning an unfair example of the secular liberal media trying to destroy conservatives? The press certainly deserves some blame for helping to dumb down the discussion. During a 2008 debate, Republican presidential candidates were asked to raise their hands if they did not believe in evolution. John McCain, after affirming his belief in evolution, wisely elaborated with a smart and nuanced observation. "I believe in evolution," he said. "But I also believe, when I hike the Grand Canyon and see it at sunset, that the hand of God is there also."

In hindsight, it was the perfect answer. Whether he knew it or not, McCain was summoning a worldview that had been around for a long time. Galileo wrote, "God reveals Himself to us no less excellently in the effects of nature than in the sacred word of Scripture."

Regardless of the media's motives, good politicians have a worldview and have thought about philosophical questions. The good thing about these "gotcha" questions is that they reveal conservatism's current incoherence. Forcing people to grapple with, and flesh out, their beliefs to comport with reality is a long-term service— especially for politicians who otherwise might never get around to doing it.

6

SURRENDERING
THE CULTURE

> *"The central conservative truth is that it is culture, not politics,*
> *that determines the success of a society. The central liberal truth*
> *is that politics can change a culture and save it from itself."*
> —Daniel Patrick Moynihan

It is often said that culture is upstream from politics, but what does that even mean? Edward Tylor, the founder of social anthropology, defined culture as "that complex whole which includes knowledge, belief, art, morals, law, custom, and any other capabilities and habits acquired by man as a member of society." Putting aside the family, there are essentially three powerful spheres of life that primarily instill and reinforce these habits in modern America: academia, news media, and entertainment.

It's reasonable to conclude that conservatives have lost all three.

It wasn't always this way. MGM studio chief Louis B. Mayer (California's state Republican chairman!) enthusiastically promoted wholesome, patriotic values in the 1920s, '30s, and '40s.

But that was then. "Cultivating an appreciation for art, architecture, and the world of beauty used to be considered by a previous generation of conservatives the mark of a civilized person," wrote Rod Dreher in *Crunchy Cons*, but "today it is often disdained by mainstream conservatives as an elitist pursuit." Somewhere along the line, people with traditional values checked out of popular culture and retreated inward. The Left filled the vacuum, in some cases, by employing a coordinated effort over decades to infiltrate these important institutions. Rather than lament this development, some conservatives look down their noses at anyone who is too interested in cultural enrichment.

It's hard to believe, but there was a time when cultural figures such as J. S. Bach, Anton Bruckner, J. R. R. Tolkien, C. S. Lewis, T. S. Eliot, G. K. Chesterton, Evelyn Waugh, Flannery O'Connor, and Walker Percy represented, to varying degrees, Christian or conservative values in the cultural marketplace. As Christian writer Mark Noll noted, evangelicals "largely abandoned the universities, the arts, and other realms of 'high' culture."

This is undoubtedly true, and the consequences were dire. But it's not just high culture that matters; pop culture matters, too. During an August 2013 interview, an unlikely source from the rock world— former Smashing Pumpkins front man Billy Corgan—shared some interesting insight. During a CNN interview, Corgan recalled having been asked, "What's the future of rock?" by a music magazine.

"My answer was, 'God,'" Corgan said. "Social security is the third rail of politics in America. Well, God is the third rail in rock and roll."

"You're not supposed to talk about God," he continued. "I think God's the great, unexplored territory in rock and roll music. And I actually said that...and, of course, they didn't put it in the interview."

Rather than complain, Corgan suggests the solution is for Christians to "make better music" and "stop copying U2."

This is good advice, but Corgan might not be familiar with the latest in Christian music. Indeed, it was once horrid, but, in fairness, it has gotten better. While contemporary Christian music of the 1990s mimicked secular music trends, newer Christian artists are refraining from compartmentalizing themselves as "Christian" artists—and are now presenting themselves as artists who are Christians. And, in doing so, they're making better music (see Hillsong United, Gungor, Chris McClarney, Matt Redman, etc.). These are musicians whose themes and lyrics are informed by a Christian worldview, which may or may not be explicitly noted. This is a positive development that actually hearkens back to a bygone era.

Similar to the constant Christian struggle to be "in this world, but not of this world," Christian conservatives must work to authentically engage the culture, instead of trying to ape what's already popular. If this feels foreign, it's partly because so many past conservatives viewed modern culture as inherently vulgar. And, of course, it is. But one wonders to what degree this was a self-fulfilling prophecy. It's a catch-22, at least. You end up with a circular argument: Christians shouldn't be involved in the culture because doing so can compromise their values. But what happens to the culture when Christians abandon it?

In the classic conservative book *Ideas Have Consequences*, Richard Weaver writes at length about the horrors of jazz music, calling it "the clearest of all signs of our age's deep-seated predilection for barbarism." Today, most young conservatives are quite well versed in the world of music, and most would view jazz as tame and old-fashioned. When one considers Weaver's rebuke, you have to wonder if this is a chicken-and-egg-type conundrum. Did we lose the culture because conservatives such as Weaver refused to accept and engage a truly American art form, or was Weaver a Cassandra in predicting jazz's pernicious and corrupting influence? The latter theory seems laughable.

Yet, ironically, many of today's conservatives are influenced by low culture. We might be enjoying a "golden age" of television, coming on the heels of excellent shows like *Breaking Bad* and *Mad Men*. But for every smart show that challenges the intellect, there are ten vapid and cheaply produced "reality" shows on air. And, it seems, this influence *has* infected both conservatism (see the conservative affinity for *Duck Dynasty*) and Christianity. The anti-intellectualism of evangelicalism today is, itself, a species of pop evangelicalism, which is a subspecies of pop culture. The average evangelical has the same intellectual horizon as the nonbeliever who's obsessed with *American Idol*. They are often one and the same. The only difference is that one has a fish and WWJD [What would Jesus do?] decal on his car and the other doesn't. The answer is for conservatives to make *good* art, not necessarily to make *conservative* art.

Look at the *Atlas Shrugged* movie trilogy, which is based on the famous 1957 Ayn Rand novel. As film critic Dennis Harvey observed in *Variety* after seeing the third installment, "The spirit is willing but the film making is oh so weak." It's unfortunate that these films flopped. I'm not a huge Ayn Rand fan (she was, in fact, an atheist), but her famous novel contains some compelling free market ideas that even those of us who disagree with her secular worldview can find appealing. And yet, they were (ahem) not great movies. Conversely, *The Dark Knight Rises*, the edgy 2012 installment of the Batman superhero series, seemed to many to be an indictment of the Occupy Wall Street movement. *Atlas Shrugged* felt like overt propaganda; *The Dark Knight Rises* like a subtle political critique. Likewise, mainstream Hollywood films like *Juno* and *Knocked Up*—with their potent mix of highbrow comedy and lowbrow raunch—have arguably done more to subtly advance a pro-life message than any overt political propaganda ever could.

All Politics, All the Time

Interestingly, while conservatives were abandoning popular culture and academia, they were *flocking* to politics. The problem is that, in a democracy, once you've lost the cultural institutions, all political victories are temporary. "Conservatives are too apt to be obsessed by politics and to cede culture to their opponents," says David Gelernter, Yale professor of computer science and author of *America-Lite*.

"For a generation, conservatives have shrugged off education, and now they face a hard slog merely to defeat a grandiose failure of a left-liberal president in a disastrous economy, in dangerous times, in what is still a center-right nation. If this isn't gross Republican incompetence, show me what is."[62]

Not long ago, it would have been easy to chart the history of evangelical involvement with the GOP, and view it as a sine qua non. With the Left having become radicalized in the late 1960s, and on the heels of the Supreme Court's ruling in favor of *Roe v. Wade* in 1973, Christian conservatives were finally ready to respond. After backing Democrat Jimmy Carter, a self-declared born-again Christian in 1976, evangelicals were brought into the conservative coalition, helping propel Ronald Reagan to the presidency. And after televangelist Pat Robertson's failed presidential bid in 1988, his activists formed the Christian Coalition, a group that was influential in helping Republicans win Congress in 1994—the first time they had controlled the House of Representatives in four decades. After George W. Bush took the White House in 2000—with the help of an energized Christian conservative base—his top aide, Karl Rove, dreamed of building a permanent Republican majority.

This dream was a mirage. And at least one man saw the writing on the wall before the rest. Back in 1999, conservative leader Paul Weyrich issued a controversial open letter declaring that conservatives "probably have lost the culture war." Weyrich wrote:

In looking at the long history of conservative politics, from the defeat of Robert Taft in 1952, to the nomination of Barry Goldwater, to the takeover of the Republican Party in 1994, I think it is fair to say that conservatives have learned to succeed in politics. That is, we got our people elected.

But that did not result in the adoption of our agenda. The reason, I think, is that politics itself has failed. And politics has failed because of the collapse of the culture. The culture

we are living in becomes an ever-wider sewer. In truth, I think
we are caught up in a cultural collapse of historic proportions,
a collapse so great that it simply overwhelms politics.

At the time, Weyrich's letter was criticized by many of his conservative pals, who had, after all, toiled in the trenches for years, first
for Goldwater and then for Reagan. They were still optimistic we
were on the verge of something big that would allow a conservative
savior to finish what Reagan started. But today, it looks as though
Weyrich was prescient. In fairness, he wasn't the first to recognize
the importance of the culture's effect on politics. Years earlier, Senator Daniel Patrick Moynihan observed, "The central conservative
truth is that it is culture, not politics, that determines the success of a
society"—a sentiment later popularized by conservative new-media
mogul Andrew Breitbart. But Weyrich was making an observation at
a time when many dismissed such reflection as needlessly pessimistic. Conservatives kept telling themselves that winning elections and
passing laws (often overturned by liberal judges) was tantamount
to victory. And indeed, a year after Weyrich penned his pessimistic
missive, George W. Bush was elected president.

It's hard to argue with results. In the 1980s, 1990s, and 2000s,
Republicans did very well electorally. And a big part of that was due
to the fact that evangelicals had joined the culture wars and were
aligning with the GOP to win elections. Evangelicals thus went from
the City of God to the City of Man—from being consumed with
spiritual matters to being consumed with political matters—all the
while largely ignoring the culture.

Since President Obama's election in 2008, and with a few exceptions
such as the 2010 and 2014 midterms, it has been especially depressing to be a conservative. In the past, one could more easily endure
the ranting of liberal commentators by taking solace in that—outside
of New York City and Washington, DC—most of the country was
center-right. Whenever a liberal commentator said something angry or

fringy, one could always console himself by saying (or at least think-ing), "I hope you push that idea, because you'll keep losing elections in real America." I'm reminded of an exchange between former sena-tor Alan Simpson and Bill Maher on HBO's *Real Time with Bill Maher*, which took place three days after George W. Bush's reelection. Simpson said, "You're making fun of Americans who have some religious bent, or a faith. Keep doing that and your people will never win an election. Because whether you and I like it or not, this is the only country on the face of the earth that was founded because of religious persecution and a belief in God—that's why they left Europe." Today, however, con-servatives have made a shocking discovery: *we are the ones in danger of appearing out of touch.* While we were busy winning elections, our civilization became less traditional and more socially liberal. For every Republican elected to office, there were a dozen films or songs selling sex or drugs—many of which were far more entertaining than any-thing heard on C-SPAN. Again, culture is more important than poli-tics, and politics will eventually reflect the culture.

Conservatives need to be able to talk about the culture without com-ing across like the angry old man shaking his fist and yelling, "Get off my lawn!" It won't be easy—there is a missing ingredient. For this to work, more conservatives will have to ditch their 5-irons, put down their remotes, and infiltrate the intellectual elite. When you lose intellectuals, you lose popular culture and, before you know it, you've lost the culture war. And that's where conservatives have been for a long time.

The Anti-Intellectual Strain in Evangelicalism

In addition to dumbing down conservatism, the anti-intellectual strain in evangelicalism is prompting conservatives to snub academia and in turn, the broader culture. The unintended consequence: a secular America where remaining both devout and relevant would become almost mutually exclusive.

For whatever reason, conservatives have an inclination toward activism that lends itself well to the worlds of politics, business, and economics, but not to the humanities or liberal arts. We saw this highlighted during the 2012 presidential campaign on several occasions. First, conservatives pounced when President Obama said, "If you've got a business, you didn't build that. Somebody else made that happen." On one hand, this is an insulting thing to say about entrepreneurs who incur risk to build a business. But, as Claes G. Ryn, a professor of politics at the Catholic University of America, wrote at the *Imaginative Conservative* website in 2011 (a year before Obama uttered the "you didn't build that" line), "If many businessmen in the Western world have exhibited admirable traits like honesty, good manners, and social responsibility, it is because, like others, they have been formed by an ancient civilization. They have been subject to the elevating pressures of priests, thinkers, aristocrats, teachers, and artists." The point here is that culture is more important than politics and even business. Western civilization gave us institutions like the rule of law. Without these institutions, a businessman would not want to risk capital, because someone could always steal his business—or someone could simply refuse to pay him, and there would be no recourse. The implication presented by the Romney campaign was that business owners were somehow superior people—that there was no nobler endeavor than building a business. "In spite of America's great universities on the intellectual side and its great symphonies and museums on the aesthetical side, to mention just a couple of relevant institutions, American life has a powerful utilitarian bias," continued Ryn. "That predisposition is exemplified by an inordinate fascination with makers and doers and an inclination to look down on persons engaged in nonutilitarian, low-paying pursuits."

Then They Came for Sports...

But it's not just the more highbrow, avant-garde worlds of entertainment, the arts, and academia where conservatives have retreated.

Aside from politics, conservatives have surrendered (or been outmaneuvered) in almost every facet of the culture, from the music industry to the worlds of food writing and travel writing—all of which are dominated by people of the Left. For conservatives, the final blow may prove to be the loss of sports as a conservative stronghold. Increasingly, it feels like liberalism is taking over our football stadiums and ballparks.

In the last few years, sports headlines have been dominated by stories like NBA player Jason Collins being celebrated for coming out as gay and Tim Tebow being derided for wearing his Christian faith on his sleeve, as well as debates over whether "Redskins" is a racial slur (with some outlets even refusing to use the name). More recently, members of the St. Louis Rams have come onto the field with their hands up—a symbol surrounding the death of an African American man in Ferguson, Missouri (a subsequent report issued by the Obama Justice Department concluded that Michael Brown did not, in fact, have his hands up). Even sports commentators are using their perch to advance progressive social engineering goals. In 2012, NBC sportscaster Bob Costas delivered a halftime gun control rant on the air (which was in response to the murder-suicide of NFL player Jovan Belcher), and in 2013, ESPN commentator Kevin Blackstone made reference to the national anthem as a "war anthem."

"It's funny to listen to sports commentators on the radio who have clearly been brought up through public schools and state university journalism programs talk about class and race and gender like a sociology major," said R. J. Moeller, a conservative who also writes about sports and culture, when I interviewed him for a *Daily Caller* column on the subject. "They hate any strong male coaches. They hate any sort of patriotism associated with the sport. They're treating sports and holding what goes on in locker rooms to the same standard they would a diversity and social justice mediation seminar on Google's campus." Moeller's not alone in feeling this way. Other conservatives worry about the "feminization" of sports and the liberal tilt of modern sports coverage.

By first rejecting the culture and turning inward, and then focusing almost solely on politics, conservatives now find themselves increasingly shut out of major conversations that average Americans are interested in. The fact that this trend is continuing into the sports world is indicative of the extent of the problem. Ironically, though, having stupidly surrendered the culture war years ago, today's culture warriors are too often employing aggressive counterproductive tactics that turn off some of the very people who ought to be cultural conservatives. In many cases, this involves overheated rhetoric, playing the victim card, and employing identity politics—in short, aping the worst characteristics conservative Americans have long attributed to the Left.

Checking Out of Politics

A couple of decades ago, the Christian Coalition provided ground troops for the conservative movement. But today, perhaps having seen what happened to their parents' generation, many young Christians are choosing to be conscientious objectors in the culture wars. Some of this may be due to changing attitudes concerning some hot-button social issues. But there's also a growing sense among young Christians that political involvement, no matter how pure the original motives, is a corrupting force. Christians, who attempt to be in this political world, but not of this political world, are constantly faced with ethical conundrums.

People have always made exceptions to their moral code in times of war. And what is politics but a bloodless war? But today, the warfare is asymmetrical. It's done on Twitter and at political rallies. The line of demarcation between "civilians" and political operatives has vanished.

And the fighting never stops.

For Christians, political involvement is a double-edged sword.

The real danger is that over time it has a coarsening effect. They are wise as serpents, but no longer innocent as doves. Many evangelicals now face a sort of catch-22. Their forefathers unwisely retreated from the culture, and now they're being told that they have to abandon their temperament and values in order to take it back. In other words, we have to destroy the village to save it.

But what shall it profit a man if he should win the election but lose his soul?

PART THREE

WHAT A MESS

7

TOO SMART TO WIN

"If a nation expects to be ignorant and free, in a state of civilization, it expects what never has and never will be."
—Thomas Jefferson

"Whatever it is, I'm against it."
—Groucho Marx

During the sweltering summer of 1776, a group of brilliant men huddled in Philadelphia to declare independence from Great Britain. Many of them—like Jefferson and Franklin—were polymaths: inventors, philosophers, scientists, theorists, and writers. Historian Richard Hofstadter described the Founding Fathers as "sages, scientists, men of broad cultivation, many of them apt in classical learning, who used their wide reading in history, politics, and law to solve the exigent problems of their time."[63] In other words—horrors!—elites.

For decades, this founding generation (Washington, Adams, Jefferson, Madison, and Monroe) presided over our young nation. John Quincy Adams, son of our second president and an incredibly accomplished man in his own right, succeeded them as our sixth president in 1825. But the nation was changing. The West was expanding, and more people were becoming enfranchised.

The time was ripe for a populist like Andrew Jackson, a Democrat and a military hero. He marked a stark break from the founding generation. With a few exceptions, populism, often with an anti-intellectual flavor (think "Tippecanoe and Tyler, Too" and the "Know-Nothings," for example), dominated American politics of this period until the rise of Theodore Roosevelt, a hybrid candidate who—despite being old moneyed, aristocratic, bespectacled, and Harvard educated—somehow managed to overcome all those "disadvantages" by virtue of advocating a strenuous life, moving to North Dakota and becoming a cowboy, leading the charge up San Juan Hill, and loving big game hunting. (The next time you see Ivy League–educated Ted Cruz wearing a blaze orange hunting jacket in a duck blind, you'll know why.)

That's not to say the presidents between Jackson and TR were all ignoramuses (many were conversant in Latin; James Abram Garfield could simultaneously write in Latin with one hand and Greek with the other). Numbered among the most important political events of our nation's first hundred years was the series of Senate debates in 1858 between Illinois's Democratic candidate, Stephen A. Douglas, and Republican candidate, Abraham Lincoln, who was a man (like Garfield) famously born in a log cabin. Just imagine it: two men—both civic-minded, both well-read—and before them an audience willing, even eager, to hear one candidate speak for sixty minutes, followed by his opponent for ninety minutes, culminating in thirty minutes for a rebuttal. Now imagine repeating that debate six more times.

Still, stylistically, populism dominated from Jackson until TR—who soon paved the way for a far less robust intellectual named Woodrow Wilson—whose involvement in the First World War effectively led to a backlash against intellectuals that lasted until FDR's "Brain Trust" of advisers came to town. A post-FDR backlash endured until JFK. After JFK's presidency and the sense that "the best and brightest" had led us into Vietnam, the pendulum again swung away from intellectuals. This third reaction lasted until the arrival of Obama. There is a historic ebb and flow between voters demanding dumbed-down populist style and intellectual elite style; the last populist phase ended with Obama, yet Republicans are still trying to win with dumb.[64]

Too many of today's conservatives deliberately shun erudition, academic excellence, experience, sagaciousness, and expertise in politics.[65] Many of the people doing so are not as dumb as they pretend to be. But many do lack wisdom—a wisdom that true conservatives from a prior generation would describe as one that embraces education, expertise, and scholarship. Today, even those rare conservatives who possess a wealth of knowledge feel obliged to *act* dumb. In 2015, Louisiana governor Bobby Jindal noted, "There is a tendency among the Left and some Republicans that say you can either be conservative or smart." He was right—so why does he keep acting dumb? It turns out there's a pretty good reason. If there's such a thing as being *too dumb to fail*, then isn't it possible a politician could be *too smart to win*?

Referring to a particularly vapid article penned by Jindal, in which Jindal criticized "bedwetting" introspection ("excessive navel gazing leads to paralysis"), *Slate*'s Dave Weigel observed, "Jindal's rep[utation] is as a wunderkind who was put in charge of Louisiana's hospital system at age 28. To be competitive in the Iowa caucuses, he needs to either pretend to be a schmuck or emphasize his heretofore-concealed schmucky tendencies."

Weigel wasn't the only one who noticed. "Jindal isn't talking to independents or Democrats in this op-ed. This is solely about telling Republicans what they want to hear," wrote Ezra Klein in the *Washington Post*. "That's how the GOP becomes the stupid party: Republican Party elites like Jindal convince Republican Party activists of things that aren't true. And that's how the GOP becomes the losing party: The activists push the Republican Party to choose candidate decisions and campaign strategies based on those untruths, and they collapse in the light of day."

Republicans have occasionally proposed a positive, substantive agenda, such as the party's Contract with America in 1994 or the more recent and ambitious government reform budgets of representative Paul Ryan. But the norm has been to eschew substance for poll-tested fluff like George W. Bush's "compassionate conservatism" (which only pretended to be an ideology) and Donald Trump's "Make America Great Again" slogan (which did not even pretend). One reason why politicians are losing their intellectual sharpness is that many have no choice but to spend about 50 percent of their time raising money. Take it from me; my wife is a political fund-raiser. Part of her job is to sit with candidates and elected officials as they "dial for dollars." The media also deserves blame for our current state of candidates. We lament the loss of access and the days of "straight talking" politicians, yet are quick to crucify any politician who dares say something interesting. The smart move for politicians is to talk in sound bites, to stay on message, and to be boring.

I'm reminded of this scene from the movie *Bull Durham*, when Kevin Costner's character—catcher "Crash" Davis, a battle-hardened minor league veteran—schools rookie phenom pitcher Ebby Calvin "Nuke" LaLoosh (Tim Robbins) on how to talk to the press:

> **Crash Davis:** You're gonna have to learn your clichés. You're gonna have to study them; you're gonna have to know them. They're your friends. Write this down: "We gotta play it one day at a time."
>
> **Nuke LaLoosh:** Got to play...It's pretty boring.
>
> **Crash Davis:** 'Course it's boring. That's the point.

Sadly, it's not just rookie ballplayers who are taught to spout insipid lines. Our nation's leaders learn the same script. And if they dare go unscripted—if they dare say something interesting—we destroy them. The result is a dumbed-down political discourse with no substance. Today, it is the GOP that is more or less the party of the disaffected populists. The party is thrashing about, suffering an identity crisis—stunned that the American public no longer reflexively supports them—and this leads to all sorts of negative consequences. As with an alcoholic who finally hits rock bottom, recovery works in stages—and denial is usually the first stage.

The final part of this book will focus on some ways conservatives can return to their intellectual moorings, and, indeed, the midterm elections of 2014 provide hope that the process has already begun. It's also fair to say that just as Ronald Reagan was able to encourage both the nation and the GOP to up their games, electing the right leader can cover a multitude of sins. Should Republicans elect a transformational president, many of these problems might right themselves.

For now, however, I have identified three symptoms of our malaise, all marked by the demise of a necessary political strength: 1) the death of experience and knowledge, 2) the death of compromise, and 3) the death of political institutions.

1. The Death of Experience and Knowledge

According to a March 2015 CNN/ORC poll, nearly half of Republicans—46 percent—want a candidate who is new to politics (conversely 77 percent of Democrats said they want an experienced one).[66] Perhaps it came as no surprise, then, when Donald Trump and Ben Carson (neither of whom had ever been elected to public office) surged to the top of the polls in the late summer of 2015.[67]

The rejection of experience and expertise parallels the history of anti-intellectualism in America. The "anti-expert" ethos is cyclical, having begun with Old Hickory Jackson's victory over John Quincy Adams, whose "learning and political training were charged up not as compensating virtues but as additional vices."[68] One contemporary newspaper described the contest as between "John Quincy Adams, who can write" and "Andrew Jackson, who can fight."[69] (In 2011, Herman Cain would unintentionally channel this sentiment, declaring, "We need a leader, not a reader.") The problem was, as

Richard Hofstadter notes, "the Jacksonian conviction that the duties of government were so simple that almost anyone could execute them downgraded the functions of the expert and the trained man to a degree which turned insidious when the functions of government became complex."[70] Donald Trump similarly convinced many conservatives that governing doesn't require any sort of expertise. Solving illegal immigration would be easy, he insisted. He would just have the Mexican government pay for a fence. Health care? Trump would simply replace Obamacare with "something terrific." Foreign policy expertise? You can get that by watching "the shows." When conservative talk radio host Hugh Hewitt tripped him up, exposing Trump's lack of foreign policy expertise, Sarah Palin came to his defense. "I'd rather have a president who is tough and puts America first than [a president who] can win a game of Trivial Pursuit," she declared. Not much has changed since the time of Adams and Jackson.

But Palin wasn't the only conservative defending Trump's lack of knowledge and experience. After videos showing Planned Parenthood discussing the harvesting and selling of baby organs sparked calls to defund the group from taxpayer support, Trump declared on CNN's *New Day*, "I would look at the good aspects of [Planned Parenthood], and I would also look because I'm sure they do some things properly and good for women." He then continued, "I would look at that, and I would look at other aspects also, but we have to take care of women. The abortion aspect of Planned Parenthood should absolutely not be funded." Despite the fact that Trump is a brilliant businessman (just ask him), he appeared unfamiliar with the basic concept that money is *fungible*. He apparently didn't realize that taxpayer subsidizing of Planned Parenthood's legitimate health care services frees up other money for abortions. More interesting than Trump's ridiculous position, however, was the fact that his conservative apologists were still making excuses. After Trump's Planned Parenthood comments, conservative provocateur Ann

Coulter actually went on Fox News's *Hannity* to defend the mogul, even if her words sounded more like an indictment of his lack of experience: "He is not a politician. He is not familiar with all the deceptive ways Planned Parenthood will sneak through funding for abortion."

Of course, Trump is merely the next step in the trend of elevating entertainers to executive positions. It's important to remember that Arnold Schwarzenegger and Jesse "The Body" Ventura have more in common than just starring in the movie *Predator*; both are also failed governors. It was only a matter of time until this trend made it to the highest office in the land.

Consider how the qualifications for president have continued to decline in the last thirty years. Yes, Ronald Reagan was an actor, too. But he didn't simply try to trade on his celebrity to attain elective office. He proved himself in the arena of ideas before becoming governor, and accumulated actual governing experience before running for president. He was married (twice), had three[71] kids (and adopted another), and had multiple careers that were punctuated by both achievement and less successful endeavors. Before being elected president in 1980, he lost two presidential bids (if you count 1968) and served two terms as California's governor. What a stark contrast to today, when seemingly fifteen minutes as a US senator from Illinois or a half term as governor of Alaska serve as qualifications. And the bar keeps getting lowered. Before she was even sworn in after her 2014 Senate victory, Joni Ernst was touted by pundits John McLaughlin and Bill Kristol as a possible 2016 presidential candidate. As recently as 2011, she served as the auditor of Montgomery County in Iowa (population 10,424), and now she's ready to be president?

Part of the problem is that, as a civilization, we no longer respect experience or revere elders. It used to be you paid your dues. The new guy on the job bided his time and spent that time observing those above him. Today, young people start a new job on Monday and are trying to take over by Friday. You've probably heard the line, "Give me six hours to chop down a tree, and I'll spend the first four sharpening my axe." How quaint. Jesus spent thirty years preparing for a three-year ministry, but today we can't wait to get behind the pulpit.

The democratization of information also deserves to be mentioned. Google empowers people to feel (incorrectly) that they no longer need experts. In politics, average voters and amateur activists can now access the same raw data as elected officials and often trust their own interpretation over that of some designated expert's. Everybody thinks he can do three things: manage a baseball team, write a book (!), and run for/hold an office. Everybody isn't always right. The "instant expert" phenomenon is choking journalism. Young people formerly worked their way up the ranks of a publication. Now, media outlets, desperate for young consumers and cheap labor, routinely make the mistake of elevating the inexperienced. In the old days, a young cub reporter might toil for years in a local market honing her craft at straight reporting before finally getting a chance to write a column. Now, a decent Twitter following might land you a TV show, as it did for twenty-six-year-old Ronan Farrow on MSNBC, despite his youth and inexperience. MSNBC canceled him in little more than a year.

Some of media's dramatic shift to youth is due to the larger trend of media decentralization and the rise of alternative outlets, giving young reporters—willing to work longer hours for less money than the middle-aged—more platforms to seize. Conservatives, who endured generations of a liberal media filter monopoly, are understandably hesitant to criticize the emergence of alternative media, but, as the late novelist David Foster Wallace pointed out in his *Atlantic* essay, "Host," "The ever increasing number of ideological news outlets creates precisely the kind of relativism that cultural conservatives decry, a kind of epistemic free-for-all in which 'the truth' is wholly a matter of perspective and agenda."

The trend gallops on even in America's most elite club—the US

Senate. Ted Cruz had barely been on the job for two months in 2013 when he pointedly challenged California senator Diane Feinstein over her support of an assault weapons ban. "I'm not a sixth grader. Senator, I've been on this committee for twenty years," she scolded Cruz.

Another particularly egregious example of pursuing instant gratification over dues paying saw former vice president Dick Cheney's daughter Liz Cheney (a former State Department official who had never held elected office) decide to challenge three-term incumbent senator Mike Enzi in Wyoming's Republican primary. Ms. Cheney had no plausible philosophical reason for opposing Enzi. He was a reliable conservative vote from a deeply red state. Even stranger, Cheney lived in Virginia, where she could have run against an incumbent Democrat. But that meant risking a loss in a swing state. Still, if she had thought her politics wouldn't play in Virginia, she might have moved westward, gotten involved in community affairs or local government for a few years until Enzi, now serving his fourth term, was ready to retire. But Ms. Cheney didn't think she had to pay her dues. She thought she could convince Wyoming voters to dump a solid conservative because of her name. Unfortunately for her, the audacity of challenging a sitting US senator of the same party *just because you can* proved unseemly. The backlash among Wyoming voters was fierce, and she dropped out seven months before the primary (citing health reasons in her family).

It was an appalling episode, but who could blame her for trying? We live in a world where both Democrat Barack Obama and Republican Ted Cruz showed up in Washington and immediately began running for president. Neither man had any executive experience (Obama had been a backbench Illinois state senator, and Cruz had never held elected office before), but both adopted a "go big or go home" mentality. It's too soon to see how this will play out for Cruz, but it's fair to say that, heretofore, both men have largely prospered professionally from their approach (even if the nation has suffered as a result).

It's not just that today's youth are disrespectful to their elders.

Our elders also fetishize youth. It was not always thus. "Young people are in a condition like permanent intoxication," declared Aristotle. We shouldn't be glamorizing the ignorance of inexperience, and the fact that we do has led us to predictable results.

The conservative movement, desperate for young people to replenish its aging ranks, has fallen prey to the cult of youth. Every once in a while, a new wunderkind emerges on the Right. Consider the case of Jonathan Krohn, best remembered for delivering a speech to the 2009 Conservative Political Action Conference (CPAC)—one of the most important annual gatherings of the conservative movement. *He was thirteen years old.* Krohn now regrets the speech, explaining that he was merely parroting what he heard growing up in conservative Georgia. "I think it was naive," he told *Politico* in 2012. "It's a thirteen-year-old kid saying stuff that he had heard for a long time."[72] So who's to blame? Over at *Commentary*, Alana Goodman took Krohn's parents to task, asking, "What were his parents thinking when they pushed him into the national spotlight as a 'conservative pundit' at just thirteen years old?" A better question: Why would a venerable institution like CPAC undermine the stature of their platform by allowing a kid to give a speech? Was it merely a novelty?

This lowering of barriers and removal of filters can be positive, but not every outcome is. Take the case of one conservative blogger who gained notoriety (or was it infamy?) during Republican senator Thad Cochran's bitterly disputed 2014 primary reelection campaign in Mississippi.

It was a story straight out of a John Grisham novel. Here's the abbreviated version: A young Mississippi conservative activist and blogger named Clayton Kelly sneaked into the nursing home where Senator Cochran's bedridden, dementia-stricken, seventy-two-year-old wife, Rose, was living, in order to photograph her. The reason? There were rumors that Senator Cochran was shacking up with one of his female staffers, and this conservative activist apparently believed juxtaposing pictures of Cochran's infirm, bedridden wife with pictures of Cochran living the Washington high life with an alleged mistress might help Cochran's primary challenger Chris McDaniel win the race. But things fell apart when the police closed in (Mississippi law prohibits exploiting a vulnerable adult), and then things really took a turn for the worse. Mark Mayfield, a Mississippi Tea Party leader who was allegedly involved in the scheme, died of an apparent suicide. (As if this story weren't interesting enough, after Rose Cochran died, Thad Cochran and his aide, in fact, got married.)

As a writer, I am sympathetic to how an ambitious yet naive young blogger might think it's glamorous and even noble to go sleuthing around for campaign dirt—and how, in that moment, he might cross a serious legal and ethical line. The incident in Mississippi represents the culmination of many things. We have the convergence of media activism (with the rise of alternative media and blogs blurring the lines between activism and journalism), the ever-present problem of campaigns and journalism being stacked full of ambitious young people like Kelly, untethered by life experience or historic perspective, and, finally, the trend of political campaigns treating losing any election as an existential threat to one's side.

And this is complicated by the fact that young people (without the benefit of a fully developed frontal cortex) are on the front lines. The adults are no longer in charge—a situation that holds true even in senior positions for major US Senate races.

Once upon a time, only a seasoned professional would serve as a spokesman for a high-profile campaign. Consider the case of the aforementioned Reagan aide Lyn Nofziger, who lost two fingers to German shrapnel on D-day,[73] two decades before going to work for Ronald Reagan. In between, he was a husband, a father, and a reporter. But times have changed. A 2014 *New York Times Magazine* piece on the two spokespersons working for the campaigns of Senator Mitch McConnell (Kelsey Cooper) and his Democratic opponent, Kentucky secretary of state Alison Lundergan Grimes (Charly Norton) makes that abundantly clear: "Norton and Cooper,

25 and 23 respectively, are typical of young political operatives at work today. Each speaks with a Southern accent, though neither is from the South, let alone Kentucky," the piece tells us. "The job now requires no special education or experience, no roots to a state, and no affiliation with a candidate."

If the lack of respect for experience, authority, protocol, and ethical standards is a problematic trend, at least it's an *informal* one. Interestingly, not only are populists unconcerned about this trend, they want to enshrine it into law with term limits—a government mandate that elected officials be inexperienced. Ronald Reagan famously opposed presidential ones, yet the 1994 Republican Revolution promised congressional term limits (not surprisingly, it's one promise they didn't keep).

Absent elected "experts" (and their presumably experienced staffs), a permanent apparatus of unelected bureaucrats and lobbyists become the go-to experts. Without experienced and tenured public servants, an unelected ruling class eventually grows more and more powerful. Conservatives usually worry about such unintended consequences, but the siren song of wanting to "throw the bums out" is too alluring to resist.

Ironically, these "outsiders" eager to replace an entrenched politician are really insiders, dumbing themselves down just to get elected. As Hofstadter observed, "Just as the most effective enemy of the educated man may be the half-educated man, so the leading anti-intellectuals are usually men deeply engaged with ideas."[74]

Who's the biggest "outsider" in the US Senate today? At or near the top of your list is probably Ted Cruz, the government shuttering, Tea Party–backed junior senator from Texas. But Cruz attended an Ivy League school, served in the Bush administration, and is married to a Goldman Sachs executive. I can hardly think of a more elite résumé. According to *GQ*, "As a law student at Harvard, [Cruz] refused to study with anyone who hadn't been an undergrad at Harvard, Princeton, or Yale. Says Damon Watson, one of

Cruz's law-school roommates: 'He said he didn't want anybody from "minor Ivies" like Penn or Brown.'"

Who's the second-biggest outsider in the GOP today? Probably Senator Rand Paul—the ophthalmologist son of a doctor and US Representative who twice ran for president. Who's the third? I'd say Senator Mike Lee, the son of Ronald Reagan's solicitor general, who once clerked for Samuel Alito, now a Supreme Court judge. Now add in a couple of the other "anti-establishment" outsiders who (along with Cruz and Paul—and numerous others) are running for the Republican nomination in 2016. You've got Donald Trump, a billionaire real estate mogul who went to Wharton, and Ben Carson, a world-class neurosurgeon with a BA from Yale. These are overdogs posing as underdogs.

This is not a new phenomenon. Politicians have long crafted careful narratives about their personal histories to help to advance their careers, which often means trying to shed their more privileged backgrounds and portray themselves as heroes of the downtrodden and disenfranchised. America falls for it most of the time.

Reinvention doesn't always equate to spinning. FDR, a patrician, contracted polio and learned to overcome obstacles, which helped him identify with down-on-their-luck Americans. Reagan, the son of an alcoholic from Dixon, Illinois, grew up to become a Hollywood movie star before being elected president. Some observers have attributed his experience as the son of a drunk to his psychological need to be liked—to be a peacemaker. Changing circumstances helped both FDR and Reagan connect with average Americans, even though they are also the very definition of elite. And sometimes the opposite happens. Over time, people with authentic credentials—in the process of bettering themselves or playing the game to get ahead—lose touch with their roots and seem to forget where they came from. As David Brooks noted a few years back, "Occasionally you get a candidate, like Tim Pawlenty, who grew up working class. But he gets sucked up by the consultants, the donors, and the professional party members and he ends up sounding like every other Republican." Was he an insider or an outsider? Sometimes it seemed like Pawlenty himself didn't know. No wonder the rest of us were confused. Four years later, another Midwestern working-class hero, Wisconsin governor Scott Walker, tried to compete with the silver spoon crowd. He won his first governor's race by bragging about how he packed a brown bag lunch every day and bought his shirts at Kohl's department stores. But on the presidential debate stage, he had little to offer but hackneyed talking points. His poll numbers tanked, and he cut his losses. Both Pawlenty and Walker are cautionary tales: a middle-class backstory is no substitute for a compelling governing vision.

It's true that William F. Buckley once famously said, "I'd rather entrust the government of the United States to the first 400 people listed in the Boston telephone directory than to the faculty of Harvard University." But what many modern "conservatives" miss is that Buckley was attacking Harvard's liberalism, not complimenting the wisdom of Mr. Aaberg through Mrs. Adkins. Buckley critiqued the *liberal* elite, not the elite conservative (and apolitical) intelligentsia whose accumulated decades of study and expertise infused their brilliance. His quip packed a punch because he was calling the liberal faculty at Harvard *even worse* than the uninformed and the uneducated. (That Buckley was, ahem, a *Yale* man might have also contributed to this assessment.)

Despite the fact that experience is sometimes a liability, the good news is that the most recent crop of newly elected Republicans in Congress boasts a plethora of experience—and it's not solely limited to experience as "career politicians," either. In a *New York Times* column titled "The Governing Party," right after the 2014 midterms, David Brooks took great pains to demonstrate the "deep roots" the newly elected Republicans had in "the dominant institutions of American society." Among the candidates Brooks cited was James Lankford, newly elected senator from Oklahoma who has a divinity degree, Larry Hogan, the new governor of Maryland who founded a real estate development firm. Brooks also noted Tom Cotton, a Harvard graduate who served in Iraq with the 101st Airborne and in Afghanistan with a Provincial Reconstruction Team. Before his 2014 election to the US Senate, Cotton had served in the House of Representatives and had worked for the respected multinational consulting firm McKinsey & Company.

2. The Death of Compromise

Conservatives rightfully revere the Founders, who faced daunting challenges in framing our Constitution. Most agreed that the Articles of Confederation were too weak, but what should any new government look like? Small states (like New Jersey) might argue that all states deserve to be treated equally, while large states (such as Virginia) might argue that, since they have larger populations, it's only fair their citizens are represented accordingly. The Connecticut Compromise solved this problem by providing each state with two Senators, but assigning representation in the lower House based on population. Of course, once it became clear that seats in the House of Representatives would be proportional, this created a dilemma for the majority of the South, which had a smaller free population. The answer was to increase the South's population numbers by counting slaves. The North balked at this. In retrospect, it seems morally repugnant, but a compromise was reached by counting slaves as three-fifths of a person (for the purposes of representation).

Another challenge: Where to locate the nation's capital? A compromise hatched a couple of years later, in 1790, solved that one. At the time, Secretary of the Treasury Alexander Hamilton wanted the federal government to assume the Revolutionary War debts still owed by the states—a bad deal for the southernmost, more agrarian states, which stood to gain little from the plan. Some Northern states such as Massachusetts owed a lot more money than some Southern states such as Virginia—which had mostly paid off its debt. As Jefferson told it, he organized a dinner attended by Hamilton and Virginia representative James Madison.[75] The deal they brokered involved Madison not opposing Hamilton's financial plan in exchange for placing the nation's capital (previously in new New York and Philadelphia) in the "south"—a swamp where I sit writing these very words now—which came to be known as Washington, DC.

This tradition continued. The Missouri Compromise of 1820 and the Compromise of 1850 helped postpone the Civil War. Some might well argue that these compromises were morally indefensible—or that they merely postponed the inevitable. Others might see them as valiant, if ultimately doomed, attempts to avert a bloody war. Regardless, it is worth noting that the Civil War coincided with the death of three statesmen and compromisers from the various regions in conflict. It is, perhaps, *not* a coincidence that Henry Clay of Kentucky, John C. Calhoun of South Carolina, and Daniel Webster of Massachusetts all died in the 1850s. With the death of compromise, the Civil War was soon to come. After the war, the Compromise of 1877 served to undermine the legacy of Lincoln and preemptively end Reconstruction, thus paving the way for Jim Crow. (Like the 2000 election, the election of 1876 between Republican Rutherford B. Hayes and Democrat Samuel J. Tilden was fiercely disputed. Democrats, who controlled the House of Representatives, broke the deadlock by assenting to Hayes becoming president; in return, Hayes pulled federal troops from the South. It's hard to overstate the harm inflicted by this compromise.)

Still, compromise has a long (if not always proud) tradition in America. The Constitution literally wouldn't exist without it. Ironically, the very people today most likely to don tri-cornered hats and genuflect at the Founding Fathers and Ronald Reagan (who cut deals with Tip O'Neil and Mikhail Gorbachev) most vociferously oppose compromise. In fairness, beginning in the 1960s, conservatives who watched in horror as America lurched leftward have valid reasons to worry that some "compromises" are just a ruse—really part of a larger, incremental plan to radically change the nation. In this instance, the side that is perpetually conceding things in the interest of comity—even seemingly small things—eventually loses. This realization was expressed well by Gun Owners of America founder and California state senator H. L. Richardson,[76] whose book *Confrontational Politics* has become a cult classic among grassroots conservatives. Writing about compromise, Richardson observes that liberals gain ground by asking for a lot; however, once opposition arises,

[t]he Liberal then offers a compromise, a partial solution is presented. Half, instead of the whole loaf, is offered. The Left suddenly creates the aura of appearing reasonable, moderating their request. Leftist dialectics is nothing more than planned retreat, a tactic used to confuse and throw the opposition off guard. Lenin called it an important tool in accomplishing overall goals.

He used the analogy of a man driving a nail with a hammer, the backward stroke being just as important as the forward thrust of hitting of the nail. Ask for much more than expected and then, when the opposition builds, give in a little, play the good guy willing to concede. Switch from bad guy to good guy, be conciliatory, be sweetness and light, offer "compromise." Initiate the conflict then strategically back off.

This might not be a big deal, but what happens when this process is repeated over and over? It helps to visualize the political world as a football field. If each side begins in their own end zone, and the Left insists on scoring a touchdown, you might compromise and meet them on the fifty-yard line. Fair enough. But the next time they try to score a touchdown, the second compromise puts them on your twenty-five-yard line. If you wonder why conservatives sometimes appear to be digging in their heels on issues that seem somewhat trivial, or even indefensible in some cases, it's because they believe that if you give the Left an inch, they'll take a foot—and then outlaw rulers.

As such, Richardson might sound like he's reflecting the paranoia of today's "hell no" caucus, which scuttles reasonable compromise and legislative accomplishment. But he is only reporting on a playbook championed by liberals such as famed organizer Saul Alinsky. In his classic book *Rules for Radicals*, Alinsky notes that the term *compromise* is generally regarded as "ethically unsavory and ugly." But he then adds that "to the organizer, *compromise* is a key and beautiful word.... It is making the deal, getting a vital breather, usually the victory." Alinsky further advises his liberal/progressive/radical readers that "if you start with nothing" to "demand 100 percent, then compromise for 30 percent, you're 30 percent ahead."

"A free and open society is an ongoing conflict, interrupted periodically by compromises—which then become the start for the continuation of conflict, compromise, and an ad infinitum," Alinsky says. Richardson less elegantly—but no less truthfully—dubs this "the 'salami' technique, one slice at a time until the whole loaf is consumed."

Not all compromises are created equal. Some are salami, and some are just plain baloney. Some things—say, giving away Poland— ought to be nonnegotiable, while others—say, where we are going for dinner—aren't worth fighting over. Some negotiators are sincere and act in good faith, while other negotiators play pernicious games. When we give in to the latter, merely in order to keep the opposition happy and return to a time of peace and civility, we become, as Winston Churchill said of appeasers, "like the man feeding the crocodile, hoping he eats him last."

It's important to differentiate between your enemies and your adversaries. Consider the statement offered up after the attacks of September 11, when President Bush famously said, "You're either with us, or you are against us." It was meant as an ultimatum to fence-sitting foreign governments who had tolerated terrorists' presence on their soil. But it quickly became the Republican Party's approach to domestic politics. Exhibit A was the Department of Homeland Security. It's hard to remember, but there was a time in the not-too-distant past when that bureaucracy didn't exist. Yet, post-9/11, President Bush decided he wanted it. And his supporters decided that if you didn't want it, too, you were anti-American. (See the attack ad on then Georgia senator Max Cleland, a disabled Vietnam vet who was compared to Saddam Hussein and Osama bin Laden for opposing some homeland security measures.)

It's nearly impossible to discuss how best to battle extremism when mere disagreement brands you as a traitor. This us-versus-them approach to politics made our debates pettier and shallower. It also eliminated *compromise* from the vocabulary of modern conservatives. In Texas, Bush was known for working across party lines, but his pledge to be a "uniter, not a divider" soon fell apart in Washington. During an interview I conducted with Reagan biographer Craig Shirley in 2015, he blamed some of this Bush-era polarization on having a "president of the United States refer to the loyal opposition as the 'Democrat' Party—which is something you would hear from a college Republican—instead of [saying] the 'Democratic' Party." Shirley went on to argue that Reagan always called them the "Democratic" Party, because he was "always recruiting."

The lack of compromise is a bipartisan problem in Washington, but it seems to hurt Republicans disproportionately. One example is John Boehner's failure to reach a "Grand Bargain" on the budget with President Obama in July 2011. The fact that neither side could agree on a budget led to the sequester—which was intentionally designed to be bad enough to force both sides to make concessions. While both sides deserve blame, Republicans deserve special blame for mishandling the public relations aspect of obstruction. The government shutdown in October of 2013, for example, instigated a precipitous double-digit decline in Gallup's favorability ratings for Republicans, arguably costing Virginia attorney general Ken Cuccinelli his gubernatorial election and postponing news coverage about the disastrous rollout of the Obamacare website for a month.

Chastened by the government shutdown, Republicans wisely averted another attempt until after the 2014 midterms. A November 2014 NBC News/*Wall Street Journal* poll showed that 63 percent of Americans favored the new Congress to "make compromises," compared with 30 percent who preferred they "stick to their campaign promises." That might not sound like a big deal, but as the *Washington Post*'s Aaron Blake noted four years earlier, "47 percent wanted middle ground and 43 percent preferred lines in the sand."

Colorado witnessed a good example of compromise in late February 2014 when Weld County district attorney Ken Buck, a Tea Party Republican seeking to unseat incumbent Democrat US senator Mark Udall, switched places with Republican representative Cory Gardner, then running for reelection to the House. Cutting a deal where a sitting congressman would run for the Senate might sound like a no-brainer, but four years earlier, when Buck was a Tea Party favorite who lost to Udall, one suspects he would have scoffed at such a suggestion. The notion that he would cut a backroom deal, as one GOP state senator also vying for the Senate seat called it, is anathema to the grassroots ethos, which decried any sort of strategic compromise as tantamount to treason. As it turns out, the move was brilliant. Ken Buck is now in the US Congress, and Cory Gardner is now a US Senator. By cutting a deal, and by being humble enough to defer to a better statewide candidate, Ken Buck not only earned a seat in Congress, but he also proved that Colorado wasn't the blue state many feared it had become. The truth is, if Udall had won reelection, a lot of people would have proclaimed that Colorado was lost. Buck, by virtue of his prudent and unselfish move, helped Republicans avoid that fate.

3. The Death of Political Institutions

The problem for conservatives—the reason there is such a thing as being "too dumb to fail"—is that even though some voters are becoming more sophisticated, the opposite feels true for the bases of both parties—neither of which want to hear hard truths and both of which demand pandering. And so, a politician who stands up to his or her own base and attempts his or her "Sister Souljah moment" (Bill Clinton's 1992 public condemnation of comments made by hip-hop artist Sister Souljah) is more often than not punished for being courageous. Meanwhile, the base often rewards the person who tells them what they want to hear—who misrepresents reality or lies to us about what is possible. And so, we have this moral hazard. Politicians who want to win their party's nomination for Senate or president—or any office—have little incentive to be truth tellers and almost every incentive to talk tough, boast about all the things they can do, and generally tilt at windmills. This plays into what is known as the "Tragedy of the Commons." For those unfamiliar, it's an economic theory that warns that individuals acting in their own self-interest can sometimes undermine the larger collective goals, thus depleting shared resources (and, in the long-run, resulting in a lose-lose scenario).

Why don't more politicians think about the broader needs of their parties? They don't partly because of the decline of institutions and respect for authority—a larger societal trend that began around the time of Watergate but has been accelerated in the political world thanks to changes in our campaign finance system. While our culture has diminished the importance of institutions ranging from marriage to the media to the office of president, the decline of the political party was merely part of a larger cultural trend. People used to get married and stay married. They used to go to work for a company, stay there for four decades, and then retire with a gold watch. They even—and younger readers may find this puzzling—used to remain one gender. Life was more predictable. Things were more permanent. Likewise, political parties once held incredible sway. People were loyal and deferential to them. And they also wielded tremendous power. This helped keep recalcitrant party members in line. But today, with the proliferation of outside groups that fund the candidates they like (and score against—and then attack—candidates who dare buck their orthodoxy) and the fact that campaign finance laws have largely neutered the political parties, the smart move for a conservative elected official might just be to "stand up to" the Republican National Committee (RNC.)

Party leaders have lost most of their institutional leverage. Keep in mind that selecting a presidential nominee by virtue of primary elections is a fairly modern phenomenon. The party bosses used to hash this stuff out in smoke-filled rooms. Now, there were a lot of problems with that, but (one suspects) they occasionally performed a service in weeding out selfish, irresponsible, incompetent, or crazy candidates.

Similarly, one can't imagine a backbench congressman in the 1950s standing up to the Speaker of the House the way backbench Republicans do now. And just imagine what might have happened to a newly elected senator who dared to mess things up for the "Master of the Senate," Majority Leader Lyndon Johnson. Again, this sort of autocratic system was far from perfect, but the trains ran on time (or, at least, not off the rails). Today, party leaders have fewer sticks and carrots. They cannot withhold campaign funding for politicians who—thanks to outside groups, the rise of SuperPACs, direct mail fund-raising, and the Internet—no longer rely on them for funding. They can't even dole out pork in the form of earmarks to the extent they once did.

Complaining about too much democracy sounds crazy—almost as crazy as complaining about too much transparency. But actually, the surplus of democracy is also a real problem, even if it sounds absurd.

If politicians are constantly pandering, maybe it's for a good reason. In the past, we elected "representatives" to essentially serve as our trustees for a set period of time. Sure, they received constituent mail and phone calls, and lobbyists visited them. And sure, they might occasionally see some polling numbers or a tough letter to the editor. And yes, on big votes, party leaders and bosses (now mostly impotent) would twist arms. But rank-and-file members generally could vote their conscience, knowing they wouldn't be called on the carpet until Election Day, which—depending on their particular office—was two to six years down the road.

This is not to say they weren't accountable. It's just that they would be held accountable at the appointed time. But until that time, they could largely act without fear or consideration of snap public opinions or an excessive immediate retribution. They were free to take a relatively long view of politics—and to sometimes take an unpopular stand. Voters had time to cool down and judge the totality of a representative's tenure: This was by design. The idea was to avoid a form of government susceptible to being swept up in the passions of the day and subverting checks and balances. The Founders wanted to avoid mob rule and the tyranny of the majority. But one senses that their concerns might be playing out as we speak.

Our system is not a direct democracy. In fact, the Founders feared it. Yet saying so sounds not only un-American but also, increasingly, un-conservative. Trends toward direct democracy represent another example of how modern conservatives have mimicked liberal tactics. Citizens do not (yet) log on to the Internet and directly cast votes on things. Some states have Progressive-era reforms like voter initiatives, referendums, and recalls (which are to blame for much political and economic dysfunction in places like California), but that's not what I'm talking about.

We still have elected officials, and they still must stand for reelection at the appointed time. But the ceaseless stream of information and input they receive from constituents, interest groups, cable news, and the Internet makes it almost impossible for them to ignore the stimuli. Today's politicians must feel more like *American Idol* contestants who survive by constantly seeking our approval rather than statesmen/community elders empowered to take tough stances. With Twitter, e-mail, constant polling, and twenty-four-hour cable news, our leaders must forever be at the beck and call of their constituents and pundits.

While many of these trends have been decades in the making, they have culminated at the very time when conservatives are without a clear leader and are suffering a form of identity crisis. It's easier to manage the decentralizing forces of social media and third-party political organizations when you're winning elections and enjoying a powerful and articulate president in the White House. Conservatives have had the opposite fortune. There are no conservative leaders who have the moral authority to put anyone in line, no William F. Buckleys who have the moral sway—the "juice"—to "write" anyone out of the conservative movement. Buckley dared take on the John Birchers and the Ayn Rands of the world, but one fears that if any prominent conservative attempted such a courageous move today, it would be he or she who is written out of the movement.

In my career covering the Republican Party and the conservative movement, I've observed a scant few such courageous acts that could restore respect for institutions. But one notable example came from Senator Mitch McConnell. In an attempt to win Republican control of the Senate in 2014, McConnell finally started playing hardball with outside groups and vendors who were supporting Tea Party candidates who were running primary campaigns against incumbent Republicans. One such group was called the Senate Conservatives Fund (SCF), founded by conservative former South Carolina senator Jim DeMint. "SCF has been wandering around the country destroying the Republican Party like a drunk who tears up every bar they walk into," Josh Holmes, then McConnell's chief of staff, told the *New York Times*. Then, referencing a scene from the film *A Bronx Tale*, Holmes continued: "The difference this cycle is that they strolled into Mitch McConnell's bar and he doesn't [just] throw you out, he locks the door."

Another courageous act came in 2013 when conservative commentator S. E. Cupp informed the *New York Times*, "We can't be afraid to call out Rush Limbaugh." This was in response to Limbaugh's rhetoric, such as his referring to Sandra Fluke as a "slut" in 2012. But acts of courage are the exception. It's generally much safer to pander to the base than the establishment these days. And, by the way, *everyone* panders. Liberals certainly pander to their base, in some cases, via the redistributive state (by giving them our money). Conservatives face the problem of pandering to a dwindling share of the future electorate. The conservative base now forces candidates to say and do things that will render them vulnerable in general elections. "I don't know if I'd be a good candidate or a bad one," said former Florida governor Jeb Bush in December of 2014 at a forum hosted by the *Wall Street Journal.* "But I kinda know how a Republican can win, whether it's me or somebody else." A successful candidate, he continued, "has to be much more uplifting, much more positive, much more willing to be practical," than recent nominees, and should also be willing to "lose the primary to win the general, without violating your principles."

Most politicians prefer winning. This leads them to tell the base exactly what they want to hear, causing conservatives to sometimes say things that are wildly unpopular with the vast majority of Americans. Consider North Carolina senator Thom Tillis, for example. He was the moderate "establishment" candidate in his Republican primary. But in 2015, just months after being sworn in, in an apparent attempt to demonstrate his anti-regulatory bona fides, he randomly volunteered that he wouldn't care if Starbucks decided to opt out of its policy requiring employees to wash hands, "as long as they post a sign that says, 'We don't require our employees to wash their hands after they use the restroom.'"

"The market will take care of that," he continued.

This same urge to overcompensate led moderate Mitt Romney to declare he was "extremely conservative"—and to spend a lot of time talking about the makers and the takers, and to make that damaging gaffe about the 47 percent. In Romney's case, he was at least partly pandering to the rich donors who write big checks. But most of the pandering is to the grassroots. And, as we are about to discover, it almost inexorably leads to a political dumbing down and to outright demagoguery. That's partly because the present-day conservative coalition increasingly harbors a hotbed of anti-intellectual fervor.

8

MEET THE VULTURES

*"The best lack all conviction, while the worst
are full of passionate intensity."*
—W. B. Yeats, "The Second Coming"

*"Every great cause begins as a movement, becomes a
business, and eventually degenerates into a racket."*[77]
—Eric Hoffer

To begin, it's important we set something straight. There's the conservative movement, and there's the Con$ervative Movement. The conservative movement is rooted in a proud intellectual heritage and is committed to protecting fundamental freedoms. The Con$ervative Movement has turned the cause into a profiteering venture, and, in the process, exploited some of the worst impulses of grassroots conservatives. For the conservative movement to survive and thrive, we need to excommunicate the hucksters and scoundrels who are running the Con$ervative Movement.

If you're unfamiliar with the problem, in May of 2015, I wrote a piece for the *Wall Street Journal* titled "The 'Conservative' PACs Trolling for Your Money." In the column, I reported on a group called the Conservative Action Fund who wanted to draft former

Florida representative Allen West to run for the US Senate there. "With Marco Rubio running for the White House, this seat is even more vulnerable," the April 17, 2015, solicitation said before asking recipients to "make a generous gift of $15, $25, $35, or even $50" to circulate a petition. There was just one problem: West was unlikely to run for the Florida Senate seat, because, as I noted in the column, he had moved to Texas.

The same group also sent out a fund-raising e-mail asking people to donate money and sign a petition to draft Condi Rice to run for California's senate seat (it's unclear which African American Republican—West or Rice—was less likely to run for senate in 2016). Around the same time, Conservative America Now, yet another group with an innocuous sounding name, was raising money to "draft Arizona representative Matt Salmon to challenge Senator John McCain." In February of 2015, Salmon's spokesman suggested the e-mail "appears to intentionally mislead potential donors."

But the problem isn't limited to groups raising money ostensibly to support hypothetical candidates. According to FEC reports, the Conservative Action Fund (a group we referenced earlier), spent less than 20 percent of funds they raised during the 2014 cycle supporting candidates and campaigns. As is often the case, most of the money went to consultants and overhead. Again, these findings are not unique.

In 2013, Ken Cuccinelli,[78] a staunch conservative who now heads the Senate Conservatives Fund (SCF), narrowly lost his gubernatorial race in Virginia. Rather than sit idly by, he filed a lawsuit alleging that much of the $2.2 million raised in 2013 by an outside group called Conservative StrikeForce PAC was the result of using Cuccinelli's name—yet the political action committee (PAC) contributed "less than one-half of one percent" of that amount to his campaign. The PAC's treasurer, Scott B. Mackenzie, responded to a request for comment in my *Wall Street Journal* column and conceded the group "fell short of our expectations and we were unable to spend as much on the race as we would have liked." In May of 2015, a settlement was reached between the parties that appeared to observers to be very favorable for Cuccinelli. Only time will tell if this has a chilling effect on this kind of activity.

Sounding the Alarm

The good news is that several media outlets—mainstream as well as ideological—have begun sounding the alarm. In February 2015, conservative blogger John Hawkins published a study of seventeen political action committees. His *RightWingNews* website found that the bottom ten PACs he examined contributed less than 10 percent of the money they raised on independent expenditures or direct contributions to campaigns. Hawkins then asked a series of depressing rhetorical questions: "How many conservative candidates lost in 2014 because of a lack of funds? How many of them came up short in primaries, lost winnable seats, or desperately tried to fight off better-funded challengers? How much of a difference would another $50 million have made last year? That's a very relevant question because the ten PACs at the bottom of this list spent $54,318,498 and only paid out $3,621,896 to help get Republicans elected."

So why do they do it? In some cases, we need to understand that fledgling groups require a lot of overhead to get started. But that excuse certainly doesn't account for all of this. Another answer might simply be incompetence. But it's also likely that some of these groups are simply bad actors whose work is a net negative for the conservative movement. Some might have started with bad motives. But many, I suspect, began with noble intentions and were seduced into the dark side. (If you're looking to make money and can't cut it in the business world or as a candidate or political operative, then this is a pretty good gig.)

And for former politicians, who says cashing in at some lobbying firm is the only way to go? Creating your own gig in the Con$ervative Movement is a great way to build a retirement nest egg. Consider the case of former House Majority Leader Dick Armey, who was essentially forced out of his position as chairman of the Tea Party group FreedomWorks in late 2012. Armey lost an internal power struggle with then FreedomWorks president Matt Kibbe, a bespectacled libertarian known for his ridiculously long sideburns, after Armey raised concerns over royalties paid to Kibbe for his ironically titled book *Hostile Takeover*. (Armey argued FreedomWorks' resources were used to write and market Kibbe's book and that Kibbe was personally profiting at the expense of the organization.) But it's hard to feel sorry for Armey. He landed softly thanks to a golden parachute. As ABC News reported, "Under the terms of the deal, Armey will receive $400,000 a year until he is 92—a total of $8 million—to be a consultant."

Interestingly, It's Almost Always Legal

Even though the examples I've cited undoubtedly harm the conservative cause, sucking up resources that might otherwise be spent on electing conservative candidates, few are illegal. And it's not just the Tea Party groups, either. Conservative consultants and vendors have aroused suspicion, too. In July of 2014, a Fox affiliate in Detroit, WJBK-TV, ran an investigative report package on conservative direct mail firms that were raising money from elderly and often ill conservatives, in some cases to fill the coffers of candidates who weren't even running for office. "Campaign finance experts say there's no law against raising money for people who don't end up running for office, and it's okay for fund-raisers to pay themselves almost all of the funds they raise as long as they fill out the proper paperwork," the report said.

Nobody should begrudge conservative candidates or organizations for paying their employees well, and it's impossible to eliminate all overhead (it takes money to make money, as they say). Nor should we criticize political consultants for earning a living. (Disclosure: As mentioned earlier, my wife is a political fund-raiser who has consulted for conservative candidates such as Ted Cruz, Rick Perry, and Ken Cuccinelli. She's damn good, and worth every penny.) But judging appropriate behavior from inappropriate behavior is sort of like the old line about pornography: you can't define it, but you know it when you see it.

The question is, at what point do these things become a net negative for the conservative movement? If you're adding value, you should, by all means, be compensated well. But the problem is that, as the Eric Hoffer epigraph at the start of this chapter suggests, this has gone from a "movement" to a "business" to a "racket" for far too many people.

And it's a racket with consequences. Even if you put aside the moral and ethical questions of lining your pockets by taking the last twenty-five dollars from an old lady who just wants to defend the life of an unborn baby, consider the possible bottom line consequences for a conservative movement whose resources are going to enrich political operatives. These groups and consultants are taking points off of the scoreboard. It's hard to quantify how much money is wasted—money that could have been used to fund an ad for a conservative candidate or to keep the phones turned on at a pregnancy crisis center. But as the aforementioned study conducted by *Right-WingNews* suggested, the worst ten PACs alone cost the conservative movement $50 million in just one election cycle.

The Pander and the Damage Done

In order to raise money from the masses, organizations and consultants are also helping dumb down conservatism. In some cases, this consists of rhetoric about taking down the establishment and the "ruling class." In other cases, it is accomplished by stirring up paranoia and anger among the base, often to get them to sign petitions (and almost every online petition is a ruse to get you on e-mail lists that can then be sold) or to clog the phone lines of House members so that reasonably conservative Congressmen can be lectured to about why shutting down the government is, in fact, a good idea that will work "if only they have the guts and courage to try."

The irony is that the people who tell the base what they want to hear are characterized as courageous, while the people willing to stand up to them are labeled cowards. And some of us have our conservatism questioned and are labeled RINOs (Republicans In Name Only).

But it's not just outside groups and venders pocketing money that should be spent on *candidates*. In 2013, a reporter for ProPublica, a nonprofit organization that specializes in investigative journalism, alleged all sorts of unethical practices by a group ostensibly set up to help support the troops. According to reporter Kim Barker, "an examination of its fund-raising appeals, tax records, and other documents shows that Move America Forward[79] has repeatedly misled donors and inflated its charitable accomplishments, while funneling millions of dollars in revenue to the men behind the group and their political consulting firms." One of the men behind the group is Sal Russo, a longtime political consultant who is chief strategist for the Tea Party Express.

When You're a Celebrity

If grifters, shysters, and flim-flam men are a problem for conservatives, love of celebrities is another. Perhaps it is because A-list conservative celebrities are so scarce that we fawn so much over the washed-up actors and musicians who end up among our ranks (sometimes seemingly after having explored every other option for resuscitating their careers). Michael Brendan Dougherty put it this way at TheWeek.com:

The conservative movement has an odd, barely admitted infatuation with celebrity. The resentment conservatives aim at Hollywood and the entertainment industry is really a back-handed way of acknowledging Hollywood's power. And so you have these odd spectacles of denouncing celebrity while craving proximity to it. See Sean Hannity dedicating so much of his show to Arnold Schwarzenegger during his first campaign for governor, rather than the eminently more conservative Tom McClintock. Or the way conservative institutions have indulged Donald Trump's fake presidential ambitions. Or Sarah Palin decrying "Hollywood leftists" on her Facebook page but having no problem joining *SNL*'s fortieth anniversary special a month later. Or Clint Eastwood's infamous conversation with a chair at the 2012 Republican National Convention.

For all the talk about "Hollyweird," conservatives go gaga over celebs. Even Marco Rubio, one of the more thoughtful conservative candidates, was boasting an endorsement from *Pawn Stars*' Rick Harrison in the spring of 2015. And for their part, A-list celebrities rarely come running to conservatives when their careers are in their primes, but instead sometimes experience a conservative political awakening as a last-ditch effort to remain relevant. In other cases, conservatives come to a celebrity's defense—not because he or she has done something noble, but because this person has done or said something stupid or controversial, angering the PC thought police. Sensing they had the right enemies, conservatives reflexively and predictably come running to the celebrity's defense.

Don Imus, the shock jock who finally crossed the line when he referred to a female basketball team as "nappy-headed hos," fits this description. He lost his MSNBC simulcast and was forced to apologize for making a joke that, while unchivalrous and impossible to defend, was nothing out of the ordinary for the crotchety old cowboy. Imus had spent years as an equal opportunity offender and contrarian, but he was never a conservative. Still, it was mostly conservatives who came to his defense, arguing that he was engaged in satire, that this was political correctness run amok, that he was victim of an organized campaign to take him down.

A similar eruption occurred when *Duck Dynasty* patriarch Phil Robertson gave an interview to *GQ* that some deemed homophobic. "It seems like, to me, a vagina—as a man—would be more desirable than a man's anus," he told them. "That's just me. I'm just thinking: There's more there! She's got more to offer. I mean, come on, dudes! You know what I'm saying? But hey, sin: It's not logical, my man. It's just not logical."

In this instance, even I became embroiled in the debate, defending Robertson during an appearance on MSNBC's *Morning Joe* program. But I have an excuse: at the time, Robertson had been placed on indefinite hiatus from his show, A&E's *Duck Dynasty*, and there was talk that he might actually be terminated. In this regard, I was objecting to the notion that someone holding politically incorrect views (and expressing them in an admittedly coarse manner) would lose his job over it. My fear was that there was a trend whereby people expressing unpopular political views are being punished, and that this would have a chilling effect on free speech (a few months after the *Duck Dynasty* dustup, the CEO of Mozilla, the web browser developer, was fired for supporting an initiative that defined marriage as an institution between a man and a woman). While I am happy to defend the principle of free speech, the notion that conservatives would hold Robertson up as some sort of hero—at least partially based on his celebrity status—was also problematic. And this, too, is a pattern.

In May of 2015, it was revealed that, as a teenager, Josh Duggar was accused of sexually molesting several girls, some of whom were his sisters, when he was a teenager. The revelation prompted the Duggar scion and costar of TLC's *19 Kids and Counting* to resign his position as executive director of FRC Action, the political arm of the socially conservative Family Research Council. Duggar was just twenty-seven years old when he resigned his leadership position.

But it was a line from a May 22 *Washington Post* story that struck me as especially telling: "Duggar was running a used-car lot before he became the new face of the Family Research Council." Celebrity infatuation syndrome had bitten conservatives yet again—but one could have said that before the molestation allegations surfaced. Duggar had no business being the face of a political activist organization without any qualifications save for being almost famous.

But you don't have to be a fresh, young face to reap the benefits of the Con\$ervative Media Complex. Conservatives have long embraced seventies rocker Ted Nugent. Nugent has always been a loose cannon, but his February 2014 comments about Obama being a "subhuman mongrel" finally earned him the rebuke of some prominent conservatives like Senator Rand Paul and Texas governor Rick Perry. Nugent didn't become controversial or uncouth overnight, but conservatives embraced him because he had all the right enemies. They do this because they hate double standards (liberal celebrities are held to lesser standards). They do this because, to them, coverage of comments like his feels disproportionate. They do this because conservatives love lost causes.[80]

Sometimes celebrities even run for office. Such was the case with former *Saturday Night Live* cast member Victoria Jackson, who lost her 2014 bid for the County Commission in Tennessee's Williamson County. When I talk about "immigrants" to the conservative movement—the activists who join the cause, but struggle to assimilate—Jackson's story serves a microcosm. According to a March 19, 2014, *USA Today* story, "Jackson said she stumbled into political activism in 2007 after spending most of her life oblivious to government and politics." After leaving *Saturday Night Live* in 1992, "she struggled to find steady work as an actress, landing roles in films that went mostly unnoticed and working stand-up comedy gigs with former *SNL* cast members." It has been noticed that some people only "find Jesus" when they hit rock bottom. Celebrities could say the same thing about "finding Reagan."

Almost Famous

But it's not just the real celebrities conservatives have a problem with. It's also that we have a penchant for making ordinary people who (to paraphrase *Saturday Night Live*) aren't "ready for prime time" into folk heroes. Who could forget Kim Davis, the then Democratic Kentucky county clerk who gained national attention in 2015 for defying a court order to issue same-sex marriage licenses? She became so famous that, fearing another politician might overshadow his candidate, an aide to Mike Huckabee physically blocked Ted Cruz to keep the Texas senator from appearing onstage with her. Depending on your perspective, Davis was either a staunch defender of religious liberty or someone who flaunts the rule of law. Either way, she made for an unlikely spokesperson for a conservative movement hoping to win the twenty-first century.

This happens because we believe the enemy of my enemy is my friend. It happens because buying into a cult of personality is easier than developing a coherent political philosophy. The moment someone stands up to our enemy, we welcome them with open arms—no vetting necessary. This is a problem. Just because someone has the right enemies doesn't make them an appropriate spokesperson for your cause. The three most obvious examples of this in recent years have been that of Joe the Plumber, George Zimmerman, and Cliven Bundy.

As you might recall, Joe Wurzelbacher (aka Joe the Plumber) gained attention when he challenged then candidate Barack Obama during a campaign stop in Ohio. Wurzelbacher acquitted himself quite well—so well that Obama's defenders started digging into his past, raising questions about whether he was even a licensed plumber. The McCain-Palin campaign started bringing him out at rallies, and McCain mentioned him during a televised debate. And then, Joe the Plumber jumped the shark. Seeking to parlay his fifteen minutes into a career, Wurzelbacher became an activist, motivational speaker, and congressional candidate. And—because anyone can do what I do—he's also a political commentator. After one mass shooting, he penned an open letter to the victims' parents, telling them, "As harsh as this sounds—your dead kids don't trump my Constitutional rights."

Why yes, Joe, now that you mention it, that *does* sound harsh.

Some conservatives likewise made the mistake of building up, and reflexively defending, George Zimmerman after he shot and killed Trayvon Martin,[81] an unarmed African American teen. After an altercation in which Zimmerman sustained head injuries, Martin was shot and killed. Zimmerman, of course, said he was acting in the capacity of a neighborhood watch volunteer. He argued he killed Martin in self-defense, and he was ultimately acquitted. It's entirely possible to believe that Zimmerman made a lot of stupid moves that night, but that he did not break the law. Having said that, I got the sense that at least some conservatives were rooting for him—that this case essentially became an example of tribalism and identity politics, with white conservatives reflexively lining up on one side, while liberals and African Americans were reflexively on the other. But whether or not Zimmerman was technically innocent, the situation should not bestow hero status on Zimmerman any more than death should automatically bestow martyrdom on Martin. Zimmerman may well have been innocent, but that did not make him a good person. The fact that he was subsequently arrested for allegedly pointing a shotgun at his then girlfriend increases the odds that he's not. Most conservatives have moved on.

Another example was of Cliven Bundy, a Nevada rancher embroiled in a decades-long standoff with the Bureau of Land Management over grazing rights and for refusing to pay grazing fees. In early 2014, tensions heightened, and an armed standoff with the Feds ensued. Playing to type, conservatives embraced Bundy, turning him into a sort of folk hero. In fairness, Bundy did represent a legitimate argument. As MSNBC's Adam Serwer wrote, "It's perfectly consistent to believe the federal government owns too much land and also believe Bundy's remarks are offensive." It's also fair to say that Fox News, and especially Sean Hannity, gave Bundy a huge platform, and that Bundy—who was shown on TV riding a horse while waving an American flag—exploited that opportunity.

The episode also tapped into something more deep-seated than grazing rights. As Josh Barro of the *New York Times* noted, "The rush to stand with Mr. Bundy against the Bureau of Land Management is the latest incarnation of conservative antigovernment messaging." This "the enemy of my enemy is my friend" philosophy is dangerous, and yet we find conservatives trapped in a cycle of abusive relationships. It usually goes like this: Government or the media oversteps its bounds, conservatives embrace the unvetted victim, who—once feted (but not vetted) on cable TV and talk radio—says or does something stupid. Then, liberal media outlets spend weeks covering the boomerang part of the story. What may start out as a boon for conservatives leaves them with egg on their face.

In the case of Bundy, not only was he technically wrong to think he could graze his cattle for free on someone else's land, but his desire for media attention ultimately got the better of him. He decided to quit talking about cattle, and instead wax not-so-eloquently about the state of race relations in America at a press conference attended by a *New York Times* reporter. "They abort their young children, they put their young men in jail, because they never learned how to pick cotton," Bundy said, referring to African Americans, according to the *Times*. "And I've often wondered, are they better off as slaves, picking cotton and having a family life and doing things, or are they better off under government subsidy? They didn't get no more freedom. They got less freedom," he continued.

In the grand scheme of things, should it matter to us that some random rancher in Nevada is a bigot? Probably not. But it's hard to make that argument after you've spent weeks building him up just so someone else can tear him down. So why did conservatives get caught up in this lost cause? Here's a theory: when the 1992 Ruby Ridge standoff resulted in the death of Randy Weaver's wife and son—and when the disastrous 1993 Federal raid on the Branch Davidian compound in Waco, Texas, took place—the fallout had a negative impact on the Clinton Administration, despite the fact that the Ruby Ridge standoff occurred in 1992, during President George H. W. Bush's watch. Both events were tragic, but they also (understandably) fed an antigovernment sentiment that was very good for the nascent Con$ervative Entertainment Complex. Could it be that conservatives are still fighting the last war? Like the aforementioned examples, Cliven Bundy had an "armed militia of supporters." (As the *New York Times* recalled in 1995, "The Ruby Ridge confrontation involved an armed separatist brigade. The Davidians were also well equipped with weapons.")

If you were a conservative talk radio host, would you not look at Bundy through the prism of Ruby Ridge? In the beginning, it might have been easy to assume Bundy would also go out in a blaze of glory, becoming some sort of martyr. And in this scenario, it would have been important to stake out a pro-Bundy position before the government turned him into a real folk hero. Instead of killing him, the Obama Administration gave him enough rope to hang himself.

Playing the Game

While the Cliven Bundys of the world do damage to the conservative brand, they are arguably not as culpable as the *politicians* who use the primary process as a résumé builder for a future TV show, or the conservative talking heads who, despite knowing better, play to the worst aspects of our human nature.

Whether the scoundrels are looking to line their pockets by fundraising off hypothetical candidates for their PAC or outside group, jumpstart their fledgling acting careers by reinventing themselves as conservative pundits, or boost their talk radio or cable TV ratings (or book sales) by saying incendiary things sure to harm the conservative cause, one thing's for sure: it almost always comes down to money for these hacktastic con$ervatives.

9

THE CONSERVATIVE ECHO CHAMBER

"After the suffering of many years of violence and oppression, the human soul longs for things higher, warmer, and purer than those offered by today's mass living habits, introduced by the revolting invasion of publicity, by TV stupor, and by intolerable music."
—*Aleksandr I. Solzhenitsyn*

"You cannot do political philosophy on television."
—*Neil Postman,* Amusing Ourselves to Death

A few years ago, my wife and I attended a popular "megachurch" in Northern Virginia. I had heard the preacher on the radio, and that's what got me in the door. But I left before he ever spoke. Our seats were so far away from the pulpit, our only option was to look at huge screens (it was like going to a Dallas Cowboys game and watching the Jumbotron instead of the game). We arrived during the music portion, which is supposed to be a time of worship, contemplation, and reflection. But when the guitar player was playing his lead, the camera zoomed in on his fingers like he was

Jimmy Page. It felt like we were worshipping *him*, not the Almighty. And it taught me something: *television makes humility hard, and technology makes intimacy difficult.*

Yes, throughout history, every new technology has faced a backlash. No doubt, there was some old guy bemoaning the fact that the printed word replaced the intimacy of telling stories around the campfire. But according to Neil Postman, author of the classic book *Amusing Ourselves to Death*, television is a uniquely problematic medium. As such, it is incorrect to think of the television as merely an extension of past media, just as it would be foolish to think of the automobile simply as a horseless carriage.

Having grown up with the television on in the background, it is almost impossible for me to imagine what life was like before its soothing glow. But as a digital immigrant—someone who was alive as the Internet became ubiquitous—I am able to appreciate the paradigm-shifting power of a new technology. My children, who are digital natives, might struggle to understand this. Television changed everything. Children would learn what was cool not from their friends and family—or even from the movie theater—but from Fonzie…or Joey and Chandler, or…*whomever*. The values that would be instilled in us would come not just from our parents and our teachers, but also from people in Hollywood with dramatically different values. A president would now also have to be an entertainer. If video killed the radio star, then TV killed the boring pol. When one considers the elections of John F. Kennedy and an actor named Ronald Reagan, it becomes pretty clear that television made image dramatically more important.

Not everyone saw the storm clouds gathering. For "good government" types, it once appeared television might be a positive force. This was not only because it helped the winsome John F. Kennedy defeat the "evil" and sweaty Richard Nixon, but also because, as Susan Jacoby writes in *The Age of American Unreason*, "Television coverage had…spelled the end for Senator Joseph R. McCarthy in the spring of 1954, when ABC devoted 188 hours of broadcast time to live coverage of the Army-McCarthy Hearings. Seeing and hearing McCarthy, who came across as a petty thug, turned the tide of public opinion against abuses of power that had not seemed nearly as abusive when reported by the print media."

Perhaps Joe McCarthy was merely unfortunate enough to have been Patient Zero? Future demagogues on both sides of the aisle would learn how to manipulate this media, as well.

The Rise of Conservative Media

I'm old enough to remember the bad old days when the mainstream media filter presented only one side of the news, but it's hard not to argue that there have been some unintended consequences associated with lifting this filter. It has become clear that the ability to perform on cable television has greatly influenced how Republican primary voters—especially early on in the election process—rank possible presidential contenders.

Additionally, new media innovations such as blogging and social media platforms like Twitter are also double-edged swords. They remove the filter and lower the barrier of entry. This lets both the good and bad actors who had been previously excluded from the establishment into the system. Like many of the trends discussed in this book, this is not an altogether new conundrum, even if the potential for using and misusing media has greatly increased. Before websites like Breitbart.com, there was talk radio. Today, we are familiar with how the end of the so-called Fairness Doctrine (which required owners of broadcast licenses to provide "equal time" to controversial political subjects) paved the way for Rush Limbaugh to become a national figure in the late 1980s. But prior to the law's inception, there were all sorts of controversial radio hosts, including religious figures like Los Angeles's "Fighting" Bob Shuler and Father Charles E. Coughlin, who spewed demagogic messages and (in some cases) anti-Semitism over the radio waves. In the 1930s, Coughlin had somewhere around thirty million listeners and was an important booster of FDR and the New Deal (both of which he later rebelled against).

Talk radio is as controversial as ever these days. And not all of the attacks come from the Left. Some conservatives are also starting to suspect that the rise of "conservative" media hasn't been solely positive. After noting that talk radio hosts were too willing to look the other way during George W. Bush's era of big government conservatism, John Derbyshire, writing in the *American Conservative* criticized "lowbrow" talk radio, calling it "Happy Meal conservatism: cheap, childish, familiar."

One of the other problems with this type of conservative punditry (and it's not solely limited to talk radio, although it is prominent there) is that it panders to angry and disaffected listeners, essentially telling them what they want to hear. Meanwhile, because these conservative pundits also become opinion leaders (not to be confused with public intellectuals in the mold of William F. Buckley), they have a certain amount of sway over voters and politicians. On the Right, this often results in a very dangerous and counterproductive outcome. Let's take the 2016 race as an example, where Donald Trump began alleging there were 30–34 million illegal immigrants in the United States—not the 11.4 million that has been commonly cited (since 2012). Where did he come up with 30 million? It turns out Trump's numbers came from conservative commentator Ann Coulter's 2015 book, *Adios America*. This number is, as PolitiFact noted, "triple the widespread consensus."[82]

But the fun didn't end there. Trump also proposed revoking birthright citizenship. This was an interesting move, for a variety of reasons. First, the argument that "Europe does it" shouldn't carry much sway with people who talk about "American exceptionalism." Second, people who care about the rule of law and define themselves as "Constitutional conservatives" probably shouldn't be so cavalier about amending or ignoring the Fourteenth Amendment. Interestingly, birthright citizenship was observed in America as an extension of English common law, but was only officially ensconced into law to overrule the infamous Dred Scott decision, which said the descendants of slaves were not citizens. So, in one fell swoop, Donald Trump found a way to offend both "the Mexicans" (as he calls them) and "the Blacks" (as he calls them). But rather than pointing out that he is wrong on both policy and political grounds, Ann Coulter tweeted a startling endorsement of Trump's immigration plan. "I don't care if [Donald Trump] wants to perform abortions in the White House after this immigration policy paper," she wrote. As previously mentioned, Coulter had, a few days earlier, defended Trump's opposition to defunding Planned Parenthood—something almost all other conservatives supported. But Coulter was so happy with Donald Trump's stand against illegal immigrants that she would be okay with him killing unborn babies... *in the White House.* Given a hypothetical binary choice between saving unborn babies and deporting illegal immigrants, Coulter comes down strongly in favor of the latter.

Media and the Dumbing Down of Politics

These trends aren't limited to shock jocks or media provocateurs. Since the advent and proliferation of TV, the power of the executive branch has increased, magnifying the power of the bully pulpit. Meanwhile, Congress has looked increasingly dysfunctional. The House of Representatives began allowing television coverage in 1979, and the US Senate voted to televise its proceedings in 1986. Not everyone thinks this has been positive. "It's probably the worst thing that happened to the Congress," Alaska representative Don Young told *USA Today.*[83] Or consider what former Reagan and Bush Administration official Elliott Abrams recalled during a June 2014 conversation with Bill Kristol[84] about his first day working for Democratic senator Henry "Scoop" Jackson of the state of Washington.

His first assignment was to cover senators marking up legislation—
the committee process where they would debate and amend legislation. Abrams described watching senators cut deals that would never
be made today. This was primarily because, back then, lobbyists and
reporters were excluded from the markup process. Then Abrams
argued that television didn't just change the process for legislative
negotiation—it changed the kinds of people who would be doing the
negotiating:

> Warren Magnuson was the other senator from Washing-
> ton State, along with Scoop. And, let me put it this way: he
> was real fat; he was slovenly. You don't have that any more. I
> mean, people in Washington State didn't care that they had
> a fat senator, because he was a great senator. He was a really
> effective legislator, Magnuson. And as I think back to the
> Senate, when I got there, the last quarter of the twentieth cen-
> tury, before TV, you had a lot of senators who were old, who
> had bad haircuts, bad suits, overweight. It didn't matter. And
> it matters now, because you have cameras now. And you got a
> lot of guys who spend, apparently, a very large amount of time
> having their hair done. The "John Edwards effect," you know.

The world has changed—and with it, so have our politicians. It
has been noted that power once came from the cloakroom, now it
comes from the greenroom. Old-fashioned politicians who could
cut deals used to wield a lot of power. Today, that power has been
transferred to anyone who wants to go on TV and raise hell against
the establishment (and then, use the video clip to raise money).
Meanwhile, little gets done legislatively. Transparency is a double-
edged sword. Sometimes, one wonders if we might be better off
with a few less blow-dried, perfectly coiffed candidates, and a few
more colorful characters in bad suits cutting deals in smoke-filled
backrooms.

How to Succeed as a Pundit (without Really Knowing Anything)

As someone who has done a good bit of political punditry, I think Neil Postman was right when he observed, "When a television show is in process, it is very nearly impossible to say 'Let me think about that' or 'I don't know' or 'What do you mean when you say that…?'…Thinking does not play well on television, a fact television directors discovered long ago." And so, we fake it. And not just the politicians. Pundits are often in error, but never in doubt—partly because, as Bill Clinton observed, "When people feel uncertain, they'd rather have somebody that's strong and wrong than somebody who's weak and right."

As a commentator, there is usually little cost to being strong and wrong. What you *cannot* be is unsure or boring or nuanced. Thinking doesn't work on television, nor does evincing any sign of ambivalence. What works really well is to be 100 percent sure of whatever it is you are saying. This is not a conservative instinct. This is not a sign of epistemological modesty. But it works fabulously on television!

Let's consider the aforementioned Bill Kristol, who once declared, "Barack Obama is not going to beat Hillary Clinton in a single Democratic primary." Or Chris Matthews, who predicted Rudy Giuliani would win the GOP nomination in 2008 and that Michele Bachmann would win the nomination in 2012. Or, even worse, let's consider Dick Morris, the erstwhile disgraced adviser to Democratic president Bill Clinton turned right-wing TV commentator and author. Just six days before the 2012 presidential election, Morris appeared on Fox News's *The O'Reilly Factor* and doubled down on his bogus prediction, assuring Bill O'Reilly that "Romney will win this election by 5 to 10 points in the popular vote and will carry more than 300 electoral votes." (Morris reiterated his prediction of a Romney "landslide" on *Election Day* in his column for the *Hill* newspaper.)

Morris's predictions were so egregious that Fox News actually dropped him as a contributor. This was remarkable. There is seldom a downside to making bad political predictions. Quite the contrary, there is only an incentive for doing so. Pundits who make dramatic or grandiose statements and predictions reap the rewards of *Drudge Report* links, and page views, and TV hits, and attention. And when they are wrong, there is little finger pointing. We mostly move on. And then the offender promptly repeats this stunt. The cumulative effect is that voters are misled, charlatans become rich, and conscientious political commentators are left on the sidelines.

Aside from feigning certainty, it also helps to *look* good on television. Maybe such superficialities shouldn't matter. But the fact is, they do. In the modern era, it's pretty clear that when it comes to the White House, we don't elect bald men (Did Scott Walker's bald spot help sink him?), diminutive men (Rand Paul's probably average height, but considered *slight* by political standards; Tom Dewey similarly suffered), men with moustaches (two strikes on Mr. Dewey, one strike on Herman Cain) or beards, men with glasses (admittedly, the least of Barry Goldwater or Rick Perry's problems), or (since Big Bill Taft) fat men. I'm not even sure if Rand Paul's curly hair passes muster.

This is unfair, but it's also reality. And it's something to consider when we examine potential 2016 contenders. Let's start with Chris Christie, who had lap band surgery. Losing weight is good for his health, but it also won't hurt his political career. Consider this question: Would a fat Mike Huckabee have done so well in the 2008 Republican primaries? Many Americans are biased against the obese—and expect their politicians and celebrities to cut dashing figures. This may not be fair, but it is true.

The Sexy and the Superficial

If television made image more important than substance, then the Internet has dumbed us down further by incessantly fueling outrage. The rise of alternative media has benefited conservatives at times.

Were it not for the *Drudge Report*, the Monica Lewinsky story might never have been known. And were it not for the blogosphere, Dan Rather's revelations about George W. Bush's time in the Air National Guard would have gone unchallenged. Instead, some conservative sleuths were able to debunk the story as a forgery.

On the other hand, alternative media has fueled a conservative outrage machine that distracts and damages the brand. Some of the outrage is even cyclical. You can almost set your watch to the Halloween columns about "slutty" pumpkin costumes and the evergreen "war on Christmas" festivities (not to say these things aren't a scourge!). Again, the tragedy of the commons is partly to blame. It is in the best interest of a given conservative diva to say something crazy or radical—like Ann Coulter using the term "ragheads" to describe Muslims. This gains her attention and buzz and book sales. And, soon enough, everyone forgets it and moves on to the next big outrage. Con$ervatism, remember, isn't just a philosophy— it's also a business. It's hard to quantify the long-term damage the Con$ervative Movement has done to the conservative movement. (In some regards, this is a bipartisan problem, but conservatives are disproportionately harmed by it. In recent years, Democrats have been able to enforce more discipline.)

Meanwhile, an entire cottage industry has sprung up, whereby conservatives use social media to mock or knock down stories. Sometimes, as with the case of "Rathergate," this is a public service. Other times, it's a net negative and evidence that the Right is aping the Left in terms of playing the victim card. There's also the problem of relying on tit-for-tat tu quoque arguments. For example, if a Republican is criticized for doing or saying something racially insensitive, the immediate response will be to remind everyone that the late Democratic senator Robert C. Byrd was in the Ku Klux Klan. If a Republican gets a DUI, the initial urge is to bring up Chappaquiddick. This reflex is brought on by a disdain for the liberal media's double standards, but it's also just about the most childish and tribalistic form of argument available. It's also a form of escapism, in which you are never forced to deal with your problems—or correct them.

Perhaps the saddest part is that there are no more civilians; we have now all been recruited into this political war where the ends justify the means. And I'm not just talking about the poor people who have had their lives ruined because of some unfortunate thing they tweeted. I'm also talking about the constant, low-grade toll that being on social media takes on all of us. If you've managed to avoid getting sucked into the Twitter vortex of false outrage and "gotcha" journalism, your days are probably numbered. To survive in the modern media industry, writers quickly learn how push people's outrage buttons and play upon their thirst for the superficial to get the requisite clicks and attention. In turn, political coverage has increasingly come to resemble gossip or celebrity coverage (think TMZ) and sports (think ESPN). It's hard to tell when this line was first crossed (maybe before the rise of the Internet, or when political operatives like James Carville started doing cameo spots in movies and TV shows?). But a prime example is the White House Correspondents' Dinner, a once dignified celebration of journalism now turned into a celebrity freak show designed to produce as much viral online content as the Beltway can muster. "The breaking point for me was Lindsay Lohan," former NBC anchor Tom Brokaw told *Politico* in 2013. "She became a big star at the White House Correspondents' Dinner. Give me a break."

In recent years, the State of the Union has even gotten in on the act. Representative Vance McAllister brought *Duck Dynasty* reality TV star Willie Robertson as his guest back in 2014. The superficial—whether that's coverage of the "horse race" aspect of campaigns or political websites that feature Kim Kardashian slideshows—now obscures the important news and conversations. Political websites know this. The dominant business model today is to provide free information (no firewalls or subscriptions) and to pay for that (and, ideally, turn a profit) via advertising revenue—which is contingent on ad impressions, which is contingent on page views. Slideshows and salacious content are one way to drive up page views. The most positive way of looking at it is to suggest that guys clicking on pictures of Kate Upton help subsidize serious reporting and analysis. This is not an absurd theory. The *Daily Caller*, where I work, won an Edward R. Murrow Award for "The Horse Soldiers of 9/11" in 2012. That same year, at the more liberal Huffington Post, a former colleague of mine named David Wood won a Pulitzer for his extensive reporting on severely wounded veterans. One suspects that piece was subsidized by the Huffington Post's less prestigious postings (such as 2012's "The Year in Sideboob"). This model isn't terribly new if you think about it. Newspapers always coupled hard news and thoughtful commentary with comic strips, advice columns, sports, gossip, horoscopes, celebrity news—you name it. Maybe today's new media landscape is merely the latest incarnation of a very old financial arrangement. There have always been P. T. Barnums in the news business, and pamphlets and tabloid journalism have a long history. Still, there is the sense that we are in an age when showmanship is no longer the exception—it's the rule.

Often this involves engaging in hyperbole. Other times, it just means making wild and outrageous predictions. In the case of Dick Morris's bogus prognostications, the results include sowing paranoia and confusion among conservative viewers who, thanks to epistemic closure and the conservative echo chamber, might only get their information from conservative media outlets. It would be reasonable for them, having been assured Romney's victory was a foregone conclusion, to suspect some sort of foul play when Obama is easily reelected. This also contributes to distrust of the media, political apathy, you name it. And I should point out that this belief in Romney's inevitability was widespread—far from being limited to people in the so-called flyover country.

Around the same time Morris was doubling down on his

prediction of a Romney landslide, I attended a meeting of conservative-movement leaders who were (to give you an idea of their confidence) preparing to launch a shadow transition office with the purpose of helping make sure conservative staffers were hired by the Romney administration. (This was a legitimate goal, inasmuch as an official Romney transition office would likely have erred toward hiring more moderate and establishment types.) At the end of the meeting—almost as an aside—the attendees were asked to raise their hands if they believed Romney would win the election on that following Tuesday. Mine was the only hand *not* to go up.

Technology and the "Sophisticated" Twenty-First-Century Voter

Having argued now at some length that technology is making us dumber, it's important to admit that there is a paradox: it's also making many of us more savvy consumers of media. Political slogans from a bygone era, such as "I Like Ike," would be laughable today. So would TV jingles—unless done ironically.

In the political realm, technology has enabled voters to learn about the issues and fact-check politicians in a manner that was unthinkable a generation ago. And this is one of the reasons why the "too dumb to fail" strategy is doomed to fail. On the other hand, it would be a dangerous conceit to suppose that we have outgrown demagoguery. New technology allows us to avoid coming into contact with opposing viewpoints. There is no common culture or consensus. It's entirely possible nowadays to go through a day and avoid hearing information that challenges your assumptions. A conservative could conceivably watch only Fox News; listen to only Rush Limbaugh, Sean Hannity, and Glenn Beck; and read only conservative blogs. There's nothing wrong with this being part of your media diet; it becomes a problem when it constitutes your entire consumption.

And while we might be more sophisticated consumers, the

demagogues are more sophisticated purveyors of propaganda than ever. Someone's always trying to sell us something, be that an idea or a candidate or a product—and it's naive to think we have finally outsmarted them. Think of this as an arms race. Just as we try to grapple with being inundated with information and adapting to new technology, the politicians and advertisers use an ever-increasingly sophisticated means to manipulate us. And it's not just the politicians and the corporations who invent devious new ways to find and seduce us; the truly bad guys do, too. Terrorists use the Internet to recruit Western jihadists. The assumption that technology would solve all our problems has always been a utopian fantasy.

Still, in some ways, it has made us better. Were it not for television, Ronald Reagan would probably not have become president. Were it not for the Internet, I wouldn't have a job writing about politics. But overall, the decline of conservatism as an intellectual movement has not been helped by the rise of TV. Inevitably, shows like Bill Buckley's *Firing Line* gave way to shows more like the political version of *Keeping Up with the Kardashians*. This is probably a moot point. We can't go back. We can't go back any more than our ancestors could go back to the days when America was protected by two oceans and we felt inviolable. The challenge for conservatives is to figure out how to maximize the positive aspects of technology so we can rise above our more primitive impulses.

PART FOUR

HOW TO FIX IT

10
ACCEPTANCE

"God, grant me the serenity to accept the things I cannot change, the courage to change the things I can, and the wisdom to know the difference."
—*Reinhold Niebuhr*

In the wake of Mitt Romney's embarrassingly lopsided 2012 defeat, the Republican National Committee commissioned a blue-ribbon panel of establishment insiders to perform what some have dubbed an "autopsy." A more positive way to look at it was as an intervention. And the GOP needed it. So how did the party hit rock bottom? You might be familiar with the narrative. As long as the party was "functional"—as long as it could keep up appearances, put on a clean suit, and act like everything was okay—the party could still fake it. At some point, though, the Republican Party became delusional. It lied to itself—and then it lied to us. Rather than accept reality, the party even said some pretty unbelievable things like, "The polls are skewed." Then, the GOP started hanging out with a bunch of hangers-on and charlatans. And if you dared to warn the party that something was wrong, you'd quickly find yourself on the outs. You only hurt the ones you love, right?

How does the party get back to its glory days? Going cold turkey won't work. Just like a person who's fallen into a harrowing cycle of dependency and addiction, the party needs a program. For those looking for help, my hope is that this book provides a path to the straight and narrow. And, as is always the case, the first step toward recovery is to accept reality. And the reality is that just 32 percent of Americans have a favorable impression of the GOP, according to a July 2015 Pew Research Center poll. (In fairness the Democrats had only a 48 percent approval rating—not exactly something to brag about, but still dramatically better than the GOP.) The good news is that this is somewhat of an improvement. One 2013 Gallup poll showed the GOP was viewed favorably by just 28 percent of Americans—the lowest rating for either party since Gallup began asking the question in 1992.

Sadly, many Republicans refuse to take the vital first step of accepting reality. It's easier to make excuses. Here's one: It is common for conservatives to hearken back to Ronald Reagan as an example of the last guy who ran as a conservative and won. It is then suggested that Bob Dole, John McCain, and Mitt Romney lost simply because they weren't sufficiently conservative. (George W. Bush presents a harder example; it is generally explained that he won because he ran as a conservative, even if he didn't govern that way.) The real answer, I suggest, is to look to the Reagan model—but not in a way that looks backward or assumes nominating a hard-core conservative is a panacea. Reagan looked to the future, and so should we. We simply cannot afford to pretend that things aren't—*haven't*—changed. The notion that we could—or *should*!—want to turn back the clock to the 1950s (or even the 1980s) is a misguided fool's errand. The idea is not to be nostalgic for some magical past time when things were better, but to use the accumulated wisdom of the past to make our future even brighter. But again, this requires taking action *now*. As Margaret Thatcher might say, "There is no alternative."

Here's why: if demographics are political destiny (and they usually are), then continuing to be the party solely of white, non-college-educated, married Americans—living in rural areas—is unsustainable. But don't take my word for it. South Carolina representative Mick Mulvaney told a group of conservative South Carolina activists in May of 2015,[85] "The largest voting demographic group in the 2016 election will be people between the ages of 18 and 30. The fastest growing demographic group will be Hispanics." But the rise of Hispanics and millennials is far from the only challenge confronting Republicans.

If you don't believe Mulvaney, then consider the following statistics:

- **The white share of the electorate is declining.** In 2012, Mitt Romney won whites by the same margin Ronald Reagan did in 1980[86]—and by a larger margin than George W. Bush in 2004. The problem is that in 1980, whites were 88 percent of the electorate, but in 2012, they accounted for just 73 percent of the voters.[87] What is more, assuming voting patterns continue to track census changes, the white share of the electorate will continue to decline.[88] In fact, the white vote has fallen an average of 2.75 percentage points in each presidential election since 1996.[89] It's important to note that the danger for Republicans is not just that whites will be replaced by Hispanic voters. In 2012, Barack Obama garnered 71 percent of the Asian American vote,[90] the fastest-growing racial group in the U.S.[91]
- **Rising educational attainment.** Although whites tend to vote Republican, those who attend college are much less likely than non-college-educated whites to do so. Putting this trend in perspective, when Reagan was elected in 1980, only about 14 percent of Americans had a college degree. Today, it's closer to 30 percent.[92] What is more, according to the *Cook Political Report*, "Non-college whites—by far [the GOP's] best-performing cohort—are slated to fall three points to 33 percent as more college-educated millennials supplant conservative seniors who didn't attend college."
- **Smaller share of married voters.** Unmarried Americans—especially unmarried women[93]—are much less likely to vote

Republican. Marriage rates continue to decline, and people are waiting longer to get married (for women, the median age is now over twenty-five—for men, it's nearly twenty-eight, according to the US Census Bureau). When Reagan was elected, about 70 percent of eligible voters were married. Today, the percentage of married and unmarried eligible voters is essentially 50–50.[94] Perhaps this is why a Republican running for president hasn't won the collective female vote since 1988.[95]

- **Fewer rural voters.** Michael Dukakis won more counties in 1988 than Barack Obama did in 2012. It wasn't even close. Dukakis, who lost by *ten* points, won 819 counties. Conversely, Barack Obama, who won just 690 counties, won the popular vote by four points.[96] It's easy to conclude that densely populated regions are gaining voters, while sparsely populated regions are losing them. In 1980, Republicans won nearly half the vote in the one hundred largest US counties. By 2012, that had shrunk to just 38 percent.[97]

- **Republican voters are dying at a faster rate.** A look at exit polls and mortality rates suggests that about 2.75 million of the people who voted for Mitt Romney will be dead by 2016.[98] Of course, some Obama voters will suffer the same fate (some fear, however, that many—especially in Chicago—will still be allowed to vote). But the numbers suggest about 453,000 more Romney donors will have died by the time the next presidential election rolls around. Do people start voting Republican when they get old, or is there something unique about today's elderly that makes them skew toward the GOP? The GOP had better hope it's the former and not the latter.

- **Republicans have lost the popular vote in five of the last six presidential elections, and the Electoral College math isn't getting any easier.** There are eighteen states (plus Washington, DC) that have gone Democratic the last six presidential elections. Assuming this holds, Republicans have to run the table, with almost no foreseeable path to the nomination that doesn't involve winning both Florida *and* Ohio. Just days after the 2014 midterm elections—where Republicans took control of the US Senate—RNC chairman Reince Priebus acknowledged this reality. "I think we've got to be about perfect as a national party to win a national cultural vote in this country. I think the Democrats can be good and win, but we have to be great," he said.[99]

These numbers matter for a lot of reasons. But consider this: Exit polls on Election Day in 2012 asked people which quality was the most important to voters, giving them four options. Surprisingly, Romney won *three* of the four qualities in the category. On questions about leadership, vision, and values, he won. But he lost big on one question. And that question was about which candidate "cares about people like me." On that question, *81 percent* of respondents answered, "Barack Obama." (Only 18 percent said, "Romney.") To be sure, part of the problem was Romney's wooden personality—but it's a safe bet that part of the problem was that, for a good chunk of the presidential electorate who are not old, white, or rural, the perception is that the Republican Party doesn't care about people like *them*.

Instead of accepting the fact that America is an exceptional and pluralistic society that values ideas and the content of someone's character over identity politics—or that, frankly, whites are simply not reproducing in numbers required to sustain a flourishing republic—a pretty sizable chunk of the conservative movement appears to want to keep the GOP a party almost exclusively for older, whiter, more rural Americans.

Simultaneously, they want to willingly ignore or otherwise antagonize a bloc liberals refer to as "the coalition of the ascendant." For Reagan-Kemp conservatives, this is a philosophical *and* mathematical problem. The mathematics are obvious; these conservatives advocate doubling down on cohorts that are losing population. But I don't want to skip over why this strays from conservative philosophy and, instead, represents a strain of populism.

In fact, some observers worry the GOP might turn into a European-style Right-populist party fueled by white-identity politics. For example, Ben Domenech, a cofounder of RedState.com who now serves as publisher of *The Federalist*, warns there's a danger America might turn into "a new two-party system which has on the one hand a center-left / technocratic party, full of elites with shared pedigrees of experience and education, and on the other a nativist-right / populist party, which represents a constant reactive force to the dominant elite.[100]

"A classically liberal Right is actually fairly uncommon in Western democracies," Domenech continues, "requiring as it does a coalition that synthesizes populist tendencies and directs such frustrations toward the cause of limited government. Only the United States and Canada have successfully maintained one over an extended period."

Whereas I see the world as Right versus Left—and right versus wrong—the scorched-earth populists see today's political paradigm as *us versus them*. They believe the defining schism in America is between the blue-collar, working-class whites—versus everyone else (the rich elites, immigrants, etc.). As such, Donald Trump's slogan, "Make America Great Again," is especially appealing. They see efforts to make conservatism more palatable to college-educated urbanites, to attract Hispanic voters, and so on, as not only a waste of time but also as counterproductive, inasmuch as it muddies the waters and postpones the day when the blue-collar union worker throws off the Democratic Party's yoke and joins the populist GOP.

The problem is that many of these conservatives have no problem with playing white-identity politics. Meanwhile, the demographic trends that are obviously so blatantly suicidal in the long term are much less persuasive in the short term. Advocates of the theory that

Republicans should double down on their traditional voters (older, white, rural)—while ignoring the "coalition of the ascendant"—have found comfort in the writings of respected elections analyst Sean Trende, whose work at RealClearPolitics.com seems to buttress the argument that, in the short term at least, the smart move for the GOP is to double down and focus on turning out more white voters.

In the wake of Romney's 2012 loss, Trende authored a piece titled "The Case of the Missing White Voters," in which he attributed Romney's loss "almost entirely...to white voters staying home." Trende is a respected analyst, and his only responsibility is to get the numbers right—and I have no reason to doubt he has. The problem is that this provides reason to postpone making long-term changes that are vital to preserve the GOP's future.

Liberal writer Bill Scher (a friend) has a theory that political parties must lose *three* consecutive presidential elections before they are finally forced to accept reality. He points to the fact that Democrats had to lose in 1980, 1984, and 1988 before they were willing to nominate a "New Democrat" governor from the South named Bill Clinton—who broke from liberal orthodoxy on welfare and the death penalty. I'm not sure if Scher is right that it takes three losses, but I do know that progress often comes only as a result of pain and that acceptance is the first step toward recovery. Only after we accept a problem do we have the motivation and courage born out of desperation to endure a season of change.

11

MODERNIZE, DON'T MODERATE

"I know that for America there will always be a bright dawn ahead."
—*Ronald Reagan*

The morning after the 2012 election, I posted a piece on the *Daily Caller* titled "The GOP Needs Modernization, Not Moderation." A few days later, I wrote another column on the same theme for *The Week*. It seemed to strike a chord. Later that week, appearing on MSNBC's *Morning Joe*, journalist John Heilemann mentioned the phrase, and GOP strategist Brad Todd later gave the idea a shout-out on MSNBC's *The Daily Rundown with Chuck Todd*. That Sunday, appearing on CNN's *State of the Union*, Representative Cathy McMorris Rodgers observed, "I don't think it's about the Republican Party needing to become more moderate. I really believe it's the Republican Party becoming more modern." And then finally, in a much-ballyhooed CNN.com column titled "How Republicans Can Win Future Elections," Governor Bobby Jindal observed, "We need to modernize, not moderate."

It's flattering to have coined a phrase—even if this moment of introspection was painfully short-lived (and even if attribution wasn't always provided)—but what does *modernize, don't moderate* even mean? In a sense, this is the political equivalent of the project Pope Francis has undertaken in the Catholic Church. He has changed the emphasis, not the doctrine—changed the tone, not the music. In short, what this means is that conservatives must recognize and accept the fact that twenty-first-century America will necessarily look different than twentieth-century America—and that this is okay. Meanwhile, conservatives must simultaneously honor and preserve our fundamental conservative principles, which, in many cases, go back to antiquity.

The way to win isn't to abandon conservative ideas or policies, but rather to adapt them to a twenty-first-century world—and explain why conservatism is the best philosophy for making the largest, most diverse number of Americans happy, virtuous, safe, and prosperous.

Before we continue, I want to be clear and transparent about something: *this involves both style and substance.*

Modernizing entails a lot of things: it means using cutting-edge campaign technology to win elections and fielding more diverse and cosmopolitan candidates (something the GOP has actually done a good job of)—and perhaps fewer candidates who look like a caricature of Boss Hogg from *The Dukes of Hazzard*. (Fair or not, some Americans are now sonically biased against a Southern accent. In the post–George W. Bush era, one wonders to what degree this bias has harmed candidates such as former Texas governor Rick Perry.) But it also means being open to adopting new common-sense policy reform positions that don't conflict with foundational conservative beliefs, as well as more effectively communicating how current policy positions can actually benefit Americans who haven't traditionally been part of the conservative coalition. Candidates won't feel empowered to promote innovative ideas that appeal to a larger swath of Americans if they fear their bases will reflexively attack them for challenging the status quo. (It doesn't do us much good to elect fresh twenty-first-century candidates if we then force them to go on the record and talk like stale twentieth-century ones.)

So, in the face of daunting demographic challenges, how can the GOP position itself to win the twenty-first century, without betraying conservative values? Here's my recipe for success:

1. Appeal to Younger, More Cosmopolitan Americans

Most of the factors that would turn off a young, college-educated urbanite to conservatism have little to do with conservative philosophy and everything to do with culture and signaling. Tell them you believe in community, and they'll nod their head. Tell them you think we should be incentivizing entrepreneurial, digitally savvy, disruptive businesses like Uber to operate without fear of onerous governmental regulations, and they'll smile. As Rod Dreher suggested in his book *Crunchy Cons*, whether it's homeschooling, living in a tight-knit community, or going to a farmers' market, traditional conservative values are pretty consistent with the way a lot of young urbanites actually live. What doesn't fly with them? In some cases, you can blame conservative policies such as opposition to gay marriage. But in many cases, what turns them off has more to do with cultural identity, not philosophical beliefs. Too many college-educated Americans write off conservatism—not because they disagree with a Burkean philosophy—but because they are repelled by what conservatism has come to *represent*. In fact, according to one study, millennials often "decided they were liberals because they really didn't like conservatives."[101]

To many Americans, conservatism isn't about tradition or Aristotelian ideas or the preservation of Western civilization, but rather watching *Duck Dynasty*, shopping at Walmart, and displaying a gun rack in your truck. The sad thing is that a lot of young cosmopolitan Americans who think they are liberal—based not on philosophy, but instead on these cultural shortcuts—are actually, in their personal lifestyles, rejecting much of what liberals have to offer. Yes, it's true that many advocate social tolerance while practicing a rather bourgeois existence, but the starkest example of cognitive dissonance probably has to do with technology: it is unrealistic to think the guy who manages his bank account on his iPhone, orders a car via Uber, buys tickets to a baseball game on StubHub, and on the way trades some stock will view government as passively as his grandfather. Nor should he; the world has changed. It's hard to imagine he will be satisfied with cavalierly outsourcing the management of his social security to a bloated bureaucracy.

I recently spent some time with Alex Castellanos, the longtime Republican political consultant who heads a PAC called New Republican. In his Alexandria, Virginia, offices—a huge factory-converted loft—the charismatic Cuban American held court, regaling me with stories while puffing cigar smoke. Castellanos is passionate about fixing the Republican brand and is astounded that the GOP doesn't already own the twenty-first century. He argues quite convincingly that big-government liberalism is tantamount to a top-down command-and-control assembly line system that worked in the Industrial Age but is antiquated in the modern era. In between puffs of smoke, he shows me a picture of Adam Smith and harrumphs, "We were right too early." A few seconds later, he continues. "This whole 'all men are created equal' thing"—he pauses to hold up his iPhone—"it's never been more true." He has a point. At some future juncture, an increasingly educated and cosmopolitan public simply will not tolerate the government being so inefficient compared with the plethora of amazing new, mostly app-based service companies that are improving so many other aspects of American life.

FedEx, UPS, and e-mail have replaced much of what the US Postal Service used to do—and they do so more efficiently. We also see this with companies like Uber, the smartphone app that connects you with a driver "at the click of a button," replacing taxicabs by providing a superior experience. As the party of labor unions who disdain the emerging gig or sharing economy, Democrats find themselves in a pinch. This tension reached a head in July of 2015, when Hillary Clinton outlined her economic policy, promising to "crack down on bosses who exploit employees while misclassifying them as contractors." Grover Norquist, a conservative antitax crusader, responded joyously, telling Business Insider, "She just declared war on the future. She just declared war on Uber." Maybe. But while technology and free market economics really could be a bridge to college-educated young urbanites, it's easy to imagine conservatives blowing this opportunity, or, at least, failing to capitalize on it. And the easiest way to miss the boat would be to nominate Republican candidates who send the wrong message. The 2016 primary really is a fight for the future of the Republican Party, and sides are already being chosen. According to a *Washington Post*/ABC News poll released in July of 2015, "Among those with no college degree, 32 percent support [Donald] Trump, compared with a mere 8 percent of those with college educations."[102] (A *Washington Post*/ABC News poll released in late September only confirmed the trend, showing Trump polling 22 points better among all non-college graduates—and a stunning 46-point education gap among Republicans. An October 2015 national Pew Research Center survey of Republican and Republican-leaning voters similarly had Trump winning 30 percent of non-college graduates, but just 16 percent of college graduates.)

2. Appeal to Hispanics

Depending on who's on the ballot, Republicans can generally figure on losing 85–95 percent of the black vote. Allowing this same thing to happen with the Hispanic vote would be mathematically catastrophic. It's vital for conservatives to compete for, and win, at least 40 percent of the Hispanic vote. To do so, conservatives must enact *some* immigration reform legislation. Whether you favor a pathway to citizenship, legalization but not citizenship, or some other form of immigration reform that addresses the 11–15 million illegal immigrants in the United States, the issue has become a *conditio sine qua non*, and something must be done to address the problem humanely.

Consider this: By 2040, whites are expected to account for just 38 percent of eligible voters in… *Texas*.[103] That means 62 percent of eligible voters in the Lone Star State will be nonwhite (Hispanics are projected to be the largest bloc at 43 percent).

The good news is that, for a variety of reasons, Hispanic voters in Texas are not yet a wholly owned subsidiary of the Democratic Party. In fact, as recently as 2014, US senator John Cornyn, a Republican, won *48 percent* of the Latino vote (his Democratic opponent got just 47 percent)![104] Rather than finding new ways to turn off even *Texas* Hispanics, Republicans might take a page from Cornyn's playbook and take solace in the fact that this voting bloc is up for grabs. But rather than competing for the Hispanic vote, it seems more likely that Republicans will antagonize them. But let me be clear about something: *if Republicans lose Texas, it's game over.*

Of course, some conservatives look at this demographic challenge and see it as further evidence we should end birthright citizenship, deport the eleven million (or so) illegals, and erect a fence (with a moat—and alligators). Others see this demographic information as proof that we had better start persuading Hispanics that our policies will help them achieve the American dream. I think most Republicans would agree that America must secure its border *and* that deporting eleven million undocumented immigrants is unfeasible. Controlling the border and wooing Hispanics need not be mutually exclusive—and yet, the rhetoric of many Republicans has made it that way. Consider the comments of Republican presidential candidate Donald Trump on June 16, 2015: "When Mexico sends its people, they're not sending their best. They're not sending you. They're not sending you. They're sending people that have lots of problems, and they're bringing those problems to us. They're bringing drugs. They're bringing crime. They're rapists. And some, I assume, are good people." It's almost as if these Republicans, in an effort to win the votes of disaffected populist Republicans, are *trying* to lose the Hispanic vote at the same clip we're losing the black vote. And make no mistake, there are real consequences for this kind of rhetoric— usually at the ballot box. As former Republican majority leader Dick Armey quipped to ABC News back in 2012, "You can't call her ugly all year round and expect her to go to the prom with you."

Earlier I noted that the Electoral College map essentially means that the only way a Republican can win is to win both Florida and Ohio. Well, in 2012, Mitt Romney garnered 39 percent of Florida Hispanics. According to prominent pollster Whit Ayres (who worked for Senator Marco Rubio in 2016), if Romney had simply done as well with Florida Hispanics as George W. Bush did in 2004 (when he got 56 percent of the Hispanic vote), Romney would have won the state by five points (instead of losing it by one).[105] But even if you don't believe Republicans can win the Hispanic vote (despite the fact that Texas senator John Cornyn did *precisely* that in 2014), simply losing it by a slimmer margin could be the difference between winning and losing a presidential election. The question for conservatives is whether or not to view Hispanic immigration as an invasion—or an opportunity. Whether to joyfully pursue their votes and contribution to America, or to stand athwart demographic changes, yelling "Stop!"

3. Change the Culture

Instead of merely adapting to the environment (like a thermometer[106]) why not seek to change the culture (like a thermostat)? For example, if Republicans have a hard time winning single women, one obvious option is to find a way to appeal to unmarried women. And I certainly think there are ways to do that. But another option is to encourage policies that incentivize marriage and childrearing. Depending on the policy proposal, this would be an appropriate and positive thing to do.

Though policies can incentivize certain lifestyle choices, when I say

we must "change the culture," I'm mostly referring to infiltrating or
influencing academia, education, and entertainment—the institutions
that, outside of the family, tend to have the biggest influence on us. These
are all tough nuts to crack. In the next chapter, I will offer some advice
for aspiring conservatives who want to support the world of the arts. The
primary answer, I think, is to *fund it*. Conservative donors with the ability to give millions of dollars to political campaigns would be wiser to
invest some of that money into helping win the future. And since politics
is downstream from culture, this is a wise investment. As Rod Dreher
wrote at the *American Conservative*, "None of the great artistic works of
Western civilization were done without patronage. Dante depended on
the charity of wealthy supporters to write the *Divine Comedy*."

4. Get Our House in Order

We must find ways to reward good behavior and punish bad actors. If
someone is engaged in scamming conservative donors (as described in
Chapter Eight), or otherwise harming the cause (for example, incendiary
rhetoric spewed by a conservative pundit for personal aggrandizement,
ratings, or buzz), there ought to be someone with the gravitas, courage,
and moral authority to call them out. For too long, smart conservatives
have abdicated this responsibility. Like adults who would prefer to be
liked and considered "cool" by their kids, they have held their tongues.
I was happy to see that Erick Erickson, a prominent conservative blogger and talk radio host took the bold step of disinviting Donald Trump
to the RedState Gathering after Trump said some inappropriate things
about Fox News host Megyn Kelly, who had moderated a Republican
primary debate featuring Mr. Trump in August of 2015. While more
famous conservative talkers were boosting Trump, Mr. Erickson rose
to the occasion and demonstrated leadership. In this respect, he was
following in the grand tradition of William F. Buckley. Because Erickson
is young and on the rise, there is reason to hope that he, and others like
him, will provide for future generations of conservatives what has been

sorely lacking in recent years—some adult supervision. Any institution worth its salt finds a way to police its own neighborhood. It needn't be a formal thing. Sometimes shaming works. Regardless, conservatism can't function—certainly can't thrive—if there are no adults willing to call out the punks hanging out on the street corner and causing problems.

5. Cast a Positive and Inclusive Vision

In an ideal world, we could take some cues from the good aspects of populism, which is to say we can be for the little guy while also embracing the optimistic brand of conservatism embraced by Ronald Reagan. It may just happen. Upon its inception in 2015, Jeb Bush's newly created Right to Rise PAC put out a statement (posted on the "What We Believe" section of the group's website) that blended elements of populism with a more optimistic brand of conservatism. "We believe the income gap is real, but that only conservative principles can solve it by removing the barriers to upward mobility," the statement said. "We will celebrate success and risk taking, protect liberty, cherish free enterprise, strengthen our national defense, embrace the energy revolution, fix our broken and obsolete immigration system, and give all children a better future by transforming our education system through choice, high standards, and accountability."

Bush, whose wife is a native of Mexico, clearly believes his brand of conservatism can compete among diverse groups of Americans. Because of his last name, Bush may be an imperfect messenger to represent twenty-first-century conservatism, but conservatives would benefit from studying this messaging. (The Right to Rise website is available in English and "Español.")

6. Reconciling Conservative Philosophy with Science

Amazingly, a lot of Americans still don't understand that one can believe in the Divinity of Christ—in creation, miracles, the Virgin

Birth, and the Resurrection—and also believe that Earth is billions of years old. In contrast, Catholics have long been open to the notion that there is no contradiction between evolution and faith, with Pope John Paul II going out of his way to reaffirm this in 1996. In October of 2014, Pope Francis drew headlines for saying "the evolution in nature is not opposed to the notion of Creation, because evolution presupposes the creation of beings that evolve." (There was so much bad reporting on this that it necessitated a *Newsweek* article titled "Pope Francis's Remarks on Evolution Are Not That Controversial Among Roman Catholics.")

Pope Francis's ability to discuss the issue provided a stark contrast with Republican politicians' inability to do so. (Recalling Francis's comments, the *New Yorker*'s Michael Specter quipped, "It would be nice if we could elect political leaders capable of that kind of thought. But, in this country, that might take a miracle.") According to a Pew Research Center poll released in January of 2014, Republicans are less likely to say that "humans have evolved over time" today than they were as recently as 2009, despite the fact that 60 percent of all American adults embrace evolution.

Yet there is a move afoot among evangelicals to reconcile the gap between their faith and science.[107] During a panel discussion in 2012, the aforementioned Pastor Tim Keller said, "The Bible does not teach that the Earth is young."[108] Keller then went on to explain that "the genealogies are not complete." (By this he means that Bible verses stating "so and so begat so and so" imply ancestry, not specifically fatherhood.) Ultimately, Keller concluded that a belief in (or against) an old Earth shouldn't be a deal breaker for salvation: "[It's] not in the Apostle's Creed, and therefore there's wiggle room."

Although this debate over evolution and Earth's age has invaded our politics for almost a century, prior to the era of William Jennings Bryan and the Scopes Monkey Trial, many Protestant Christian theologians thought evolution was acceptable as part of God's plan.

In his 1908 classic *Orthodoxy*, the future Roman Catholic convert

G. K. Chesterton observed, "If evolution simply means that a positive thing called an ape turned very slowly into a positive thing called a man, then it is stingless for the most orthodox; for a personal God might just as well do things slowly as quickly, especially if, like the Christian God, he were outside time."

Indeed, as Baylor professor Barry Hankins told me, "Some of the best conservative, evangelical theologians of the late nineteenth century were willing to consider ways in which evolution—not Darwinism or Darwin's theory of how evolution took place—but evolution, itself, could be part of God's plan. But by the 1920s, the categories had hardened."[109]

Science sometimes seems to contradict faith, but sometimes it can also turn an atheist toward God. In a 2014 *Wall Street Journal* op-ed, Eric Metaxas wrote, "Fred Hoyle, the astronomer who coined the term 'big bang,' said that his atheism was 'greatly shaken' by scientific developments quantifying the incredibly long odds of our universe randomly supporting life." What is more, Metaxas continued, "theoretical physicist Paul Davies has said that 'the appearance of [intelligent] design is overwhelming' and Oxford professor Dr. John Lennox has said that 'the more we get to know about our universe, the more the hypothesis that there is a Creator...gains in credibility as the best explanation of why we are here.'"[110]

Christians should probably be a little more open to the notion that evolution was part of God's plan—*and so should atheists and intellectuals.*

A similar fear of science undermining faith holds conservatives back in the debate over climate change. But the solution is not to surrender to liberals, whose environmentalist alarmism is quickly becoming the secular version of an apocalyptic, snake-handling, end-of-times prophecy. Conservatives may be saddled with the anti-science label, but liberals, too, put their ideology before science.

Conservatives should first understand that much of the Left is more interested in smearing conservatives as "climate science deniers" than they are in convincing people to accept the science. To win the climate change argument is to gain the added political cudgel that conservatives are stupid and, beyond that, more interested in politics/ideology than in actually solving not only climate change, but also immigration reform and other issues. In this regard, liberals deserve a good bit of blame for why our political process is broken.

The liberal notion that conservatives are all climate science deniers is misleading. Sure, some deny scientific consensus outright. But with this exceptionally broad brush, liberals tar those who constructively question the most alarmist interpretation of the data and criticize heavy-handed government solutions to the problem. To the extent that ignorance is defined as credulously adhering to a reductionist doctrine, and intelligence is associated with skepticism and a nuanced understanding of things, it is perhaps ironic that conservatives are labeled stupid. It is today's liberals—not conservatives—who all too often forget that science is not a creed but a process.

The subject of climate change—and conservative views about it—is much more diverse than most people appreciate. First, we must acknowledge that some examples of global warming alarmism and doomsday hysteria have simply proven not just marginally, but wildly, overwrought. Conservatives should hardly be penalized for "denying" such "facts." It's also true that liberals have made a quasi-religion out of environmentalism. This hearkens back to Rousseau and his belief that man, in his natural state, was pure. His Eden was destroyed by property, religion, and (you guessed it) capitalism. So a natural liberal bias exists toward believing that civilization causes problems; whereas, I would argue, the true conservative believes that civilization makes us better (that's why we call things "civil" after all). And while both sides have their inherent biases, it's hard to argue that environmentalists have been exactly consistent, or even honest, in their presentation of what we have now taken to calling "climate change." There were, of course, warnings throughout the twentieth century about "global cooling" and a "little ice age." "If present trends continue," declared ecologist Kenneth Watt on the original Earth Day in 1970, "the world will be about four degrees colder for the global mean temperature in 1990, but eleven degrees colder in the year 2000." A more recent story, known as "Climategate," raised questions about the agenda of scientists studying climate change. After a hacker released a trove of e-mails, Forbes.com's James Taylor observed that three themes had emerged: "(1) prominent scientists central to the global warming debate are taking measures to conceal rather than disseminate underlying data and discussions; (2) these scientists view global warming as a political 'cause' rather than a balanced scientific inquiry; and (3) many of these scientists frankly admit to each other that much of the science is weak and dependent on deliberate manipulation of facts and data."

But not all conservatives are skeptics. In fact, a handful of prominent conservatives like former representative Bob Inglis (R-SC), who now heads the Energy and Enterprise Initiative at George Mason University, and conservative economist Art Laffer—inventor of the Laffer curve, which spawned "Reaganomics"—support policies to slash carbon emissions. Both advocate swapping the income tax for a carbon tax. Inglis is a devout Christian who says his faith calls us to be good stewards of the earth, and, as he told me, we have a "moral obligation to restore Eden wherever possible." Laffer is a conservative economist who remains agnostic on the science of climate change, but who argues taxing carbon makes more sense than taxing income.

Even if one believes in anthropogenic global warming (the fifth Intergovernmental Panel on Climate Change [IPCC] concluded that "it is extremely likely [95 percent confidence]" that humans are responsible for more than half of the observable global warming), it is not unreasonable to insist on studying the issue further before decreeing sweeping public policy decisions. There are still good questions worth asking: To what degree can we change things? Should we focus more on reducing carbon emissions or adapting to inevitable climate changes? What's the cost-benefit analysis for either approach? If we could lower the temperature by a fraction of one degree over the next century, but the cost would be millions of jobs over the next decade, would it be worth it? There's also the question of unilateral disarmament: unless China and India agree to a legally binding, long-term climate agreement, our efforts to control climate change would amount to little more than a drop in the bucket.

Conservatives should be capable of translating science into evidence-based policy—in other words, accepting the science, noting its limitations, and putting forth market-oriented policies to address potential problems according on what is *known*.

It's easy to suggest Republicans seek safe harbor by adopting the positions of their adversaries. But that's simple moral cowardice. Properly executed strategies do not capitulate to the Left. They expose the Left's hypocrisy while restoring the reputation of conservatives as clear-eyed problem solvers.

It's become increasingly clear that politics clouds the minds of conservatives and liberals alike. A study released in the March 2015 issue of *The Annals of the American Academy of Political and Social Science* suggests that both liberals and conservatives are susceptible to having their political views bias their belief in science. Liberals were less likely to believe the science on hydraulic fracturing, while conservatives were less likely to believe the science on evolution and global warming. If conservatives put scientific blinders on, then environmentalists also seem allergic to the science of natural gas, the energy source most responsible for our increased energy independence and our reduced reliance on coal. Liberals skew paranoid about nuclear energy (which some experts like Carol Browner, who served as administrator of the Environmental Protection Agency under President Bill Clinton and director of the White House Office of Energy and Climate Change Policy in the Obama administration, believe could actually reduce carbon emissions) and have been known to be susceptible to the antivaccination hysteria, and "Trutherism" (the notion that 9/11 was an "inside job," and alarmism over genetically modified foods). Writing at *Forbes*, Jon Entine, founder and director of the Genetic Literacy Project and senior fellow at the Center for Health & Risk Communication and STATS at George Mason University, took to task Chris Mooney, author of the one-sided *The Republican War on Science*, for his past opposition to hydraulic fracking. "Don't expect Mooney to come clean," Entine wrote, but there are more Democrats who reject the science of fracking than there are Republicans who reject evolution. Conservatives could potentially trump liberals with a science-based, market-based approach to climate: recognize that fossil fuels can't be eliminated anytime soon and get government out of the way of the Keystone XL Pipeline, fracking, and nuclear projects, while implementing revenue-neutral carbon taxes that allow market incentives to drive greener consumer behavior.

7. Let Go of Cultural Identity Preferences That Have Nothing to Do with Conservatism

In Chapter Four, we talked about how South Carolina Republicans were wise to throw the Confederate battle flag under the bus, so to speak. Some Palmetto State conservatives might feel a cultural connection to the flag, but it is deeply offensive to many African Americans and is historically connected to the Democratic Party. It's sometimes hard enough to justify carrying your own baggage; why carry someone else's?

Having already made this point about shedding oversimplified images of the South, let's examine some of the suburban stereotypes. As previously noted, conservatism has become associated in the popular imagination with McMansions and gas-guzzling SUVs. Meanwhile, liberalism evokes images of public transportation or bicycle commutes from high-rise lofts to open-floor workspaces.

It is assumed that conservatives, if they must live near a city, will seek to buy the biggest house they can possibly afford with the longest commute they can possibly endure and purchase the biggest, least fuel-efficient car to take them back and forth. And you know what? Based on our choices, it's pretty clear that we conservatives believe this, too. Never mind the fact that conservative icons such as William F. Buckley rode a motor scooter and that Russell Kirk (as previously mentioned) refused to drive a car, which Kirk referred to derisively as a "mechanical Jacobin" that would increase rootlessness in America. While I have no problem with the country or the suburbs, for a long time now I've been a proponent of something called New Urbanism. The name is unfortunate, inasmuch as it makes people think I'm suggesting we all live in urban areas; I'm not. Essentially, the concept promotes walkable, mixed-use neighborhoods with narrow streets and retail shops on the sidewalk level and apartments above. And it's not just about high-density, high-rise buildings. The New Urbanism concept promotes living within a safe walking distance of our churches, schools, shops, restaurants, and more.

A couple of years ago, I interviewed two modern New Urbanists on my podcast and wrote about it at *The Week*. Sid Burgess calls himself a "Coolidge Republican," and Kerry S. Decker, who considers himself a Tea Partier, briefly worked as a city planner. Their stories illustrate why modern conservatives should embrace ideas like New Urbanism. But the conversion won't be easy. "Whenever I start mentioning any kind of New Urbanism items—for conservatives and Republicans who I talk to who don't know me personally—I'm instantly branded a Communist," Decker confessed.

Burgess became a champion of this movement after hearing James Howard Kunstler's 2004 TED Talk.[111] During his presentation, Kunstler showed slides of urban sprawl and then declared, "These are places that are not worth caring about [and] when we have enough of them, we're going to have a nation that's not worth defending." Kunstler then asked his audience to think about the American soldiers who, at that very moment, were dying in Iraq, and said, "Ask yourself, what is their last thought of home? I hope it's not the curb cut between the Chuck E. Cheese and the Target store." Just back from Iraq himself, this hit home with the conservative Burgess.

"To make us love our country," Edmund Burke said, "our country must be lovely." Burke was also talking about the spiritual attributes of a people—something Kunstler doesn't deal with. But it's not out-of-bounds to think that aesthetics—and the search for the sublime—are somehow interrelated to the intangible and spiritual aspects of a people. Or another way of looking at it: the place we physically inhabit is an outward and visible manifestation of the inward.

Ironically, government regulation (the tax code, zoning, a federally financed highway system, a failing public school system, and so on) helps explain America's post–World War II push for sprawl. What is more interesting, though, is that conservatives so readily embraced this modern fad as being tantamount to the American Dream.

Americans may be uniquely fond of cars, but most humans long for family and community and beauty. According to a Swedish study,[112] people who endure more than a forty-five-minute commute are 40 percent more likely to get divorced. A study of German commuters conducted by University of Zurich economists Bruno Frey and Alois Stutzer found that people had to earn 40 percent more money to be as satisfied as someone who can simply walk to work.[113] In truth, it's probably impossible to quantify the spiritual and psychological cost associated with endlessly frustrating commutes, disconnection from a community, and ugly buildings. And there is certainly an economic cost of taxpayers maintaining low-density areas and infrastructure that yields relatively little revenue.

If you worry that wanting to live in a walkable community makes you some sort of hippie Leftist, have no fear. In a report titled "Conservatives and the New Urbanism," Heritage Foundation cofounder Paul Weyrich joined the *American Conservative*'s William S. Lind and New Urbanist Andres Duany in making a pretty compelling case for why more conservatives ought to embrace these communities:

On the face of it, it is hard to see why conservatives should oppose offering traditionally designed cities, towns, and neighborhoods as alternatives to post-war "sprawl" suburbs. As conservatives, we are supposed to prefer traditional designs to modern innovations in most things (and we do). We hope to demonstrate traditional designs for the places we live, work, and shop to encourage traditional culture and morals. This should not surprise us. Edmund Burke told us more than two hundred years ago that traditional societies are organic wholes. If you (literally) disintegrate a society's physical setting, as sprawl has done, you tend to disintegrate its culture as well.

To be sure, any suggestion that Americans should encourage these local polices will be greeted by some as proof that there's a vast conspiracy dedicated to undermining our freedoms. I suspect this goes back to Eden and our long national preference for all things rural. "Liberals in power produce more mass transit because they hope more mass transit will produce more liberals," wrote conservative columnist Terence Jeffrey in a piece titled "The Conspiracy Against the Car."

Nobody I know is suggesting big government—or the UN— ought to mandate or impose these sorts of development policies. The idea is that local governments should think of these things— and that conservatives who actually hold traditionally conservative values may want to live in such communities. Conservatives—who often talk about states' rights and local control—tend to stick to their antigovernment views even at the local level. To some degree, this is admirable and appropriate. But sometimes, it's a bad thing. Conservatives ought to be involved in making local government work well, proving that the heavy hand of the federal government isn't needed for smart planning and growth. We've all heard that famous line about a shining city on a hill. Did you ever notice there is no shining cul-de-sac on a hill?

The GOP was able to thrive in the latter part of the twentieth century, partly because they dominated this constituency of the South, rural America, and suburbia. But since turning out voters at the polls who already agree with you is easier than either finding new voters or persuading voters who disagree with you to change their minds, the base drives policy.

The real culture war taking place is one of ideas, pitting conservatism against liberalism. Unfortunately, we have simplistically conflated ruralism with conservatism and urbanism with liberalism. To use a term Rush Limbaugh likes, this is sloppy signaling—it's "symbolism over substance." (Read about Brooklyn's large and thriving Orthodox Jewish community, if you find urban conservatism unimaginable.) And there could be negative long-term consequences. The problem is that a party that relies solely on non-college-educated rural and suburban white men and married white women might eventually run out of them.

But it's not just ostentatious suburban McMansions that feel increasingly repellent. A recent business story regarding the fate of McDonald's might serve as a microcosm for the struggles of a conservative movement that is culturally the political equivalent of the fast-food chain. The company is undergoing a slump, and while McDonald's has been culturally associated with conservatives, they have apparently seen the writing on the wall. In 2015, a new CEO came in to help turn things around and promptly declared the franchise a "progressive burger company." Only time will tell if this appeasement will pacify the company's critics, but it just might work—at least, it did for another once hated company. Having fended off attacks from the Left in the 2000s, Arkansas-based Walmart, has, in recent years, worked to ingratiate themselves with their erstwhile liberal oppressors. In 2015, Walmart's CEO spoke out against an Arkansas religious freedom bill and, in the wake of the horrific church shooting in Charleston, South Carolina, they pulled merchandise featuring the Confederate flag from all stores.

It's unclear whether it's wise to try to make friends of your enemies by making enemies of your friends. Conservatives argue McDonald's slumping sales are due to switching from beef flavoring to pure vegetable oil in their French fries—a concession they made to health-conscious progressives. Others argue they were just doing what they had to do to keep up with the times. As the *Wall Street Journal* pointed out, "Customers in their twenties and thirties—long a mainstay of McDonald's business—are defecting to competitors." While McDonald's was resting on its golden arches, pricier (but cooler, trendier, healthier, tastier, and more flexible) competitors like Chipotle and Five Guys exploited the demographic and cultural changes.

Sound familiar? Like the GOP, the once savvy McDonald's failed to adapt to changing times (they also both revere a guy named Ronald, but that's a different story). But change is hard, and—for the GOP, at least—solutions won't be as simple as deciding to serve breakfast all day.

Growing the Tent without Burning It Down

If Republicans can add these seven ingredients called for in my recipe, they'll be well on their way to success. Of course, every action has an equal and opposite reaction. While Republicans simply must appeal to segments of the population that are growing, attempts to modernize the GOP into a brand that is capable of winning the twenty-first century also risk alienating loyal supporters. Sometimes this is unavoidable. But while the GOP must win more urban and cosmopolitan votes, Republicans would be foolish to mock or undermine their current base. Writing off the South or evangelicals, for example, would be unwise. By the same token, writing off Hispanics, unmarried women, and college-educated Americans is also stupid. (Quick! Ask yourself, who did Reagan write off?) If conservatism is really the best philosophy, then it can win the free market of ideas among a diverse audience. If we are to turn off voters, then let it be because they disagree with our ideas—not because they drive a different kind of car, or their skin is a tone lighter or darker than ours, or they live in a more or less urban area, or we have allowed them to wrongly believe the worst stereotypes about us.

While the larger umbrella of conservatism must be coherent and consistent, conservative leaders, especially at the local and state level, should stress different aspects of the conservative perspective to different regional audiences. In a 2013 *New York Times* column, David Brooks made the case that the GOP should "build a new division that is different the way the Westin is different than the Sheraton.... Would a coastal and Midwestern GOP sit easily with the Southern and Western one? No, but majority parties are usually coalitions of the incompatible. This is really the only chance Republicans have. The question is, who's going to build a second GOP?"

It's unclear what the exact Boss Hogg–to–Bill Buckley ratio *should* be in a big tent party. But if the Democratic Party can stress different values in different regions of the country, why can't the GOP?

12

WHAT CAN I DO?

"And He gave some as apostles, and some as prophets, and some as evangelists, and some as pastors and teachers, for the equipping of the saints for the work of service."
—*Ephesians 4:11*

"With great power comes great responsibility."
—*From* Spider-Man

America is better off when conservatism is a thriving and thoughtful force for good, contributing to the great debates of our time. Otherwise, the Republic suffers. Such a renaissance is both possible and within our power to achieve. Of course, the next question is, how do we make it happen? The previous chapter dealt with how and why conservative leaders and politicians must adapt conservatism to win the twenty-first century at the macro level. This chapter examines how we, as individuals and groups, can do our part at the micro level. This requires each of us to accept responsibility for the movement. And, in a sense, this is really just a microcosm of what is required of a healthy nation. "We have no government armed with power capable of contending with human passions unbridled by morality and religion," wrote John Adams.

"Avarice, ambition, revenge, or gallantry would break the strongest cords of our constitution as a whale goes through a net. Our Constitution was made only for a moral and religious people. It is wholly inadequate to the government of any other." A well-run movement operates the same way. It can function only if people *voluntarily* behave appropriately and set aside personal ambitions for the good of the cause. It can happen only if there are leaders and "adults" who accept their responsibilities to serve.

The problem is that this is sort of like voting. Just as one person's vote (I hate to break this to you) rarely matters, our votes are *collectively* very important. If everyone acts as if his or her vote doesn't count, that will have serious ramifications. So we each have a responsibility to vote, but the truth is that this won't amount to much unless others join in, too. But this is easier said than done. How should conservatives comport themselves if we are to end the "too dumb to fail" conundrum?

In the remaining pages, I will provide some advice—first, general (for all of us), and then more specific (for individual roles, such as columnists, talk radio hosts, political consultants, etc.). But let's start with some things we can probably all work on...

For All of Us...

1. Be a Happy Warrior

Passion is a vital ingredient to success, but blind anger makes us stupid. People who are mad don't think rationally. Instead, they take unwise risks, are susceptible to traps laid by their enemies, and make otherwise foolish mistakes. Look again to Ronald Reagan, the quintessential happy warrior. One of conservative leader Morton Blackwell's "Laws of the Public Policy Process" is: "Don't get mad except on purpose." To be sure, Reagan could feign anger ("I am paying for this microphone!"), but like Fonzie, he almost never lost his cool. Getting mad also plays into the stereotype that conservatives are mean. "I'm a conservative, but I'm not mad at anyone about it," former Arkansas governor Mike Huckabee once quipped. It was funny because it was true.

But especially since President Obama's election and the rise of the Tea Party, the trend has been toward anger. In fact, we now conflate passion with ideological purity to the degree that one's level of anger has become *the* litmus test for judging one's conservative credentials. To some, "fighting the Left" has become the only core value. It's always fun to pretend that your tribe is simultaneously right on all the issues—*and* yet perpetually victimized. If liberals are bullies, then conservatives are aping the Left and becoming bullies... *with persecution complexes.*

Positive optimism is important for all of us hoping to win converts and preserve our own sanity. But it's even more important for leaders. It's hard to follow someone who believes your side is destined to fail. Can you imagine a football coach rallying his team at halftime by saying, "Look, they got us beat. And I don't see how we can come back in the second half"? Great leaders are also great inspirers. That doesn't mean they ignore problems or pretend they will fix themselves. But if your leader doesn't provide hope, then you've got problems. Why would you want to follow that leader?

2. Reject Anger

It's easy to simply decree that we should be happy warriors, but pulling it off in the midst of political battle is another thing. Devout Christian conservatives (or, for that matter, other people of devout faith) can especially face tension between their faith and their political activism. We are called to love our neighbors and bless those who curse us, which works for a happy warrior—but not for an angry warrior. If you truly believe that the spiritual world is eternal and vastly more important than this carnal world, it's easier to endure the slings and arrows of losing an election. Fear is the opposite of faith. Nevertheless, there is a sort of religious *tenor* to this fear and anger, and I suspect it is based on an apocalyptic sense that time is running out.

Where do we get the sense that things are so bad? Talking heads make careers out of whipping us into a frenzy, like an old man stocking up at a supermarket before an imminent snowstorm. (If you listen to talk radio, you're no doubt familiar with the ads for survivalist food storage, stockpiling gold, etc.) Scarcity leads to hoarding, which is a far cry from living an abundant life where God supplies all your needs "according to His riches in glory." If you believe, as Jack Kemp did, that we can grow the pie, then you're likely to be more generous with what you've been blessed with. But if you believe that you (and your children and their children) could lose your already-small piece of the pie, you will become fearful and angry. So which are you? Even for those who put their trust in the Lord, there *are* some things worthy of fear. Sometimes bad things do happen to good nations. However, it's important to realize that huge industries called "Politics, Inc." and "Media, Inc." profit from pushing our emotional buttons to extremes.

Aside from the professional button pushers, I have another theory to help explain the ubiquity of anger. Some of the people now passing judgment on everybody else were asleep for the last thirty years. These people woke up one day and realized America was in trouble, and all of a sudden, *they* have become the arbiter of everything conservative. I think some of these people are angry at *themselves*. They were asleep at the switch, and they're trying to make up for lost time, so their "no compromise" position is a result of going from zero to sixty—from zero involvement to overindulgence—and they now feel that if they don't do something, the world is going to collapse. And that they'll be partly to blame. This is zealotry of the convert, or what novelist David Foster Wallace called "the 'moral clarity' of the immature." Unfortunately, this "making up for lost time" is often counterproductive. Politics is important—even noble—but it's important to find balance in your life. Family, friends, faith, and hobbies can keep us grounded.

3. Find Your Calling

One of my favorite actors was Philip Seymour Hoffman. Though he got his Academy Award for his starring role in *Capote*, it was his supporting work as a character actor in films like *Scent of a Woman*, *The Talented Mr. Ripley*, and *Charlie Wilson's War* that I loved. Hoffman was at his best when you didn't even know he was the actor. Everyone wants to be the star, but Hoffman was humble enough to accept supporting roles. And often, he stole the show. I suspect the conservative movement needs more people willing to be Phil Hoffman, and fewer wanting to be Tom Cruise.

The existence of role players was vitally important during the rise of the conservative movement in America, too. There were intellectuals like Bill Buckley, statesmen like Reagan, Senate rabble-rousers like Jesse Helms, conservative activists and organizational entrepreneurs like Paul Weyrich, operatives like Pat Buchanan (and even direct mail guru Richard Viguerie), journalists like Robert Novak, and columnists like George Will. Each of these men had their part to play in the conservative movement. They didn't always agree, but they *did* work in complementary fashion. Today, these players might instead step on one another's toes, wade into the other guy's turf, and "troll" the other guys on Twitter. They would all probably try to run for president—or, at least, float the notion in order to generate buzz. I'm not suggesting that there weren't fights during the "good old days" (there were), but I am suggesting that we can take a page from that generation. Not everyone needs to run for president. We all have our role to play.

4. Stay Humble

Another good piece of advice is to embrace humility. It is a virtue that should come naturally to conservatives who, unlike liberals, suffer no illusion that we have all the solutions or can fix all the world's problems. Epistemological modesty is one of the hallmarks of conservatism. Liberals may think their utopian schemes and "comprehensive" plans can manage an economy or fix health care, but conservatives are supposed to be humble enough to realize this is a fatal conceit. There's a reason Greek tragedies warned us against flying too close to the sun. Today, there is such a need for humility that *New York Times* columnist David Brooks even taught a course on it at Yale, with a syllabus that featured required readings of Edmund Burke, Reinhold Niebuhr, Augustine, Montaigne, Samuel Johnson, and Martin Luther King Jr. Talk about a countercultural topic. More than one observer thought it ironic that Brooks, who has been accused of being haughty and self-righteous by his critics, would teach a course on humility. But the truth is that this is a value that has sadly receded from our culture. In fact, in a world where you have to hustle and be a "rugged individualist," it almost sounds like bad advice to tell someone to be more humble. It goes against both today's "conservative" ethos and the mainstream commercial culture. As Hillsdale College's David J. Bobb, author of *Humility: An Unlikely Biography of America's Greatest Virtue*, points out, rapper Kanye West once said, "People always tell you, 'Be humble. Be humble.' When was the last time someone told you to be amazing? Be great! Be great! Be awesome! Be awesome!"

Unfortunately, this attitude has transcended the entertainment world and infiltrated our elected leaders. From Kanye to Cruz (is it a coincidence that Kanye West was called a "jackass" by President Obama—and Ted Cruz was called that exact same word by then Speaker John Boehner?), one gets the sense that some of the most talented figures in America—the "stars" we worship—too often embrace humility's opposite: arrogance. Consider some of what Donald Trump has said: "I'm really rich," "I'll be the best jobs president God's created," "Sorry, losers and haters, but my IQ is one of the highest," and (during one *Meet the Press* appearance, in which he said that it is hard for women to attack his looks) "because I'm so good-looking." Today everyone craves fame and attention and riches. Nobody wants to be a respected character actor; everyone wants to play the lead. In a strict hierarchical organization (think the US Marines) people are forced to subjugate their personal whims and follow orders. There is a proper chain of command. Until recently, much of civilization functioned via an informal pecking order. Today, that's out the window. This trend is not only bad for our country, but it's also bad for the conservative movement.

5. Go to School

How can a conservative movement leader—or even a foot soldier—avoid the pitfalls of ignorance and narcissism inherent in the political word? *Go to school.* I don't just mean get a college degree (although that's not a bad idea); rather, bone up on the issues long before you write a letter to the editor, pop off on Facebook, speak out at a town hall, volunteer on a campaign, or even run for office yourself. Someone who wants to work effectively in conservative politics should devote hundreds of hours to studying a wide variety of subjects. Even someone who simply wants to be a more informed voter or a more effective activist would benefit greatly from investing this time.

Former Texas governor Rick Perry learned this lesson during his failed 2012 presidential run. "I did not prepare," Perry confessed to Joe Scarborough during a 2014 episode of MSNBC's *Morning Joe*. "I was a bit arrogant," he conceded. "To run for the highest office in this country, and the most influential position in the world, requires an extensive amount of preparation. Whether it's domestic policy, whether it's monetary policy, whether it's foreign policy. And I did not prepare." It was a remarkable admission. In fairness to Perry, his star-crossed 2012 campaign can be partly blamed on the back surgery he endured weeks before jumping into the campaign. Still, give him credit for "going to school" and boning up on the issues before pursuing the nomination again. I wish Sarah Palin had done that in 2008. Had she spent a few years gaining expertise, Palin might have parlayed her charisma and name recognition into something extraordinary. Instead, she chose the route of populist firebrand at Tea Party rallies, a Fox News contract, and the allure of a reality TV show. She made money, but one wonders what might have been.

For those looking to increase their knowledge, an obvious place to start is the conservative canon (see my reading list in the afterword of this book). Being a "gut" conservative—someone who listens to talk radio, agrees taxes are too high, and hates abortion—is fine. That's what I was for much of my early life. But to advance you must supplement this with a coherent worldview that will hold up when you are confronted with opposing viewpoints or adverse conditions. Having a passable understanding of conservative philosophy is good; possessing that alongside an understanding of the practical side of politics is even better. Political philosophy is important, but how do you run an effective "Get Out the Vote" operation or raise enough money to win on Election Day? Understanding the nuts and bolts of a political campaign will not only help you understand the process, but it will also help explain some of the compromises and calculations that inexorably led to the dumbing down of conservatism.

What else? Any educated person should have a good understanding of history. A rudimentary knowledge of religion and theology is helpful for anyone who wants to understand Western civilization. This is especially good advice for secular readers who weren't brought up in a faith tradition. And don't forget popular culture. It would be a mistake to waste your life watching TV, but anyone who wants to positively impact the culture had better know something about it. You don't have to be an expert, but anyone who doesn't know who Jennifer Lawrence is will appear out of touch. Aside from books, read some newspapers (the *New York Times* and *Wall Street Journal*), magazines (*National Review*, the *Weekly Standard*), quarterly journals (like Yuval Levin's *National Affairs*), and as much online material as you can find (might I suggest the *Daily Caller*, TheWeek.com, the *Daily Beast*, and the *Telegraph*). Although I am sometimes critical of Twitter (it's "garbage in, garbage out"), if you follow the right people, you'll find it's a terrific way to curate the content you *must* read every day.

Those who want to do more than just dabble in politics need to go one step further. Instead of getting all their information from behind a media filter, they should try building policy knowledge closer to the source by reading white papers from think tanks on topics like economics, monetary policy, foreign policy/international relations, health care, governmental bureaucracies, entitlement spending, policing, and prison reform. For politicians, academics, and journalists, think tanks can be a big help. Unfortunately, some think tanks are moving away from their core missions. When one considers the struggles required to launch these bastions of conservative thought to obtain intellectual parity with the Left, that's a real shame.

In Lee Edwards's *The Power of Ideas: The Heritage Foundation at 25 Years*, the veteran conservative writer recalls how activist Paul Weyrich, with the help of then Nixon aide Lyn Nofziger, persuaded beer magnate Joseph Coors to invest in starting the Heritage Foundation—even though another conservative think tank, ostensibly dedicated to the same mission, already existed. As Edwards writes, after a meeting with Coors,

> Weyrich was excited about how well the presentation had gone until he learned that Coors was also considering "investing" in the American Enterprise Institute. His high hopes collapsed. How could an unknown, untested research firm compete with a respected think tank that had been operating for nearly thirty years? Casting about for help, Weyrich arranged for Coors and [Jack] Wilson to talk with fellow conservative Lyn Nofziger, a deputy assistant to President Nixon for congressional relations. Along with Ed Feulner, they met in Nofziger's large pastel-blue office in the Old Executive Office Building next to the White House.

"So, what about AEI?" Coors asked Nofziger.

"AEI?" repeated the White House aide. And, according to Weyrich, he strolled over to a bookshelf and blew some dust off an AEI study. "That's what they're good for—collecting dust. They do great work but they're not timely. What we need are studies for Congress while legislation is being considered."

At the time, conservatives had enough mere thinkers; they needed some doers. Today, the situation is almost 180 degrees in reverse. There's no shortage of activist groups. Meanwhile, AEI has not strayed from its core intellectual mission. Conversely, in January of 2013 the Heritage Foundation was taken over by former South Carolina senator Jim DeMint, a fiery Southern conservative known more for his conservative political stances than for any academic credentials. In 2013, the group reportedly spent $100,000 on online advertising attacking former DeMint protégé Marco Rubio for his support of "amnesty."[114] "The ad campaign reflects the ongoing debasement of think tanks: nominally, these groups are supposed to be engaged in policy research, but they look increasingly like tax-advantaged vehicles for political activism," wrote Business Insider's Josh Barro.

Heritage doesn't just "look like" an activist group; it started a full-fledged activist arm called Heritage Action for America, which uses a "scorecard" and "watchlist" to pressure members of Congress. The danger is that this sort of lobbying might make it harder for Heritage to serve as an impartial and reliable resource for conservatives. Though there was once a real need for conservative activist organizations that could lobby politicians and hold their feet to the fire, in recent years numerous groups dedicated to this very cause have emerged. By the time Heritage decided to make this move, there were already activist groups like Americans for Prosperity and FreedomWorks—and there were already conservative pressure groups like the Club for Growth[115] and Senate Conservatives Fund that scored legislation and ranked politicians (something the

American Conservative Union has done for years). Why get into a business that is already saturated? One supposes there are ulterior motives, such as expanding the base of donors.

6. Teach Your Children Well

According to popular evangelical author Nancy Pearcey, "The main reason people abandon their Christian upbringing is unanswered intellectual questions."[116] This was her experience, at least. Raised a Christian, she lost her faith. "Eventually I concluded that Christianity must not have any substantial answers," she said during a recent interview, but "after several years as an agnostic, I finally stumbled across L'Abri, the work of Francis and Edith Schaeffer in Switzerland. There for the first time I met people who offered reasons and arguments supporting the truth of Christianity."

Why bring this up? Whether or not you accept evolution or climate change, if you're a conservative reading this book, you probably at least believe in free markets. And, as such, you would probably agree that protectionism makes for lousy economics. And—I would argue—for equally lousy theology. A young Christian who has been exposed to various theories ranging from young earth creationism to intelligent design to Darwinian evolution will be better prepared to handle an atheistic college professor than a young student who has been sheltered from these sort of debates (who then might suddenly find his entire worldview crashing down around him or her as soon as he or she leaves for college).

Today, I see plenty of examples where conservatives end up looking foolish because they are ill equipped to answer these questions in an intelligent manner that persuasively makes the case for a conservative worldview, and does so in a manner that is intellectually honest and defensible. A one-hour-per-week faith simply will not last longer than a generation.

During the Christmas of 2014, an open debate took place

amongst those who write "think" pieces about whether kids should be taught about Santa Claus. I didn't weigh in, but when I was a kid, my dad (when asked) opted to tell me the truth. "I'm telling you this because I want you to know that I tell you the truth," he said. "Then, you'll know I'm not lying to you when I tell you God *is* real." I'm not suggesting your parents were wrong if they allowed you to entertain this fantasy or that you suffered some sort of identity crisis upon learning (spoiler alert!) that a jolly fat man did not, in fact, slide down your chimney each year. But I am suggesting that credibility matters. Even if—perhaps especially if—you are steeped in faith.

We walk by faith, not by sight. But the head matters, too—and fealty to the facts is essential to establish credibility. My dad never read Augustine's *The Literal Meaning of Genesis*, but I think he'd agree with what Augustine had to say about the importance of being known as an honest broker that deals in reality:

> It is a disgraceful and dangerous thing for an infidel to hear a Christian, presumably giving the meaning of Holy Scripture, talking nonsense on these [scientific] topics; and we should take all means to prevent such an embarrassing situation, in which people show up vast ignorance in a Christian and laugh it to scorn....
>
> If they find a Christian mistaken in a field which they themselves know well and hear him maintaining his foolish opinions about our books, how are they going to believe those books in matters concerning the resurrection of the dead, the hope of eternal life, and the kingdom of heaven?

Conservatives must be more rigorous than our ideological opponents. Not just for ethical reasons, but also for practical ones. With the Left in solid control of the media and academia, the Right is simply outgunned. It *has* to be better, stronger, tougher, smarter. Propagating information we know to be false—or failing to fact-check out of fear of finding out we've been wrong about something all along—is intellectual protectionism. And it's as effective as was the Smoot-Hawley Tariff Act.

For Leaders...

Now, let's turn to some specific advice for specific role players in the conservative movement.

1. Politicians

Once you've "gone to school" and become a well-rounded, constantly learning conservative, you may be tantalized by the prospect of running for office yourself, whether it's US representative or local city councilperson. It's a noble impulse, but also a huge commitment and responsibility. First, think long and hard about whether this is the right move for you and your family—and for the conservative cause. Is there anything about you or your past that could come out and tarnish your reputation or make the movement look bad? Second, as always, bone up on the issues. Lastly, don't be a Liz Cheney and try to start at the top. Pay your dues. Maybe even as a precinct committeeperson. That's where Calvin Coolidge started—though it's not where he finished. In the process, you'll earn people's respect, join civic and volunteer organizations in your community, and gain knowledge and experience that will come in handy once you're in higher office.

We each have a role to play. While it was appropriate and heroic for Bill Buckley to take on the John Birch Society, Ronald Reagan's take on the group was entirely different: "They're buying my philosophy. I'm not buying theirs." Likewise, the next Republican nominee should leave it to people like me to take the slings and arrows from fringe elements in the base. His or her job is to win the election—and then lead.

Is there a role for some good old-fashioned "bomb thrower" in politics today? There is a proud tradition of the gadfly, truth-teller pol who eschews backroom deal making, fights for ideological purity, stands on principle, and employs all means at his or her disposal, including the filibuster, to resist the tyranny of the majority. Whether you agree with him, or not, former senator Jesse Helms comes to mind. In the past, however, politicians accepted their roles. And, as a rule, they didn't try to run for president (though Helms was sometimes rumored to have presidential ambitions). And therein lies the problem. Today's bomb throwers are simultaneously running for president. This clouds their judgment, and makes their motives questionable.

When Ted Cruz leads an effort that ultimately shuts down the government, you have to wonder if he's doing it to score points with the base. America needs principled politicians who are willing to rock the boat and even occasionally take on an unrealistic and impractical mission. But problems arise when these role players want to star in the film. Not only do we question their motives, but their eccentric excesses are now magnified by a twenty-four-hour news media. Such bomb throwers have come to define what conservatism is to a lot of Americans. If you are emulating that model in your community, you are only confirming the worst caricatures of conservatism to your friends and neighbors.

These candidates are empowered by the rise of outside groups. These are the outfits that endorse candidates, bundle for them (collect checks from member donors), and run independent expenditure ads on a candidate's behalf. The biggest problem these groups seem to face is in vetting their candidates. So my advice is this: before investing your donor's hard-earned money into a campaign (or a group that financially supports candidates), it's prudent to do a little research. Is this a winnable race? Does this person have a track record (and even better, a voting record) of supporting the causes important to you— or is he or she telling you what you want to hear because this year it's popular to be a grassroots conservative? And last, but not least, is this a person of honor with whom you want to be associated?

It's easy to get caught up in the maelstrom of a political war, but don't go too far with this. Always put honor and integrity first. Remember that your enemies are also children of God. And even if you want to be purely Machiavellian about it, keep in mind that a lot of people who get caught up in political warfare end up harming themselves, as well as the cause they love. Remember the blogger who broke into the nursing home of Thad Cochran's bedridden wife? Not only did he land in hot water, and not only did one of the alleged coconspirators commit suicide, but his actions arguably helped cost Chris McDaniel—the candidate the blogger supported—the chance to win his primary outright, thus avoiding a runoff.

Take some advice from Richard Nixon, a man who got caught up in pointless political warfare and games (I say pointless, because his campaign was destined to win, making the shenanigans the Watergate burglars engaged in not only stupid and morally bankrupt, but also superfluous). This is what Nixon had to say the day he left office in disgrace (it's actually solid advice): "Always give your best. Never get discouraged. Never be petty. Always remember others may hate you, but those who hate you don't win unless you hate them and then you destroy yourself."

2. Strategists and Political Operatives

People who work in campaigns—especially the decision makers—all have a part to play, too. During a 2007 interview with conservative bloggers Rob Bluey and Ed Morrissey, former Speaker Newt Gingrich said this:

> I think Republican consultants are mostly very stupid. I think they have no education. I think they have no sense of history.... If I throw away African Americans, and then I throw

away Latinos, and then I throw away suburban women, and
then I throw away people under forty, and then I throw away
everything north of Philadelphia—there's a morning where
Republicans can't get to a majority.

This quote is kind of amazing. Here is Gingrich in 2007, wor-
rying about the GOP writing off Latinos—and young people—and
suburban women. He was ahead of his time. But what did he mean
when he said that consultants "throw away" suburban women, African Americans, and others?

With all due respect to Newt, political consultants aren't stupid,
so much as they are obsessed with short-term thinking (and making money). Their immediate goal is to win a November election,
and all their strategies and tactics are seen through the prism of that
deadline. A campaign is an operation that knows it's going out of
business the first Tuesday in November, which means they aren't terribly worried about repeat customers. The trouble is that sometimes
the things that are good for you this November are death for your
cause beginning ten Novembers from now—and then, possibly in
perpetuity.

Let's take the concept strategists refer to as "targeting." Generally speaking, this process involves identifying eligible, persuadable,
likely voters, winning them over to your side, and then making sure
they actually turn out to vote for you.

Because time and money are limited quantities, campaigns typically husband most of their resources on this select group, and devote
almost *zero* resources to people outside this rubric. It is incredibly
hard to persuade someone who actively opposes your candidate to
vote for your candidate, so any Republican campaign premised on
wooing loyal Democratic voters is in grave danger. Likewise, it is
much easier to get someone who is a frequent voter (and this is public
information) to vote for your candidate than it is to persuade someone with no track record of voting to go to the trouble of registering

and showing up at the ballot box (and then, to actually vote for *your* candidate), so any campaign whose victory plan is contingent on registering new voters is essentially throwing a Hail Mary. That is to say that it could theoretically work, but it is an unorthodox act of desperation, only to be attempted after all other strategies have been exhausted.

In the short run, targeted voter contact is wise and efficient. If your liberal opponent is knocking on the doors on the conservative side of town, and you're knocking on the doors of likely voters who are undecided, you're being more efficient and productive. But there's a catch. Targeting certain voters means *ignoring* others. That's what Newt means when he says consultants "throw away" certain voters. Consultants make a strategic decision to ignore certain types of voters. At the micro level, this might be based on one's personal voting history (or perhaps even which magazines one subscribes to). At the macro level, this could be based on strategists making assumptions about a voter based on factors such as geography (where you live), age, marital status, or race.

What if year in and year out, election cycle in and election cycle out, campaign strategists were to do this? It's easy to envision a scenario where increasingly large swaths of the electorate are conceded for decades. What I've just described is a real conundrum. Winning individual elections is important—it's what strategists are hired to do. People who care about the long-term growth of a party or movement must realize that consultants have this conflict of interest. It's important to win elections. But by ignoring so much of the electorate, Republicans may be setting themselves up for a far greater problem in the future: obsolescence. (Note: A similar dynamic occurs in the world of sports. This is why managers and general managers should never be the same person. Managers and coaches focus on today; general managers are responsible for the long-term health of a team.)

Cycles of abuse and dependency are usually broken when one person stands up and decides to break the cycle. Ultimately, you can't blame the consultants or advisers, as they work for the candidates. My hope: the GOP will nominate a candidate who will run the kind of campaign that flips the script on the consultants.

3. Conservative Writers

Conservatism can be like a ghetto, but it's an alluring one. Can't make it as a comedian? Hang out in the ghetto; become a *conservative* comedian. Want to start a social media platform but don't have a hook? How about being the *conservative* Facebook? By wearing our ideology on our sleeves, we simultaneously use it as a crutch and limit our potential. "They put warning labels on packs of cigarettes and pesticides because they can be dangerous to your health," writes reporter turned columnist Bernard Goldberg. "And, as far as many liberals—both in and out of the media—are concerned, conservatives need warning labels because their ideas can be dangerous to your health."

If you want to really do some good for the conservative cause, here's what you do: Don't be a conservative political writer—be a writer who happens to have conservative ideas. Don't try to be the next William F. Buckley—try to be the next Joan Didion. Don't try to be a Christian rock band—try to be a really good rock band that *happens* to consist of believers.

This requires, I think, three ingredients. First, you have to be rooted firmly enough in your philosophy so as not to become unmoored when you're in the world. Second, while you can be ideological, you must fight like the devil to avoid overt partisanship or politicization. And lastly, you actually have to be very talented at your craft; you have to work at actually being a good writer, musician, whatever. And the work has to come first. The art has to come before the politics.

This is not easy, but I would argue that if more young conservatives went this route—instead of overtly becoming involved in politics—conservatism would be vastly advanced. (So do as I say, not as I do.)

But what if you want to do what I do? What if you want to write about politics for a living? How can you do the most good for the conservative cause?

Seek the truth.

For years, the knock on conservative journalism was that it was too heavy on opinion and analysis and too light on reporting. Everyone wanted to be the next George Will, when what we really needed were more Robert Novaks. The good news is that, in recent years, conservative outlets have started doing much more original reporting and helping to break stories, advance stories, and drive the debate (rather than merely retroactively commenting on the stories the mainstream media had decided were newsworthy). This has led to a huge change. The most insidious form of liberal bias was always selection bias. In other words, mainstream reporters might cover a given story fairly, but the question never asked was, why is this the big story in the first place? The rise of center-right new media outlets like the *Daily Caller* and the *Washington Free Beacon*, to name two, have gone a long way to alleviate this problem by focusing on important stories that might otherwise have been ignored. Another tremendous benefit of the rise of center-right reporting is that it has become a stepping-stone to mainstream media jobs. In recent years, *National Review*'s Robert Costa has landed at the *Washington Post*, and several of my former colleagues at the *Daily Caller* have moved on to mainstream gigs: Alexis Levinson is now at *National Review*, by way of *Roll Call*; Will Rahn serves as Washington bureau chief at the *Daily Beast*—where I sometimes contribute columns; Jon Ward (who departed the *Daily Caller* just before I arrived) is now at Yahoo!; and Chris Moody is now at CNN.com.

Now, this is not to suggest that these conservatives have infiltrated the mainstream media. But what this does mean is that these mainstream outlets have now hired folks who are not openly antagonistic to a conservative worldview—people who have conservative friends—and whose knowledge of conservatism will help inform their straight reporting.

4. Talk Radio Hosts

"In political talk radio," wrote David Foster Wallace, "the emotions most readily accessed are anger, outrage, indignation, fear, despair, disgust, contempt, and a certain kind of apocalyptic glee." Rather than summoning our better angels, the temptation is to stoke these primal urges; the challenge is to occasionally rise above them. Just as center-right reporters are arguably more needed than conservative pontificators in print, most of my favorite talk shows are now blending opinion and analysis with breaking news. "I'm interested in reporting news and making news," radio host Hugh Hewitt recently told the *Washington Examiner*. "I think the [radio] medium's got to be more about news show, breaking news with commentary. Not the amplification of old memes."

"You have to provide breaking news," Hewitt continued. "It has to be reliable and it has to be fast. That's what people want. Some old-time hosts can't do that. They want to talk about immigration every day."

Times have changed. During his heyday, Rush Limbaugh, who essentially pioneered the art of talking (without a guest or taking many calls from listeners) for three hours, was fresh and irreverent and funny. He clearly didn't take everything quite as seriously as the Mark Levins of today. I just dusted off my copy of his 1992 book *The Way Things Ought to Be* for some inspiration and noticed how he explained big ideas (crime, feminism, etc.) simply, instead of just talking about simple ideas. Limbaugh still cites facts and books, but he uses very basic language to describe the issues and makes them accessible for a passive radio audience. I think it's a good model. There is a place for middlebrow or even lowbrow content.

Not everything has to be (or should be) aimed at intellectuals. Some things should be fun and politically incorrect. In my case, Limbaugh was a sort of gateway drug that got me hooked on deeper conservative writers.

But I think it's also worth noting that the world has changed, and the media will now exploit things said on talk radio, using them to limit other conservatives and to drive narratives. For example, if Rush Limbaugh had called Sandra Fluke a "slut" in the pre–digital media days, that probably would have remained a bit of hyperbole that fans of Limbaugh's show understood as a sort of gag. Today, however, other media outlets pick that up, run it ad nauseam, out of context (not to suggest there was a good context for this one), and it becomes a key piece of evidence to reinforce the bogus Republican "war on women." Talk show hosts who truly care about advancing the conservative movement (not just about ratings and stirring up controversy) must adapt to these changing times and train themselves not to provide fodder for their political enemies. Talk radio can serve a vital role to help advance the cause of conservatism—as it has in past years (remember: the class of 1994 dubbed Limbaugh the "Majority Maker"). But doing so will require the most prominent hosts to be more prudent and to accept the fact that they have been granted a huge responsibility and a big megaphone, with the knowledge that their words have consequences.

Of course, it's not just the ad hominem attacks that have consequences. Occasionally, I'll hear a commentator describe himself as "only a comedian" or "only an entertainer." But what does that mean? If politics and news is just entertainment, then I suppose the stories are just material? Is a dead man in Ferguson, Missouri, an entertainment project? How about the beheading of a journalist in the Middle East? Is that just content? People are, after all, entertained by all sorts of bad things. Someone slipping on a banana peel is funny to a lot of people. People watch soap operas and horror movies for entertainment. But politics? Not to sound like a scold, but this is a pretty serious business. Telling people the end of the world is nigh has consequences.

I've focused mostly on the macro impact of talk radio punditry, but what about the long-term micro impact apocalyptic punditry has on individual listeners? Those of us who have been around politics for a long time are a little more cynical about these "the sky is falling" predictions. For example, I remember hearing things about Bill Clinton that essentially went like this: "Bill Clinton is the most liberal president in history—and the Republic might not survive if he's reelected." He ended up being a fairly moderate liberal who was willing to deal. When I hear those same warnings regurgitated today, I am a little more cynical. Take them with a grain of salt. My guess is that the doom-and-gloom stuff is more damaging to listeners who are already struggling with issues like depression.

Conclusion

One last piece of advice for everyone—candidates, strategists, think tankers, and individuals alike—subject yourself to opposing viewpoints. Doing so poses risks if you're not firmly rooted in your core beliefs, but I've found that necessity is the mother of invention. The more I have appeared on liberal interview shows, the more I have fleshed out why my conservative beliefs actually are best for America. By attempting to understand the other side, I have become more knowledgeable and better able to communicate my conservatism.

In the old days, the liberal media monopoly meant that conservatives (and the rest of America) were constantly subjected to liberally biased information. As previously noted, this was often in the form of selection bias. In other words, the media bias was manifested most acutely not in terms of any individual story's slant but instead by virtue of which stories were deemed to be "newsworthy." It's understandable why conservatives, finally freed of this, would never want to go back to the "bad old days." Fair enough. But one significant downside of today's new media environment is that it is tempting to never leave the echo chamber that reinforces our preexisting ideas. We must resist that urge.

The fancy term for this is *epistemic closure*. It's a problem I've mentioned before, but it bears repeating. You could, theoretically, watch only Fox News, read only RedState.com, and listen to only Rush Limbaugh, Sean Hannity, and Mark Levin. By doing so, you would be taking in a tremendous amount of political information, but you wouldn't be forced to confront troubling ideas with which you disagree. In fact, someone on a media diet such as this might have awakened the day after the 2012 election utterly stunned that Mitt Romney had not been elected president.

Someone who avoids confronting inconvenient information will have a very difficult time winning over Americans who *are* consuming information from different media outlets. If the San Diego Chargers played only home games, they might think they are a pretty good team. But what happens when they have to go into New England's Gillette Stadium in Foxborough, Massachusetts? All of a sudden, they realize they aren't as good as they think they are. Conservatives should celebrate the rise of friendly media outlets, but conservatives who are only good at playing games in the comfy confines of their home field—who never play "road" games—are often not as smart as they think they are.

Now the good news: Despite all the serious problems laid out in this book, Democrats are also being asked to do something that is very hard to do, and that is to win a third consecutive presidential election. The last time this happened was 1988, when George H. W. Bush was essentially awarded Reagan's third term. It's also important to recognize that even though the trends all look disastrous, things can change. And fast! Just as past predictions about the GOP being a "permanent governing majority" turned out to be laughable, notions that the conservative movement is dead might also turn out to be absurd. It's entirely possible that in 2017 Republicans will control the presidency, the house, and the senate. I'm not predicting that, but it's well within the realm of possibility.

To paraphrase Reagan, we aren't automatically victims of some fate that will befall us no matter what we do. A political party is never more than one generation from extinction. Or rebirth. It's our responsibility to seize the mantle—to make the hard choices. Conservatives must be proactive to ensure these demographic trends do not become destiny. The solution is not to water down the brand with, to paraphrase Reagan one more time, pastels instead of bold colors. The last thing we should do is betray conservatism's first principles—or its base of supporters. On the other hand, conservatism must evolve if it is to survive and flourish in the twenty-first century.

AFTERWORD

"Someone has said that heroes may not be braver than
anyone else, they're just braver five minutes longer."
—Ronald Reagan

Conservatism is at a crossroads. Will this generation decide to double down on angry populist rhetoric that stirs up aging, rural, white voters—or will we seek to make the conservative philosophy appealing to all Americans? This book highlights the problems—the negatives. And so, there are villains such as Donald Trump, Ann Coulter, Scam-PACs, and others who are (in my view) moving us in the wrong direction. You might have noticed that talk radio hosts are a pet peeve of mine, but this in no way is meant to impugn the many terrific hosts out there who raise the level of intellectual discussion. I go on many talk radio shows, and I find most of them stimulating. Among the best is Hugh Hewitt, who is widely considered to be one of the most important conservative commentators covering the 2016 Republican primaries.

Having said that, there does tend to be a contrast between many of the most famous talk radio hosts and the conservative columnists and journalists who focus on the written word. For example, sage conservative columnists Charles Krauthammer and George Will continue to churn out enlightening copy. And there are several young writers who have taken on the fever swamps of late. *Commentary*'s

Noah Rothman, *The Federalist*'s Ben Domenech, and *National Review*'s Charles C. W. Cooke are among the smart, young, up-and-coming conservatives to keep an eye on.

It's important to end the book on a hopeful note and to point out some of the thoughtful people who are challenging the movement's stasis. Genuine conservative leaders are making a strong case for why conservatism is the best philosophy for anyone who wants to pursue the American Dream. Today, Christian or conservative institutions of higher learning provide better academic opportunities. Examples such as Hillsdale College, Biola University, Houston Baptist University, and the King's College (in New York City!) abound. Other accomplished conservative intellectuals like Robert P. George, a Princeton University professor the *New York Times* has dubbed "this country's most influential conservative Christian thinker," provide an intellectual inspiration for conservatives. Some important and effective organizations and leaders are helping to bring the conservative movement forward. Among my favorites: the Club for Growth, the Leadership Institute, and the Federalist Society. Here, I have chosen to highlight a few groups and individuals who are specifically focusing on the kinds of projects this book calls for—the work of restoring conservatism to its rightful place as a proud, intellectually coherent philosophy.

Arthur Brooks

A French horn player turned Syracuse professor—turned head of the American Enterprise Institute (AEI)—the bespectacled Brooks has continued to make conservatism look hip and smart. Championing what he calls the *moral* case for free markets, a message he has continued to promote in his capacity as a contributing columnist at the *New York Times*, Brooks has greatly influenced prominent Republican politicians and conservative leaders to reject the dark side. As a book author, he is prolific and his columns typically have illuminating themes like "Abundance without Attachment," "The Trick to Being

More Virtuous," "Love People, Not Pleasure," and "Breaking Out of the Party Box." Brooks is also a devout Catholic, one who even New York hipsters would appreciate—and might even learn something from. And they wouldn't be alone. Brooks's evangelizing of the free market is so effective that he can persuade people who have fully formed, and opposing, worldviews. "After [listening] yesterday and to the presenters today, I developed more respect about capitalism," said the Dalai Lama, who was part of a February 2014 panel Brooks hosted at AEI. In short, the Dalai Lama, a *Marxist*, discovered capitalism is not just about money and exploitation, thanks to Brooks. How many fire-breathing conservatives could have accomplished that?

Dr. Russell Moore

Russell D. Moore is a Southern Baptist, but he's not what you'd think of when you think of *either* part of that term. President of the Southern Baptist Ethics & Religious Liberty Commission, Dr. Moore is a devout believer, but he's more interested in loving people into the Kingdom of God than in preaching fire and brimstone. He combines old-fashioned Baptist theology with a younger generation's appreciation for pop culture, sports, and entertainment. Though Dr. Moore sees some troubling aspects to fighting the culture wars, during an October 2013 conversation with me, Moore lamented that more young evangelicals are eschewing politics. And he stressed the importance of taking one's faith into the public square. When asked how to be in this world but not of this world, he references Johnny Cash's song "Walk the Line," telling me, "I keep a close watch on this heart of mine." It turns out that Moore is a huge Cash fan. "He always presented himself as a sinner—a sinner who was in need of mercy and in need of grace," he says of the late country star. Cash didn't revel in his sin—but he also didn't push the kind of "sappy sentimental Christian testimony" that can turn off people who are hurting or paint an overly optimistic picture of Christian life, either, Moore avers.

"Cash came in with this sense of a great hurt," Moore says, "a sense of a past that he was carrying with him, the sort of 'man in black' sort of mythology that was there—that I think resonated with people to say, 'the love of God extends to you.'"

Koch Industries and the Charles Koch Institute

Despite being blamed for all sorts of evils by Harry Reid, billionaire industrialists Charles and David Koch are actually incredibly generous philanthropists. What is more, many of the organizations they run and fund are committed to reforming conservatism. This book has generally avoided providing a specific policy recipe, focusing instead on more fundamental questions. But it is clear that modernizing will require some substantive changes. Along those lines, the Koch Brothers are active in pushing conservatism toward certain policy reform goals. For example, they are committed to immigration reform. But it might be in the area of criminal justice reform where they are making the most inroads. Mark Holden, general counsel at Koch Industries, and Vikrant Reddy, senior fellow for criminal justice at the Charles Koch Institute, are among the most eloquent advocates for reforming criminal justice (reducing mandatory minimum sentences and mass incarceration—and seeking to reform offenders who are amendable) to ensure that people don't come out of prison worse than when they went in. Many of these reforms don't just receive bipartisan support—they also unite social conservatives (who stress compassion) with libertarians (who stress civil liberties) and fiscal conservatives (who find our bloated incarceration rates to be inefficient and costly).

Ross Douthat

As the youngest-ever op-ed columnist for the *New York Times*, Ross Douthat reaches Americans who otherwise might never come into contact with a conservative worldview. But rather than revel in his early success, Douthat went to work churning out insightful columns that don't just preach to the choir, but expose liberal readers to a smart, Christian, conservative worldview they might not otherwise know exists. In the process, he also manages to expose liberal hypocrisy, and he does so in a manner that liberal readers might actually not find inherently repellent.

Take his July 5, 2014, piece on Hobby Lobby, a chain of arts and crafts stores. Upon discovering that the Affordable Care Act would mandate providing birth control products, the company decided to supply just sixteen of the twenty FDA-approved contraceptive options. The point was to cover only the drugs they viewed as "preventative," and not the ones they believed to be abortifacients. The case went all the way to the Supreme Court, and Hobby Lobby narrowly won. Conservatives saw it as a victory for religious liberty, while liberals framed the conflict as a corporation "denying birth control" to its employees.

Douthat framed his column differently, noting that liberals have long "bemoaned the disappearance of the socially conscious corporation, the boardroom devoted to the common good." To the intellectually honest liberal, this should have been a thought-provoking column. How is it that the Left has suddenly gotten on the wrong side of socially conscious companies—that don't allow profits or the desire to avoid controversy to trump their core values? There are other Douthats out there doing this kind of interesting writing. While it might be more fun (and easier) to pen a blog post attacking the Left for being evil hypocrites, Douthat's method is more persuasive. "Anyone can lie to the press," quipped former Reagan aide Lyn Nofziger, "but confusing them with the truth is an art I am proud to have mastered." Likewise, anyone can tell liberals to "go to hell," but Douthat has a way of making them look forward to the trip.

Dr. Francis Collins and BioLogus

If you're not familiar with the story of Dr. Francis Collins, then get this: one of the nation's top scientists is also a believing Christian. Dr. Collins was director of the Human Genome Project when he wrote a 2006 book called *The Language of God: A Scientist Presents Evidence for Belief.* In 2007, Dr. Collins established the BioLogus Foundation, a 501c3 organization to spread his message, and in 2009, he was appointed by President Obama to be director of the National Institutes of Health. As the BioLogus website notes, "In [his book] Collins recounted his own development from atheism to Christian belief, and argued that science is not in conflict with biblical faith but actually enhances faith." Collins subsequently stepped down from his official role with BioLogus, but the mission of helping "the world to see the harmony between science and biblical faith as we present an evolutionary understanding of God's creation" is ongoing, and the organization continues to grow.

Eric Metaxas

With books like *Amazing Grace: William Wilberforce and the Heroic Campaign to End Slavery; Bonhoeffer: Pastor, Martyr, Prophet, Spy;* and *Miracles: What They Are, Why They Happen, and How They Can Change Your Life,* Eric Metaxas, who is in his early fifties, has emerged as one of the most important Christian writer-historians of our time. During a recent conversation about his book *Miracles,* I asked Metaxas whether he thought his status as an urban intellectual who sports hipster glasses helped advance his message.

> I think that I am, you know, I'm a Yale graduate, I live in Manhattan, and I don't fit the stereotype of "person of faith"—which actually tells you how little we really think about this stuff rationally. I mean, the idea that we have this stereotype, based on what? You know, some of the smartest people who have ever lived are people of profound faith. So this is just kind of a recent thing that has crept into the culture, and we basically go with it out of intellectual sloppiness.

Not everyone can or should aspire to be like Metaxas. But I would suppose that there are a lot of fire-breathing conservative pundits who are more famous but much less effective at winning converts—at winning the intellectual or theological arguments.

The Faith Angle Forum

Rather than lamenting the fact that few journalists have a deeply rooted understanding of religion and that this ignorance of theology and apologetics is often demonstrated in coverage of religion, the Ethics and Public Policy Center's vice president, Michael Cromartie, has, since 1999, hosted twice-yearly meetings, called the Faith Angle Forum, in places like Miami, Florida.[117] These meetings bring together respected journalists and top scholars to discuss issues related to faith and culture. This is only one aspect of the EPPC's mission, but it's a simple and important one. My guess is that this outreach to influential mainstream journalists and opinion leaders is more effective and efficient than 99 percent of what conservatives spend money on when they're trying to impact the culture.

Tim Keller

Pastor Tim Keller is not a political conservative—at least, not as far as I know. He believes that faith has a moderating impact on us, essentially making us less political (or, at least, putting politics in proper perspective). But Keller serves as a suitable example for many of the ideas summoned in this book, for combining a deep-abiding faith with urbanity and intellectualism. A 2004 *Wall Street Journal* profile noted that most of the people who show up for his services "are single and under thirty-five, whether bankers, lawyers, actors, or artists. Mr. Keller has a growing national following and is often described as a Christian intellectual who takes on the likes of Nietzsche, Marx, and Freud in a sermon rooted in a specific biblical text."

Keller might well have decided that he could become an even more successful preacher by going the "televangelist" route—or by opening one of those megachurches in the suburbs, where land is cheap. Instead, he followed his calling to (again, of all places) New York City. And, in order to put people in the pews, he didn't tone down his message about Jesus's divinity or miracles or sacrifice, or any of the sacraments and traditions of believers. Nor did he dumb down his message. Instead, he went the other direction on both counts. He's not afraid to preach about spiritual matters, and he's not afraid to invoke philosophers or academics in order to make his point.

In fact, Keller argues that pastors should incorporate a certain amount of teaching on apologetics into sermons, because even if everyone in the room is already a Christian, people are more likely to bring friends and family to church if they hear the pastor teaching and explaining things in a manner that would appeal to someone who isn't already a believer.

In short, Tim Keller's model of starting a church is very close to what Republicans should consider doing when it comes to winning converts. This doesn't mean that we should abandon rural areas any more than having a thriving church in New York City means we should close up the churches in the South or in suburbia. This isn't an "or" thing, but an "and" thing.

Conservatism should be able to appeal to lowbrow, middlebrow, and highbrow audiences. If presented correctly, it can play in every geographical region in the nation—North or South, rural or urban. This is the gospel truth.

Too Dumb to Fail Reading List

If you're committed to helping turn this around, you'll need some intellectual reinforcements. This is by no means a definitive reading list, but here are some books that I think are important for conservatives to read. This list generally includes three types of books: 1) those that are considered part of the conservative canon, 2) those that specifically influenced my thinking and the philosophy of this book, and 3) a few books about how politics is played. (Note: You might also want to check in with the Bible and the Constitution at some point.)

Important conservative books

The Conservative Mind by Dr. Russell Kirk

Politics by Aristotle

The Conscience of a Conservative by Barry Goldwater

The Road to Serfdom by F. A. Hayek

Reflections on the Revolution in France by Edmund Burke

Ideas Have Consequences by Richard Weaver

Books that greatly influenced Too Dumb to Fail (not a comprehensive bibliography)

The Conservative Heart by Arthur Brooks

Reagan's Revolution by Craig Shirley

When Character Was King by Peggy Noonan

The Great Debate by Yuval Levin

The Scandal of the Evangelical Mind by Mark Noll

Crunchy Cons by Rod Dreher

Anti-intellectualism in American Life by Richard Hofstadter

Amusing Ourselves to Death by Neil Postman

Upstream by Alfred Regnery

10 Books That Screwed Up the World by Benjamin Wiker

Some books on how the political game is played

Hardball by Chris Matthews

Buck Up, Suck Up...and Come Back When You Foul Up by James Carville and Paul Begala

All Politics Is Local by Tip O'Neill

Nofziger by Lyn Nofziger

ACKNOWLEDGMENTS

Writing a book can drive one mad, so I want to thank my wife, Erin, for tolerating me and for being a constant inspiration in everything I do. I also thank my mom, Hope Lewis, for always insisting that I "be somebody," even when I resisted (and for proofreading, too).

My friends Bill Scher, Kristi Speights, and David Pietrusza deserve special recognition. They graciously spent countless hours helping brainstorm ideas and editing this book (I can only imagine the number of hours they contributed to this effort).

This book wouldn't have happened without my book agents at Javelin, Matt Latimer and Keith Urbahn, who encouraged my efforts and were intimately involved in helping craft the initial book proposal. Kudos are also in order for my editor, Paul Whitlatch—who believed in this book and worked tirelessly to see this project through to completion—and the entire team at Hachette Books, including Mauro DiPreta (publisher), Michelle Aielli (executive director of publicity), Betsy Hulsebosch (marketing director), Lauren Lavelle (publicist), and Emily Caldwell (publicity assistant). They have been amazing to work with.

I also want to thank the following people for their ideas, edits, time, memories, expertise, support, and various contributions to this effort: Tucker Carlson, Morton Blackwell, Craig Shirley, Vince Coglianese, Adam Hasner, Brian McGuire, Jim Eltringham, Rachel Motte, Andrew Walker, Daniel Darling, Josh Finestone,

James Strock, William Beutler, Yuval Levin, Chuck Warren, Chris Meekins, and R. J. Moeller.

Thanks also to Neil Patel, Jamie Weinstein, Alex Pappas, and everyone at the *Daily Caller* for their continued support and friendship. And lastly, a special thanks to Jon Avalon and Will Rahn at the *Daily Beast*, Ben Frumin at *The Week*, and the *Telegraph*'s opinion editorial team (especially Peter Foster), all of whom have been generous enough to publish my columns while I was writing this book and who, along the way, became cherished friends and allies.

NOTES

1. From *Speaking My Mind* found at the Reagan Foundation website: http://www .reaganfoundation.org/tgcdetail.aspx?p=TG0923RRS&lm=reagan&args _a=cms&args_b=1&argsb=N&tx=1736.
2. According to James C. Humes's *The Wit and Wisdom of Ronald Reagan*, page 182.
3. According to a *Vanity Fair*/CBS News poll conducted in 2011.
4. From Reagan's speech to the 1992 Republican National Convention.
5. Truman never attended "regular" college. He did, however, attend two years of law school—but he never graduated.
6. From *Anti-Intellectualism in American Life*.
7. Amitai Etzioni's January 8, 2015, piece in the *Atlantic* was titled "The Left's Unpopular Populism."
8. The crux of Etzioni's piece is that "populism becomes much less popular—once Leftist themes join the mix."
9. This was a May 9, 2006, article in *National Review* titled "Pick Up Your Own Crap."
10. From a 2004 interview with the author on FrontPageMagazine.com.
11. While it is unclear whether Rousseau specifically influenced Paine, he profoundly influenced the thinking of the French Revolution's leaders—most famously, Robespierre.
12. Years later, to the consternation of Burkean conservatives who understood the historical context and worldview implications, Ronald Reagan would quote this line. It should, however, be noted that the unique experience of American democracy—the entire experience of the New World, and later, the Wild West—imbued in Americans a greater sense of reinvention. European conservatives would be shocked by Reagan's citation of Paine.
13. Yuval Levin responded to my inquiry, e-mailing this to me on May 18, 2015.
14. The French Revolution directly inspired Communism. For example, Marx and Engels studied the revolutionary French journalist and agitator

François-Noël Babeuf, going so far as to acknowledge him in the *Communist Manifesto*.

15. Craig Shirley and Donald Devine in the *Washington Post*, April 4, 2010.

16. Ironically, largely first spearheaded by such disenchanted Democrats as former Democratic presidential nominees Al Smith and John W. Davis.

17. Ludwig von Mises, George Stigler, Milton Friedman, et al.

18. In his book *The Maker of a Movement*, Lee Edwards notes that William F. Buckley, a devout Catholic, "adamantly opposed Communism all his life not just because it was a tyranny, but also because it was a heresy."

19. Like, Chambers, Edmund Burke had similar fears, evidenced by the fact that he asked for an unmarked grave.

20. From Tanenhaus's *Whittaker Chambers*, page 487.

21. Traditionalists such as the University of Chicago English professor Richard Weaver, author of *Ideas Have Consequences* in 1948, and other conservatives like Berkeley sociologist Robert Nisbet's (*The Quest for Community*) made great strides.

22. In recent years, *National Review*'s Jonah Goldberg has argued that the Muslim world needs a Pope. One could probably make the same argument about the conservative movement. (Or, at least, a commissioner.)

23. The John Birch Society was named after the man thought to be the first casualty of the Cold War.

24. Penned by the equally brilliant conservative wunderkind M. Stanton Evans.

25. Actually, Morton Blackwell made this point in a handwritten note on an early version of this manuscript he was helping to fact-check.

26. Early in his career, Will served as *National Review*'s book editor.

27. The line was authored for Goldwater by Dr. Harry V. Jaffa.

28. It was also widely—and perhaps quite correctly—interpreted as Goldwater's defense of the indefensible John Birch Society.

29. Disclosure: I serve on the board of trustees of the Blackwell Family Trust.

30. In the preface of Lionel Trilling's *The Liberal Imagination*.

31. I worked there for four years.

32. From an August 17, 2015, e-mail with Reagan biographer Craig Shirley.

33. From Deroy Murdoch's *National Review* article, "Egghead Reagan," published June 15, 2004.

34. A decade later, Reagan's political team would attempt to do the exact opposite—persuade insiders and donors that Reagan was sophisticated enough to be president. The solution was to bring on respected Beltway strategist John Sears. As Michael Deaver told journalist and Reagan biographer Lou Cannon, "We had a western inferiority complex." The attempt failed miserably.

35. George P. Schultz in the foreword of "Reagan In His Own Hand."

36. From the "Conversations with [Bill] Kristol" podcast, April 13, 2015.

37. Ibid, May 25, 2015.

38. This story, retold in Nofziger's memoir *Nofziger,* wasn't meant to make Reagan look bad. Nofziger, a rumpled old journalist turned operative, was a loyal aide. But the point is that Reagan and his image-makers downplayed the Hollywood aspect to Reagan, and played up his folksier image. Both were authentic parts of the man.

39. Via Hofstadter's *Anti-Intellectualism in American Life.*

40. Peggy Noonan's June 7, 2004, *Wall Street Journal* column was titled "Thanks from a Grateful Country."

41. Ironically, this paved the way for Speaker of the House Dennis Hastert. He got the job because he was supposedly squeaky clean. But while I was writing this book, Hastert was indicted for attempting to conceal he was paying hush money to cover up alleged sexual misconduct.

42. Christine O'Donnell's speech took place at the Family Research Council's Values Voter Summit.

43. Because the line "In Birmingham they love the governor…" is followed by "boo-hoo-hoo," there is an argument that this line was meant to be sarcastic—that Birmingham really didn't love Gov. George Wallace. That doesn't seem to comport with a line later in the song about "where the skies are so blue and the governor's true." Regardless of where the band stood on Wallace, the line "Watergate does not bother me" suggests they were generally pushing back at the liberalism of the day.

44. According to NPR's Ron Elving.

45. It was *Virginia senator* George Allen who famously said "macaca." But that's another story.

46. Some may date that to 1964, but LBJ still bested Goldwater six Southern states to five. Goldwater only looks so strong in Dixie because of LBJ walloping him 38–1 elsewhere.

47. Goldwater had voted for the 1957 and 1960 civil rights bills, but opposed the 1964 bill based on Constitutional concerns over two provisions. Additionally, a larger percentage of Republicans than Democrats in both houses supported the Civil Rights Act of 1964.

48. It's worth noting that Democrats made a big shift toward civil rights in 1948, adopting a civil rights plank in the platform and Truman's desegregation order, dividing the party and sparking Strom Thurmond's National States Right Democrat ("Dixiecrat") bid.

49. It'll be interesting to see how people fleeing liberal states like California for Texas will impact Texas's political landscape. One imagines that, eventually, they will reach a tipping point where the increased population produces negative consequences.

50. Southern politicians are still punching above their weight. Some, like former South Carolina senator Jim DeMint and Texas senator Ted Cruz are bona fide fiscal conservatives, but still embody many of the cultural

stereotypes associated with Southern pols, including a penchant for lost causes.

51. There is a debate as to whether the Lone Star State should qualify as Southern or Western.

52. Troy's actually understating the case. "W" and his adviser Karl Rove actually engaged in prodigiously reading "contests" during their White House years.

53. Bush, of course, lost the popular vote in 2000.

54. Steven Conn was being interviewed on the "New Books in History" podcast by Peter Aigner.

55. *Wired* magazine columnist Matt Ridley delivered a TED Talk titled "When Ideas Have Sex." During a later TED Talk, author Steven Johnson referenced Ridley, noting that cities are places "where ideas could have sex."

56. Secular humanists might well ponder how their increasing self-righteous jeremiads against the sins of Christians reads like the infamous (and unheard) prayer of the Pharisee: "O God, I give thee thanks that I am not as the rest of men, extortioners, unjust, adulterer…"

57. Morton Blackwell e-mailed me this on January 9, 2015.

58. From a May 14, 2013, article by Ed Stetzer in *Christianity Today* titled "Recovering Classic Evangelicalism: An Interview with Gregory Thornbury."

59. The Scopes case remains interesting on numerous levels, being as it was a purposely choreographed test case to challenge the validity of Tennessee's law—and also to provide publicity for the small town which hosted the trial. It was all very much "reality TV"—minus television.

60. When it comes to evolution, Bryan comes across looking poorly today. Score one for the intellectuals, right? Maybe. But it's also worth noting that while Bryan opposed teaching biological evolution, he was also vehemently opposed to social Darwinism, the "survival of the fittest" philosophy that was embraced by an alarming number of intellectuals of the day. This pernicious philosophy led to eugenics and helped inspire some of the atrocities of Nazi Germany. Bryan deserves credit for standing against this at the time—even if he (and his intellectual adversaries) wrongly conflated Darwin's theory of evolution with social Darwinism.

61. George W. Bush nominated his friend and adviser Harriet Miers, an evangelical, in 2005, but withdrew her nomination after conservatives voiced strong opposition.

62. From a July 18, 2012, interview with *National Review*'s Kathryn Lopez.

63. From page 130 of Richard Hofstadter's *Anti-intellectualism in American Life*.

64. History is messy. Reagan was incredibly smart, but downplayed his intelligence. Both Bushes had Ivy League credentials, though George W. Bush

downplayed them. George H. W. Bush, with his preppy image, certainly didn't fit the populist profile—and his inability to play the populist card probably contributed to his reelection loss to Bill Clinton. Though Bill Clinton was a Rhodes scholar, his "aw shucks" demeanor and his Arkansas "Bubba" upbringing prepared him to play both sides of the elitist-populist card like a Hot Springs, Arkansas, casino dealer.

65. A notable exception was Indiana's former governor Mitch Daniels, but even he ostentatiously tooled around the state on a motorcycle.

66. This is an interesting reversal of traditional party roles. Traditional Republicans have opted for the "next in line" candidate: Nixon, Ford, Reagan, G. H. W. Bush, Dole, McCain, Romney; while Democrats have more often flopped down for outright novelty: Stephenson (at least the first time), JFK, McGovern, Carter, the saxophone-playing Bill Clinton, Obama.

67. In the twentieth century, Republicans elected three candidates who had never previously run for a single office: William Howard Taft, Herbert Hoover, and Dwight Eisenhower. The first two proved to be unmitigated political disasters.

68. Hoffstadter's *Anti-Intellectualism in American Life*, page 160.

69. Ibid, page 159.

70. From page 170 of Richard Hofstadter's *Anti-intellectualism in American Life*.

71. In 1947, Reagan's first wife, Jane Wyman, prematurely delivered a daughter named Christine, who died nine hours after birth. As such, Reagan technically fathered four children (and adopted another).

72. Of course, in 2012, Krohn was then a seventeen-year-old, parroting what he had heard for a *short* time.

73. "A recollection of D-Day," written by Craig Shirley in the *Washington Times* on June 6, 2013.

74. From page 21 of Richard Hofstadter's *Anti-intellectualism in American Life*.

75. In Joseph J. Ellis's *Founding Brothers*, he suggests that Jefferson's "version of the story" (page 48) was "essentially true" (page 50). Essentially, there were other conversations taking place at the same time, and Jefferson's account "vastly oversimplifies the history that was happening at that propitious moment" (page 51).

76. Richardson may have also foreseen the messy passage of Obamacare, when in 1978 he wrote a little book too honestly entitled, *What Makes You Think We Read the Bills?*

77. Okay, Eric Hoffer didn't actually say this! What he actually said in his 1967 book *The Temper of Our Time* was, "Up to now, America has not been a good milieu for the rise of a mass movement. What starts out here as a mass movement ends up as a racket, a cult, or a corporation." Having

said that, this pithier, bastardized misquote has been cited so many times that I've chosen to recycle it here—with this note of explanation.

78. My wife previously consulted for Mr. Cuccinelli, though not on his gubernatorial campaign.

79. In the past, I voluntarily appeared in a few of their "TroopAThon" webcasts, which were ostensibly online telethons to raise money and awareness for the troops.

80. In fairness, both sides do this. Unlike conservatives, the Left has plenty of A-list celebrities, so they don't have to go scraping the bottom of the barrel for them—unless you count Clay Aiken, who did run for Congress as a Democrat recently. On the other hand, liberals *have* been known to lionize dictators, cop killers, and domestic terrorists, so there's that.

81. In fairness, conservatives were partly reacting to what they deemed as unfair media favoritism toward Martin. Martin was seventeen when the incident occurred, but as Poynter noted, "The dominant photo of Martin shows him thirteen or fourteen years old." Meanwhile, "[t]he most common photo of Zimmerman is a 2005 police mugshot."

82. This is from a July 28, 2015, PolitiFact story titled "Donald Trump wrongly says the number of illegal immigrants is 30 million or higher" by Amy Sherman.

83. From a *USA Today* story in March of 2014, noting the thirty-fifth anniversary of cameras in the House of Representatives.

84. From the "Conversations with [Bill] Kristol" podcast, which aired on June 30, 2014.

85. From David Drucker's *Washington Examiner* column, "Mick Mulvaney: Republicans Need to Appeal to Hispanics," on May 9, 2015.

86. From Philip Klein's November 6, 2012, column in the *Washington Examiner* titled "Romney Wins White Vote by Same Margin as Reagan Did in 1980 Landslide."

87. Via the University of Connecticut's Roper Center, this based on exit polling conducted by CBS News and the *New York Times*, with a "[s]ample of 15,201 voters as they left voting booths on Election Day, November 4, 1980."

88. The Cook Political Report's "Mapping the 2016 Electorate: Demographics Don't Guarantee a Democratic White House," published by David Wasserman on June 19, 2015.

89. Whit Ayres's *Wall Street Journal* column, "A Daunting Demographic Challenge for the GOP in 2016," March 4, 2015.

90. According to the survey by the Asian American Justice Center, Asian & Pacific Islander American Vote and the National Asian American Survey.

91. According to a 2012 Pew Research Center report titled "The Rise of Asian Americans."

92. Via Dan Balz's February 28, 2015, *Washington Post* column titled "For 2016, Candidates Count, But Don't Ignore Fundamentals." Balz's statistics were culled from a study produced by the American Enterprise Institute, the Center for American Progress and the Brookings Institution, called "States of Change."

93. Via ABC News' "Put a Ring on It: Obama Wins Women, but Not the Married Kind," published April 3, 2012, by Matt Negrin.

94. The "States of Change" study produced by the American Enterprise Institute, the Center for American Progress and the Brookings Institution, published February 24, 2015.

95. *Tampa Bay Times* PunditFact: "Republican presidential nominee hasn't won over women since 1988, says progressive pundit," August 21, 2015.

96. "25 Interesting Facts about the 2012 Elections," written by Jennifer Duffy in The Cook Political Report on December 20, 2012.

97. According to James Gimpel, a University of Maryland political scientist, cited in the Reuters article: "In US Cities, Republicans Are Looking for a Few Good Losers for 2016."

98. "The GOP Is Dying Off. Literally," published by Daniel J. McGraw in *Politico* magazine on May 17, 2015.

99. Reince Preibus's comments came at a breakfast organized by the *Christian Science Monitor* on November 7, 2014.

100. Ben Domenech's column "Are Republicans for Freedom or White Identity Politics?" at *The Federalist*, August 21, 2015.

101. From Reason.com's "Millennials Tell Us What Their Political Ideology Means to Them," by Emily Ekins on July 16, 2014. Findings are based on the Reason-Rupe public opinion poll of millennials conducted in February of 2014.

102. A *Washington Post* column "Donald Trump and the Anger of Conservatives," written by Ruth Marcus, July 21, 2015.

103. From Ronald Brownstein's February 11, 2015, piece in *National Journal*, titled: "The States That Will Pick the President: the Reach States." This was based on historical data and future projections by the States of Change project.

104. According to the *Houston Chronicle*'s Kevin Diaz, whose column "Texas Latino Vote Splits" was published November 4, 2014.

105. Fred Barnes's *Wall Street Journal* op-ed, "Avoiding the Trump Trap on Immigration," from July 20, 2015.

106. Dr. Martin Luther King Jr. uses the thermostat-versus-thermometer analogy in his "Letter from a Birmingham Jail."

107. Or might we say the supposed gap? Consider that Copernicus, Gregor Mendel, Roger Bacon, and William of Ockham were not merely religious. They were all *priests*.

108. This was the "fireside chat" that took place during the New Canaan Society's 2012 Washington Weekend.
109. From a 2012 discussion I had with Baylor professor Barry Hankins. Just as the death of antebellum statesmen and compromisers like Webster, Clay, and Calhoun directly preceded the Civil War, the 1921 deaths of three prominent theologians who were open to evolution—B. B. Warfield, George Frederick Wright, and A. H. Strong—seem to have ushered in the culture war over evolution. For example, in David N. Livingstone and Mark A. Noll's "B. B. Warfield (1851–1921): A Biblical Inerrantist as Evolutionist" it is noted that "Benjamin Breckenridge Warfield of Princeton Theological Seminary, the theologian who more than any other defined modern biblical inerrancy, was throughout his life open to the possibility of evolution and at some points an advocate of the theory." http://www.jstor.org/stable/236917?seq=1#page_scan_tab_contents.
110. Science vs. faith? Again, it was the Belgian priest, Father Georges Lemaître, who developed that "big bang" theory.
111. It might be noted that Kunstler resides in Saratoga Springs, New York, a quite workable example of the New Urbanism—and, perhaps surprisingly, a city governed quite often by Republicans.
112. This is based on a dissertation by social geographer Erika Sandow at Umeå University.
113. This is from the *Scandinavian Journal of Economics* 110(2), 339–366, 2008. DOI: 10.1111/j.1467-9442.2008.00542.x. "Stress that Doesn't Pay: The Commuting Paradox."
114. From Conn Carroll's *Washington Examiner* column titled "DeMint vs. Rubio: The Heritage Foundation goes all in against amnesty."
115. Note: I have attended and spoken at several Club for Growth meetings in Palm Beach, Florida, as a guest of the Club.
116. From an April 14, 2015, interview with ChristianPost.com.
117. I have attended two such meetings in Miami.